A New Cold War

Celebrating
30 Years of Publishing
in India

A New Cold War

Henry Kissinger and the Rise of China

Edited by

Sanjaya Baru *and* Rahul Sharma

HarperCollins *Publishers* India

First published in hardback in India by HarperCollins *Publishers* 2021
4th Floor, Tower A, Building No. 10, DLF Cyber City,
DLF Phase II, Gurugram, Haryana – 122002
www.harpercollins.co.in

This edition published by HarperCollins *Publishers* 2023

2 4 6 8 10 9 7 5 3 1

P-ISBN: 978-93-5699-361-7
E-ISBN: 978-93-5422-789-9

Typeset in 11.5/15.5 Adobe Garamond Pro
Manipal Technologies Limited, Manipal

Printed and bound at
Manipal Technologies Limited, Manipal

MIX
Paper from responsible sources
FSC® C043100

This book is produced from independently certified FSC® paper to ensure responsible forest management.

Contents

Introduction to the Paperback Edition

THE YEAR IN WHICH WE compiled these essays, 2020,[1] to mark the fiftieth anniversary of President Richard Nixon's historic 1971 visit to China, the strategic community in Washington DC was still echoing President Donald Trump's call for a 'decoupling' of the United States (US) and Chinese economies. 'China is spending the money we give them to build up their military,' Trump told a gathering at the White House on Labour Day, September 2020. 'So when you mention the word "decouple", it's an interesting word. So we lose billions of dollars, and if we didn't do business with them, we wouldn't lose billions of dollars. It's called "decoupling". So you'll start thinking about it. You'll start thinking.'[2]

Trump's views echoed the thinking of two eminent Harvard scholars, Edward Luttwak and Robert Blackwill, who had canvassed the idea of a 'geo-economic containment' of China. In *The Rise of China vs the Logic of Strategy*, Luttwak advocated that such a containment of China aimed at preserving 'the world's equilibrium without worse forms of conflict'.[3] 'The only remaining means of resistance [to China] would then be "geo-economic", to apply the logic of strategy in the grammar of commerce,' concluded Luttwak. He suggested that the US restrict trade with China; deny China access to key raw materials; and stop technology transfers that China would still need. All this aimed at 'impeding China's growth'.[4]

Where the Cold War had been about 'containing the Soviet Union', we felt there was a 'New Cold War' afoot to contain China, albeit economically. Robert Blackwill and Jennifer Harris explored the role of geo-economics in the US 'grand strategy' and asked, 'Is China changing the rules of the game more quickly than the existing rules are changing China?'[5] If the answer is 'yes', then what is the US prepared to do, they asked. 'What geo-economic resources are we willing to commit to tip this ratio back toward more favorable balance for the United States?'[6]

Advocating 'returning geo-economics to the helm of the US foreign policy', Blackwill and Harris suggested that the US policy makers ought to ask three questions with respect to the country's relations with other countries: 'How does it affect America's economic position in the world? How can we use geo-economic tools to advance our strategic interests? And, how can we shape emerging economic trends to produce geopolitical results beneficial to the United States, to our allies and friends, and to a rules-based global order.'[7]

Trump followed up his rhetoric with policy action on trade, raising tariffs of several products, imported from China, worth over $300 billion. Beijing retaliated, targeting some $100 billion worth of mainly agricultural goods from the United States.[8] President Joe Biden retained all these tariffs and by the middle of his tenure used industrial policy to hurt China. Biden's CHIPS for America Act imposed export controls and offered subsidies aimed at benefitting the US companies and curbing high tech exports to China. The act specifically sought to support domestic production of semiconductors and limit China's capacity in this area. China called it technology blockade and said it was aimed at controlling their rise.

Despite increasingly tense bilateral trade relations and political chatter on the need to decouple the US economy from China's, trade between the world's two biggest economies has only flourished. Numbers tell the real story. Trade in goods hit a new record in 2022, rising by 2.5 per cent year on year to touch a staggering $690.6 billion. The previous record was $658.8 billion in 2018, the year when Trump launched his 'trade war'. What is interesting to note is that not only did US imports of Chinese goods increase, but the trade deficit is also vastly in favour of China, again indicating how difficult it is for the US to 'decouple' from it. The US trade deficit grew by 8.3 per cent year on year to touch $382.9 billion in 2022 with the US imports of Chinese goods hitting $536.8 billion and exports at $13.8 billion. China was the United States third-biggest trading partner, but the biggest source of imports.

The recent US hard-line on technology and sanctions on Chinese technology companies has only intensified the rhetoric on trade and security issues in the run-up to the 2024 US presidential elections; but what is clear is that there is an effort in Washington DC to send a subtle message that they did seek 'de-risking' rather than 'de-coupling'. And that has been visible in the statements made by several senior US officials, including US National Security Advisor Jake Sullivan.[9]

Janet Yellen, secretary of treasury of the US, was the first to convey the message when she ended a long list of complaints, warnings and threats aimed at China with an interestingly conciliatory, albeit realistic, appreciation of the nature of inter-dependence between the world's two largest economies. She was quoted in media as saying, 'The US will assert ourselves when our vital interests are at stake. But we do not seek to "decouple" our economy from China's. A full separation of our economies would be disastrous for both countries. It would be destabilizing for the rest of the world.'[10]

Her message, said in passing, was quickly reiterated and imparted gravitas by the US National Security Advisor Jake Sullivan. On 27 April 2023, at the influential Washington DC think tank—Brookings Institution—Sullivan ended a long and substantial address on the US economic strategy aimed at reviving and revitalizing the country's economy, reasserting their global economic leadership, and so on, with the categorical statement, 'we are for de-risking and diversifying, not decoupling' from China.

Yellen and Sullivan were not just articulating a new line of thinking on China supported by President Biden, but also echoing the words of a US corporate leader and former president of the American Chamber of Commerce (AmCham), Ken Jarret. Jarret told *Forbes* magazine in March 2023, a month earlier, that while the US–China relationship is defined by 'rivalry, mistrust and suspicion … The one thing that hasn't changed [after the pandemic] is that the level of economic interdependence between the United States and China is still quite deep. US companies want to "derisk", not "decouple".'[11]

Underlining the influence of the US business interests on the bilateral relationship—a point elaborated later in this book—a White Paper published in early 2023 by the AmCham China showed that the US firms remained 'optimistic' about their business prospects in China. As many as 37 per cent of the 109 respondent companies 'gave a positive response when asked about their business profitability outlook in China, an increase of 4 percentage points from a previous survey'.[12] Thus, even as politicians in Washington DC were talking of 'decoupling' and think tanks echoed these views, the big businesses in the US continued to view their prospects with China in a positive, albeit cautious, light. Like any smart firm they would derisk, not decouple.

The new 'derisk' strategy is not just a departure from Trump's 'decouple' plan that had gained so much traction both in the US and around the world, but a definite retreat from the bravado of the 'geo-economic containment of China', which was in vogue barely a decade ago and influenced our thinking as we brought this collection of essays together.

India, too, will take some time to extricate itself from the Chinese trade trap. Despite frosty diplomatic relations and India's tough stance on Chinese businesses, trade between the two giant neighbours grew by 8.4 per cent in 2022. China's exports to India rose to $118.5 billion, which is an increase of nearly 22 per cent while its imports fell by nearly 40 per cent to $17.48 billion, pushing the overall trade deficit to more than $100 billion in favour of Beijing for the first time.[13]

India's border conflict with China has made many Indians view the neighbouring country primarily through the prism of military conflict. However, the fact is that China is still more of a 'geo-economic' power than a military power. While China's geopolitical reach has widened, as was recently witnessed in West Asia, which poses a geopolitical challenge to many of its neighbours, the US–China rapprochement of 1971 and the post-Tiananmen growth in their bilateral economic relations has established China as a manufacturing and trading superpower. It has emerged as a geo-economic power and the West is still not clear how to deal with this challenge.

More importantly, there is a bigger question: Will China buy into the new US rhetoric? It seems unlikely, as the Middle Kingdom seems sure of its place in the sun and firmly believes that the West is in decline. China doesn't see itself as a junior partner to the US; it wants an equal partnership.

In its design, a Xinhua commentary said, on 26 April 2023, that the US wants (in the post-Cold War era) to manage China's development and turn the country into its junior partner—a huge market for US products, services and capital, a source of affordable resources for US industries, and most importantly, 'a minion' who could deliver on America's priorities. China can grow but must grow on the track set by the US, and certainly not to the extent that the US' supremacy might be challenged.[14] 'To put it simply, the Chinese should just keep their feet on the ground and manufacture T-shirts and socks for American consumers, instead of trying to move up the "smile curve",' the commentary added.[15] China strongly feels that the US is hurting its interests and interfering in its internal matters while expecting that Beijing will be open to discussions and cooperation. The view in Beijing is that the US can't have it both ways.

This book records the historic role of decisions taken in the US that helped contribute to the rise of China, posing a new challenge to the West. If during the 'Old Cold War' the former Soviet Union (USSR) was sought to be 'geopolitically contained', a 'New Cold War' would entail the 'geo-economic containment' of China. The former Soviet Union had spread its ideological and military tentacles around the world. Today, it is China that has spread its economic arms around the world. It is now clear that battling the Soviet system was easier than overpowering China. What is the difference? China is the world's biggest manufacturing and trading nation and almost every country around the world has economic relations with China. There are few economies that can grow without doing business with China.

Introduction

XINTIANDI—A NAME THAT TRANSLATES AS 'New Heaven and Earth'—is today an upmarket, pedestrian-only district of Shanghai, full of trendy shops, restaurants and bars. A China tourist guide says it is 'the place that youngsters love the most'. A century ago, in July 1921, the Communist Party of China (CPC) came into being in a small building in this neighbourhood. In July 2021 the People's Republic of China will mark two historic anniversaries. First, the centenary of CPC's formation and the convening of the First Party Congress. Second, the fiftieth anniversary of a historic reconciliation between the world's most populous communist country and the world's most powerful capitalist country. China's supreme leader and the Great Helmsman, Mao Zedong, was present in that Xintiandi house when the CPC was formed in 1921. Fifty years later he met with the emissary of the president of the United States of America, Henry Kissinger, to redefine China–US relations and the global balance of power.

Ironically, China marks these two anniversaries at a time when the onset of a 'New Cold War' with the US looms large. Even as geopolitical analysts were writing newspaper columns and addressing online webinars recalling the events of 1921 and 1971, the US Secretary of State Anthony Blinken met his Chinese counterpart, State Councillor Wang Yi, in snow-covered Alaska in an icy interaction in which no punches were pulled. In an exchange marked by mutual recrimination, Blinken and Wang traded barbs and charges that prompted several analysts around the world to say that the Alaska meeting was the defining moment of a New Cold War.

Against this background, it is relevant to recall that the 'reset' in the US–China relationship in July 1971 played a vital part in finally bringing to an end the 'Old' Cold War. That Cold War, between the US and the Soviet Union, came to an abrupt end as several parallel political and economic developments of the late 1980s across Europe resulted in the fall of the Berlin Wall and re-unification of Germany, the upheavals in the Soviet and European communist parties and the failure of 'perestroika' in preventing the fallout of 'glasnost'. The US–China reset of 1971 played its own role altering the geopolitical environment within which the Soviets, the European and Asian communists were acting. A China intent on recovering its own national status as a civilizational power, abandoned the principles of communist internationalism and embraced what has euphemistically been dubbed 'socialism with Chinese characteristics'.

The new development path that China pursued under the leadership of Mao's old comrade and detractor, Deng Xiaoping, with the enthusiastic support of the US, enabled it to emerge as the second-most powerful nation today, next only to the US. In seeking to vanquish one challenger, the US sowed the seeds, so to speak, that have since blossomed into a new challenger. China's historic rise, enabled partly by US investment and business opportunity, has created the basis for a New Cold War as Beijing rejects the existing balance of global power and seeks a greater say for itself in Asian and world affairs.

The transformation that China underwent in the first fifty years of the past century was historic and of great significance for its own people. It was globally significant, too, as the ruling Communist Party worked towards enhancing China's economic heft that also allowed it to build a new social contract with the citizens—prosperity in return for political status quo. Beginning with the 'reset' of bilateral relations between China and the US, following Henry Kissinger's July 1971 visit and the subsequent visit of

President Richard Nixon in February 1972, communist China set itself on the path of modernization. Looking back at the Nixon–Kissinger outreach of July 1971 and the reset in the US–China relations over the past half a century, these essays seek to understand the role played by Kissinger, both as a senior US government functionary and as a lobbyist for China in global corridors of power. The essays are divided into two sections: those that examine the global implications of the US–China reset and those that look at this process from the perspective of select countries.

It was in a 1968 speech that he had drafted for Nelson Rockefeller that, says **Teresita Schaffer**, Kissinger first drew attention to the need for a relook at the US policy towards China. The event that prompted this was the border conflict between the Soviet Union and China for it indicated clearly that the 'Sino–Soviet alliance' that the West had taken for granted until then was now coming apart. While the US policymakers had, after 1968, devoted considerable time to thinking about establishing diplomatic relations with the People's Republic, concrete steps in this direction were taken only after Nixon and Kissinger entered office. Schaffer offers a US diplomat's perspective and an interesting peek into Kissinger's preparation for his China visit. In Schaffer's reckoning the US–China equation established in 1972 altered the post-war bipolar balance of power system irrevocably, creating in its place a new tripolar order. Over the years, however, China utilized the space it secured, thanks to US policy towards it, to build itself up and emerge as a stronger power. While Kissinger helped create a tripolar world order out of a bipolar system, a new bipolarity may yet be emerging.

Henry Kissinger belongs to the pantheon of textbook realists in international relations. Paying tribute to his policy oeuvre, the ardent practitioner of realism, **Kishore Mahbubani**, asserts 'the biggest damage done by the abandonment of Kissingerian realist-pragmatism is that the US has become severely weakened both domestically and externally'. Mahbubani views the 1971 moment as one of the US coming to terms with Asian reality and argues that it is presently in denial with respect to China's inevitable rise as a Great Power. Successive US administrations pursued an effective foreign policy as long as Kissingerian 'realist-pragmatism' reigned supreme in Washington, DC. After the end of the Cold War, both hubris and misplaced liberalism took over, contributing to declining US power and influence. Mahbubani believes President Donald Trump not only got China wrong but, by the end of his tenure in office, has left it a stronger power. American liberals, argues Mahbubani, have to come to terms with China's inevitable rise and, to remain globally competitive and in a position to deal with a powerful China, the US must look inwards and invest in the capabilities of its own people and in the institutions and infrastructure needed to build those capabilities.

Kanti Bajpai offers an incisive recounting of the events of 1971 and argues that while Nixon and Kissinger 'kowtowed' to Mao and Zhou, the Chinese duo were more comfortable in their skins and took the new equation in their stride. Bajpai, too, points to the more enduring American fascination with China and warns India that it must keep a watch on any US return to a policy of accommodation with China, preferring to manage the more familiar bipolar world. While Nixon–Kissinger opened up to China, it was the administrations of President Ronald Reagan and Bill Clinton that in fact helped build China up. The US contributed to the modernization not just of the Chinese economy but also its military. The US strategy towards China, suggests Bajpai, was 'carrots for good behaviour' and when that did not work then it was 'more carrots'. Bajpai rejects the Indian view that the world order in the twenty-first century would be characterized by multipolarity. Nor would it be a Chinese century. It would yet again be a bipolar system. The question is whether the US and China would pursue a G-2 condominium or a conflict-ridden bipolarity. Bajpai believes the American elite remain fascinated by China, even if their past indulgences have come home to roost and bedevil the US, and that they have less regard for an India that is still not getting its act together.

Samir Saran and **Kalpit A. Mankikar** situate the Nixon–Kissinger outreach within the context of the longer history of the US–China relations and also see this as the point of departure for China's rise in the twenty-first century. The 'amplification of its comprehensive power', they believe, is a consequence of, among other things, Kissinger's foreign policy principles 'that privileged ends over means'. The 'Nixon Doctrine', as they put it, of outsourcing the fight against communism to regional partners meant that China was no longer in the line of fire, so to speak, as was the Soviet Union until its end. This helped China hide its capacities and bide its time.

While recognizing that the Nixon–Kissinger reset of the US–China relationship was a hugely important development, **Rana Mitter** points to earlier missed opportunities in the 1940s and '50s when this reset could have been done. Kissinger only made up for the lapses of his post-war predecessors who ought to have come to terms with the reality of China's status. However, the economic and political circumstances of the early 1970s were more propitious for a reset. The China of 1972, argues Mitter, was in the 'right state at the right time' for the Kissinger mission to succeed. Grand strategy is important, but it needs economic and political strength and stability to operate. Like many of our other authors, Mitter also believes that the US assumption, most recently articulated by former US secretary of state, Mike Pompeo, that a normalization of relations with China would contribute to a weakening of the communist regime and to China's evolution into a plural democracy was flawed. Whatever the US motivations, Mitter believes Mao's was not to make China a democracy but to make it rich and powerful.

Necessity rather than choice may have motivated the US–China reset of 1971 suggests **Chung Min Lee**, given the US concerns about Soviet assertiveness and the quagmire in Vietnam and China's own internal problems at the time and its external weakness. Nixon and Kissinger dealt with the Soviets at the 'height of their power', says Lee, and with the Chinese at the 'height of their isolation'. Neither imagined at the time that the reset would set in motion the secular rise of China. The reset did, however, provide China with the time and space required for its emergence as a global player and a challenge for the US.

Lee argues that Kissinger may have imagined that the US and China could manage Asia together, but President Xi Jinping has changed the terms of engagement. An assertive China is claiming Asian leadership.

The response to it in the form of a quadrilateral grouping of Australia, India, Japan and the US may help check this. The more the Quadrilateral Security Dialogue or the Quad (the US, India, Japan and Australia) and like-minded partners speak with a united voice, says Lee, and the more clearly they articulate their core interests, the costlier would it become for China to test or antagonize them. The Quad could help China's adversaries win without fighting.

However, the rise of China poses the same security dilemma for Asia that Soviet power posed to Europe—how to deal with a powerful neighbour next door while dealing with the even more powerful but distant friend. The US had long pooh-poohed any talk of collective security in Asia, but has China's rise provided an incentive for other Asian nations to seek collective security? While Europe's security dilemma was resolved by the implosion of the Soviet Union, Asia's is just beginning to manifest and define itself.

Kissinger had famously drawn a distinction between power and legitimacy as defining principles of the status of nation states. The US reset with China in 1971, allowing the People's Republic to claim its chair in the United Nations Security Council, was the final seal of international approval that confirmed the legitimacy that Mao's regime sought, says **Sanjaya Baru**. However, far more significant than this seal of legitimacy was the economic empowerment of China thanks to the supportive US trade and investment policies. Here, too, Kissinger played his part encouraging the Clinton administration to normalize trade relations with China, supporting China's application for membership of the World Trade Organization (WTO) and advising US companies to invest in China. Kissinger Associates Inc. became an influential pro-China lobbyist facilitating Chinese access to US technology, talent and markets, even as US multinationals moved. China's emergence as a trading superpower and the 'factory of the world' has in turn enabled its rise as a global power. If the US faces a China challenge, it is in part a problem of its own making.

Rahul Sharma captures the dramatic sequence of events that led to Kissinger's secret visit to Beijing and poses the question whether Nixon and his successors viewed relations with China in a purely tactical manner, while China's leaders always had a more strategic view of the 1971–72 reset and the subsequent US–China relationship. The 'Kissingerian approach', as Sharma puts it, continued to define the US approach to China through successive administrations, both because his intellectual disciples proliferated in the Washington, DC establishment over the years and because of the influence of business lobbies that benefited from the China relationship. It was not until President Trump declared a trade war and finally identified China as the principal adversary of the US that US analysts began taking a more long-term view of China. Until then it was almost always tactics and business interests that scored over strategic thinking about China. This past, says Sharma, haunts the present. Sharma blames Kissinger, his disciples and generations of their successors for viewing China as a 'status quo power', and enabling China's sustained rise till China's revisionist intentions became all too clear. While Trump succeeded in giving the US a wake-up call on China, the US requires a longer term for strategic thinking, not altered from administration to administration, to deal with China's rise, which will inevitably alter the world order and the global balance of power.

Sujan Chinoy situates the US view of China within the wider context of America's historical fascination with the Middle Kingdom. Kissinger's very European obsession with the Soviet power encouraged him to reach out to China. This diplomatic and economic outreach by Nixon set in motion a process over which the US later lost control, says Chinoy, with vested political and commercial interests driving the US policy towards China. The US has either repeatedly misread China's strategic intentions or has chosen to sacrifice reality on the altar of political expediency and commercial interests. Chinoy faults the US for not standing firm in its support for Tibetan autonomy or Taiwan's freedom. While complimenting President Trump for demonstrating greater resolve in dealing with China, Chinoy wonders how committed President Joseph Biden would be in his resolve to confront Chinese assertiveness.

Frédéric Grare questions the view that Kissinger and Nixon's visit to China in 1971 and 1972 helped unleash China's phenomenal rise, contributing to its perceived emergence as a threat to the existing world order. Indeed, says Grare, China was already seen as a potential threat by some of its neighbours at the time of the US–China reconciliation. Also true that the reconciliation itself added to China's heft. However, Grare rejects the hypothesis that the subsequent rise of China was a consequence of the Nixon/Kissinger's diplomacy. It is not 'Mao's China' that has challenged the US. It in fact enabled the US to emerge stronger with the division of the communist bloc. The US has been challenged by Deng Xiaoping's China and that is thanks to the accommodative stance pursued by President Bill Clinton.

Going beyond the geopolitical and geo-economic analysis of the US–China reset of 1971 and its global consequences, these essays also offer a range of country perspectives on what the US–China reset meant for different countries around the world. We present perspectives from Australia, France, India, Japan, Pakistan, Russia, Singapore and the United Kingdom.

The country that triggered the desire for a reset of the US–China equation was the Soviet Union. Today Russia's new equation with China has come to define the thinking about a New Cold War. **Igor Yurgens** offers a Russian perspective not just on the events leading to the 1971 moment but also on its consequences. The rising geopolitical clout and military power of a nuclearized Soviet Union in the 1960s on the one hand, and growing Sino–Soviet rivalry on the other, were without doubt the factors that spurred the US outreach to China. Yurgens does not credit Kissinger with any originality in strategic thinking given that the US was merely using the tested principle of making an enemy's enemy a friend. Yurgens believes Vietnam was very much on Nixon and Kissinger's mind; but while the US succeeded in splitting the Sino–Soviet axis, it failed to win the war. China, on the other hand, secured the US assurances on Taiwan which were more tangible.

Yurgens records the movements of the pendulum in the China–Soviet Union/Russia–US triangle, concluding that while the US got the better of the two in the 1970s, the pendulum has swung the other way with the Xi–Putin China–Russia alliance posing a challenge to the US. Yurgens suggests that Kissinger's strategic calculations of the 1970s may well have been upset by the implosion of the Soviet Union and the Tiananmen Square incidents. Yurgens is not optimistic about the prospects for a new global balance of power that would ensure geopolitical stability and peace, and hopes a latter-day Kissinger will come forward with some ideas to avert conflict between an East strengthened by 'a dynamic mix of autocracy, technocracy and nationalism' and a West weakened by 'the loss of common purpose'.

If the Soviets were the proximate cause for the US–China reset, it was Pakistan that made the most of it, having been preferred over European options as the intermediary that facilitated Kissinger's secret visit. Pakistan, says **Ayesha Siddiqa**, has tried to benefit from its relations with both powers, developing a closer and a more strategic equation with China. From bridging the gap between Washington, DC and Beijing in the early 1970s to sharing Western technology with China during the 1980s and developing a defence-industrial partnership, Siddiqa suggests that Pakistan and China have bolstered each other's strategic capacity and advantage. This two-way connection with China makes this bilateral equation fundamentally different from Pakistan's relations with the US. Nonetheless, concludes Siddiqa, Pakistan's key interest remains in maintaining ties with both powers and avoiding any collision between the two big powers that would impose a cost on Pakistan.

Bill Emmott takes the straightforward view that in establishing diplomatic ties with the People's Republic in 1972, the US was only catching up with history. Britain, India and many other nations had come to terms with reality long before the US. Why was Britain quick to recognize PRC? Emmott attributes it to the role of British interests in Hong Kong and to the fact that for over a century Britain had acquired Asia-wide interests that it now sought to protect, recognizing the potential importance of China to the preservation of her Asian interests. Emmott also points to more clear-headed strategic thinking in London compared to Washington, DC. He reminds us that Winston Churchill had taken the view at the time that 'the natural thing for all western powers to have done would have been to recognise the new government, not as a compliment but as a convenience'. Why then did the US hold back till the 1970s? Emmott offers three hypotheses: the power of anti-communist ideology; policy inertia born out of the lazy thinking of vested interests; and the fact that non-recognition of PRC in 1950 imposed few costs on the US, and the US was not as concerned about the costs this might have imposed on allies like Britain and Japan. When maintaining the fiction that Taiwan was China had become counter-productive, Nixon took the logical next step.

The country most directly and immediately impacted by the US–China reset was Japan. **Tsutomu Kikuchi** delves into China's impact on Japan's foreign policy. Japan was acutely embarrassed when it was informed only at the eleventh hour about Nixon's visit to China. For Tokyo, it meant the US didn't recognize Japan as a major player in power politics. However, Japan also saw it as an opportunity to normalize its own relations with China and work around the past historical baggage between the two nations—building an economic and business bridge that helped both. The Nixon Doctrine highlighted the importance of Japan's role in Asia's peaceful development. Japan, as we know, has supported China's economic reforms and helped it adjust smoothly in the international community. However, there is a past—the humiliation of history—that still sits between the two neighbours, triggering fears in Japan that China might want to redeem itself now that it is a major power. Kikuchi looks at how Japan could handle a China that is fast becoming aggressive and assertive. How does it address the larger concerns about the future of the Indo-Pacific region?

It has been long since China shed its 'hide and bide' policy and began pushing and executing its strategic and economic expansion. The transition from Deng Xiaoping's worldview to Xi Jinping's idea of China's place in the world has brought about a dynamic change in Beijing's global outlook. It has also proven that China considers itself to be more powerful than it might seem to the rest of the world. **Peter Varghese** analyses this adjustment in Chinese framework through an Australian lens, as Beijing's engagement with Canberra reshapes rules of the strategic culture in the Indo-Pacific region. China, an authoritarian one-party state, has made its rise less peaceful and more about exhibiting the price that needs to be paid by nations that cross its path. Varghese discusses the rigidity in China's trajectory and how that makes it difficult for Beijing to get allies. He goes on to dissect how the aggregate weight of the Quad will always be superior to China. Australia isn't stuck on maintaining a hold on strategic primacy like the US, so could it make peace with China? Decoupling from its largest trading partner seems impossible but trade diversification is a worthy policy objective for Australia.

The world begins to look very different when two adversaries join hands, but decades later again become one another's primary strategic competitors. Was the Sino–American rapprochement sparked by Kissinger–Nixon America's greatest geopolitical folly? **Hoo Tiang Boon** and **Quah Say Jye** write about the contemporary relevance of this historic visit to Southeast Asia. The communist flagbearer in this region was China and Mao's foreign policy centred on the desire for China to be the base of communist revolution in Asia. Ethnic factors too coloured the relationship between China and other Southeast Asian nations. The antagonism between China and the Soviet Union in the 1960s compelled Beijing to consider Moscow a principal security threat instead of the US. Boon explores the power calculus of the region, which is in constant tension with China—fearful of its military and economic might and unable to build trust, given past history. All Southeast Asian nations have had a good ride on the Chinese growth train, deepening linkages and prospering as they built their own economies. However, as it becomes clear that China is unlikely to make an ideological shift many hoped for, none of them is sure whether they can count on China, which is now flexing both its economic and military muscle.

The rapprochement with China was not only crucial for strategic reasons, but also for Nixon's re-election prospects. **Tanvi Madan** discusses the geopolitical complexities that made Nixon deeply consider the global impact of developments around India as he fine-tuned his China policy at the peak of the Cold War. The US considered friendship with China would improve its chances for a better deal with the Soviet Union and also in managing the Vietnam War that was getting out of hand. There were other questions too. Would it be possible to discourage the Soviet Union from hitting out at China when the engagement became public knowledge? Should Beijing make military moves against India on Pakistan's behalf?

Madan assesses the public proclamations and secret diplomacy in the US policy towards China. In 1971, the US objective was to maintain Pakistan's goodwill to preserve the channel to Peking. She analyses the formation of Bangladesh and the US–China role in it. This tilt towards Pakistan resulted in India leaning towards the Soviet Union and the signing of the India–Soviet peace treaty. America's approach in 1971 even helped erase memories of the US aid to India during the 1962 Chinese War. Indian policymakers learnt that it was important to diversify strategic relationships in the larger interest of national security.

The US outreach to China altered India's geopolitical environment dramatically. **C. Raja Mohan** explores India's adaptation to the challenges presented by Henry Kissinger's visit to China in 1971. India's first Prime Minister Jawaharlal Nehru and Sardar Patel had differences over assessing China's character. The tension between Nehru's 'Asianism' and the legacy of the Raj realpolitik only exacerbated the discord in India's ideological scaffolding between the East and the West. Raja Mohan goes on to assess the various factors that weakened India's role in geopolitics in the 1970s. Kissinger's visit to India in 1974 provided means to rebuild the Indo–US relationship post the bitterness of 1971 and the stiff US reaction to India's nuclear tests. Indira Gandhi, who returned to power in 1980, reached out to the US, Europe and China to diversify India's foreign and security policies. Despite that, the engagement with the West remained tentative and hesitant. The end of the Cold War and India's rapid economic growth enabled geopolitical restructuring. Successive Indian leaders invested a lot of capital and time in strengthening diplomatic relations with the US. Still, India finds itself in a tricky spot as Washington, DC looks for its support to contain China and New Delhi seeks to maintain its relations with Russia. India's challenge is to find its place in the world given the constant shifts in great power politics.

South Asia as a whole also felt the impact of the US–China reset and, more specifically, of the US decision to use Pakistan as a conduit in its outreach to China. **Suhasini Haidar** analyses the shifting power dynamics in Pakistan in the 1970s, the political environment in India and the 1971 Indo–Pakistan war that led to the birth of Bangladesh. Haidar also assesses the tumultuous events in the rest of South Asia, such as Bhutan's entry into the United Nations, the renegotiation of the trade and transit treaty with Nepal, and the emergence of Bangladesh. Five decades later, how do Indo–Pak ties compare with the US–China relations pre-1971? How different could South Asia have been if the US had used Romania as the conduit, and not Pakistan? Kissinger once termed Indians as 'the most aggressive goddamn people around [South Asia]'. However, the shift from India's once heavy influence in its South Asian neighbourhood to China's current pole position has changed the region. China's clear strategy to openly interfere in matters of other countries has altered the stakes dramatically.

It is clear from a reading of recent history that the US–China reset of 1971 was historic and has left its imprint on international relations, the global balance of power and the destiny of many nations over the subsequent half century. Equally, it would seem, the recent deterioration in their bilateral relationship and the resumption of Great Power competition would have global implications. Given the nature of this moment, with the world at the threshold of a New Cold War, it is relevant and instructive to look back at the impact of the 1971 reset. How the US and China manage their bilateral relations and their relations with other major powers will define the course of history in the coming decades. This is a good moment, therefore, to ponder over the lessons of history over the past half century that this collection of essays draws attention to.

Sanjaya Baru and Rahul Sharma

GEOPOLITICAL & GEO-ECONOMIC PERSPECTIVES

1

Kissinger and China

Strategy, Diplomacy, and the World Order

TERESITA C. SCHAFFER

WHEN RICHARD NIXON APPOINTED DR Henry Kissinger as his national security advisor in 1969, the main reaction was 'What an interesting choice!' He was a refugee from Nazi Germany, a dyed-in-the-wool intellectual, a Harvard professor whose PhD dissertation focused on the world order that followed the Congress of Vienna. At a time when American politics were roiled by a land war in Asia, his background led people to assume he would follow a strategy focused on Europe and the transatlantic scene. But the area where he helped give birth to a new world order was China.

The Backdrop

Kissinger came to Washington with a clear view of what was desirable in a world order. The goal, most of the time, was stability. The configuration most likely to produce that, he had argued, was a balance of power, preferably a triangle, with broadly comparable levels of power among three parties. And yet since the mid-seventeenth century, he wrote, only two arrangements had been known for their stability: the Concert of

Europe, which arose out of the Congress of Vienna in 1815; and the liberal international order that followed World War II. But neither was a classic balance of power. The former had too many players; the latter had two superpowers, and no plausible 'balancers'.[1]

Kissinger also had well-documented convictions about what ought to drive a nation's foreign policy, which he spelled out most clearly some years later in *Diplomacy*. National interests and the major features of national geography came in the first place. But even this student of Metternich acknowledged that in the case of the US, a third factor had to be included: some measure of idealism. He looked on Theodore Roosevelt as the ultimate American realist, and on Woodrow Wilson as the exemplar of messianic US foreign policy. Theodore Roosevelt and others had implemented realist policies. However, without something to respond to the idealism in the US collective ethos, he argued, foreign policy would not command the popular support needed in a democracy.[2]

Unsurprisingly, Vietnam and the doomsday potential of US–Soviet relations occupied him most intently when he took up his position as national security advisor. But close observers might have noticed his attention already on China. Kissinger had mentioned the importance of a dialogue with China in a 1968 campaign speech he had drafted for Nelson Rockefeller.[3] Before Kissinger had finished three months in the White House, Soviet–Chinese military clashes along the Ussuri river provided an early indication that the cracks in the 'Sino–Soviet bloc', as it was often known in those days, might be serious. As more intelligence came in, it became apparent that the Soviet military had built its forces all along the border, strongly suggesting that a crisis was imminent.[4]

Kissinger pinpoints this as the moment when both he and Nixon started thinking seriously about an overture to China, taking up the opportunity created by this manifestation of Sino–Soviet mutual hostility. Working up to a relationship with China would be advantageous to the US. It might also provide a chance to achieve the stability offered by a triangular balance of power. Since the post-World War II order was set up, the distribution of global power had shifted so that the US by itself could neither withdraw from the world nor dominate it.[5] Balancing was now possible.

The opening

The story of Kissinger's trip to Beijing via a feigned intestinal flu in Pakistan is well-known—and the stuff of legend. His memoirs describe in elaborate detail the cloak-and-dagger manoeuvres involved in opening communications. Kissinger was famous among those who worked on US foreign policy during his time for his love of secrecy.

The opening actually began more conventionally, with messages buried in what must have been achingly familiar talking points for scheduled formal meetings between the US and Chinese ambassadors in Warsaw. For fifteen years and 134 meetings, this dialogue had been the only official communications channel between China and the US. Until that point, its main accomplishment was that it existed. The actual content of the meetings went through a complicated bureaucratic clearance process in Washington, and they were not intended to make news. The same was presumably true in Beijing.

In early 1970, a new message was passed: the US ambassador was instructed to raise the possibility of a US envoy visiting Beijing. This message and the careful but encouraging Chinese reply were reinforced by messages between the US and Chinese governments, hand-delivered to Kissinger by the Pakistan ambassador in Washington. A few months later, the US incursion into Cambodia sparked international outrage—and led the Chinese to cancel the Warsaw talks. This was 'providential', to quote Kissinger. It enabled Kissinger to use his channel through Pakistan into the sole means of high-level communication between China and the US. Plenty of room to innovate—and no bothersome bureaucratic clearances.[6]

From that point on, things moved relatively quickly. The last piece to fall into place was formally naming Kissinger as President Nixon's special envoy in May 1971. His formal invitation to visit Beijing arrived in June, once again hand-delivered by the Pakistan ambassador. Kissinger handed it to Nixon, calling it the 'most important communication that has come to an American president since the end of World War II'.[7] Kissinger now had his triangle: China would be the third participant in a balance of power that already included the US and the Soviet Union.

Thus far, China had primarily been a valuable piece on Kissinger's strategic chessboard. Starting in early 1970, Kissinger began reading up on China, consulting academics, commissioning studies from experts inside the US government, and starting to think about China as a country rather than a chess piece.[8] His fascination with China and its leaders grew with his increasing contact with them.

Kissinger's pathbreaking secret visit to Beijing took place in July 1971. The announcement of Kissinger's mission a few days later dominated the news. Two events in late 1971, before Nixon's visit to Beijing, made clear how far-reaching the resulting changes were. The first was the annual debate in the United Nations over who should represent China there. The Republic of China, or Taiwan, had held the China seat since the beginning of the United Nations, and the yearly vote count had been sliding slowly towards the People's Republic. The critical vote for the 1971 debate was scheduled for 25 October. The US had been pushing a compromise solution that would bring the PRC into the world body without expelling Taiwan. As the US government had anticipated, neither Beijing nor Taipei was willing to accept that. A further coincidence, and an embarrassment to the officials assigned to push for the 'ChiRep' resolution (including Taiwan's retention), was that as the vote took place, Kissinger was once again in Beijing, advancing Nixon's visit. The vote to bring in Beijing and expel Taiwan was overwhelming.

The second incident came to public view only some years later. On 10 December, as India and Pakistan were a week into a war that would eventually conclude with the former East Pakistan becoming the independent Bangladesh, Kissinger met in New York with the Chinese ambassador to the United Nations. His message was startling: 'If the People's Republic were to consider the situation on the Indian subcontinent a threat to its security . . . [the US] would oppose efforts of others to interfere with the People's Republic.' The Chinese took no action, but certainly registered that the US was prepared to act as China's quasi-ally, and to do this in the face of incontrovertible evidence that the Pakistan army had conducted a genocidal massacre in their Eastern wing.[9]

Finding the 'new normal'

Nixon's visit to Beijing in February 1972 ratified and formalized what the two countries had accomplished: the end of the bipolar division of the world. Television coverage brought the glamour and majesty of the visit home to the American public—the visit to the Great Wall and other memorable sites, the spectacular banquet, and the encounters with Zhou and Mao. The State Department members of the visiting delegation handled the litany of issues from decades of Cold War. By Kissinger's account, the president's top-level meetings, especially with Zhou, focused on the global balance of power and the emerging international order.

The concluding document, the Shanghai Communiqué, summarized the basis for relations between the US and China. Each side stated its position on the most neuralgic bilateral issues, including Taiwan, and on Asian security issues. They pledged to implement scientific and educational exchanges and undertook to open trade. They agreed to move towards establishing full diplomatic relations, to avoid international conflict and not to seek hegemony.[10] It also started the process of building the emerging world order. Kissinger made six more visits to Beijing, deepening the strategic dialogue and preparing for eventual normalization.

In 1973, both sides set up 'liaison offices' in each other's capitals, charged with handling the US–China relations. These were 'non-embassies', embassies in all but name. The US liaison office was headed by a galaxy of prominent people, including David Bruce, long-time US ambassador to Britain; George H.W. Bush; and the former president of the United Auto Workers, Leonard Woodcock. Six years later, the US formally recognized the People's Republic and established diplomatic relations with it. By that time, Jimmy Carter was president, and Woodcock negotiated the agreement on opening diplomatic relations. It required the US to break off diplomatic relations with Taiwan, terminate the mutual defence treaty with Taiwan, and withdraw the US military personnel from the island. The US and Taiwan established private institutions to carry out their 'non-official' relations. The US office was called the American Institute in Taiwan (AIT).

Two episodes illustrate how this process affected relatively junior officials in Washington. The first is the elaborate structure of rules governing the relations between the US and Taiwan. Most of the staff of AIT were drawn from the US Foreign Service. In deference to the unofficial character of the office, they were required to submit a technical resignation when they were assigned to Taipei. This would then be rescinded when they finished their assignment. Some of the special arrangements for AIT were much more convenient than the conventional ones. Most embassies, for example, have to thread their way through three different appropriations when they spend official money; Taiwan got all its funding in one pot. There was a whole vocabulary that was required (or forbidden) for dealing with Taiwan, starting with no references to 'government', or 'official'. The US government officials travelling there on business were forbidden to travel on diplomatic or official passports. When I travelled to Taiwan in 1980 as part of a trade negotiating delegation, I was told to apply for a non-diplomatic passport. On the application form, I was not to give my occupation as 'Foreign Service officer' or even 'US government employee'. I was simply an 'economist'. I was also cautioned not to claim the passport fee on my travel voucher. However, the State Department lawyer who was the ultimate authority on Taiwan vocabulary told me, 'You can submit a fake taxi voucher in the same amount.' The opening of relations and the Shanghai Communiqué were high strategy. By the time the implementing regulations had been written further down the bureaucratic food chain, it seemed more like *Alice's Adventures in Wonderland*. One of the early heads of AIT, Ambassador Charles T. Cross, told me that despite its unofficial character, this assignment was 'the most diplomatic job I ever had'.

About two years later, the textile industry in the US petitioned the Commerce Department to impose countervailing duties on Chinese-made textiles, arguing that China's multiple exchange rate system amounted to a prohibited export subsidy. The US system for adjudicating such petitions involves an elaborate process of computing the unsubsidized price, and the regulations prohibited the Commerce Department from taking foreign policy considerations into account. So, the Commerce Department, with clearances from half a dozen other agencies, instructed the US embassy in Beijing to distribute a questionnaire to the major textile exporters, asking them for the details of their cost structure. Unsurprisingly, the Chinese foreign ministry took umbrage at this intrusive procedure. When the US embassy explained that the Commerce Department was prohibited from treating this like a foreign policy issue, the Chinese government in effect said, 'That is YOUR problem.' Thus were the Chinese textile industry and the Chinese government introduced to the inscrutable ways of the US bureaucracy.

Kissinger's approach to diplomacy

Strategy and policy are what one does to advance one's country's interests. Diplomacy is how one does it. Achieving an objective requires both the 'what' and the 'how'.

Kissinger was clearly more intellectually interested in strategy than in diplomacy, but recognized that he needed both. In writing about his opening to China, he spelled out his strategic thinking but devoted far more space to the details of his diplomacy. This involved not only the special communications channels but also his thinking about how best to make sure that his Chinese interlocutors accurately heard the message he was trying to transmit. His memoirs reflect at length on the subtlety of Zhou Enlai. Forty years after his first visit, Kissinger wrote a lengthy book about China.[11] His analysis of Chinese culture and history is regarded as a bit facile by China scholars, but his personal contact with Chinese leaders, starting with Zhou, engaged him deeply. These are the most basic elements in diplomatic tradecraft, and the time he spent reading up on China before his first trip was a critical investment in his success.

Kissinger was much admired, but not as much loved, by the US Foreign Service.[12] By all accounts, he was frustrated with many of his diplomatic subordinates. According to one story that was widely repeated in Foreign Service circles, Secretary Kissinger was chatting at the end of a long day on a visit to a large US embassy with the senior diplomats assigned there and asked them what they thought about relations with the Soviet Union. No one wanted to answer the question; they explained that they were not Soviet specialists. Kissinger was shocked at what seemed to him like a scandalous lack of strategic thinking. That was a reasonable criticism, but it also reflected their fear of saying something wrong in the presence of the secretary of state, especially one with a reputation for blackballing those who crossed him. Foreign Service officers are known to be risk averse.

There is an irony here. From Kissinger's perspective, career diplomats spent too much time becoming experts on a narrow slice of their country's foreign relations and were too focused on other individual countries. And yet, when one looks at Kissinger's diplomatic accomplishments—not just the opening to China, but also his negotiations in the Middle East—he relied heavily on members of his team who possessed precisely this kind of granular, focused expertise on the countries they were dealing with. Kissinger prided himself on his understanding of China, but his knowledge owed much to the members of the team that worked with him at the NSC, some of them Foreign Service China experts, in particular John Holdridge. Similarly, in Kissinger's Middle East negotiations, he leaned heavily on Hal Saunders's encyclopaedic knowledge of the countries involved. Saunders was a career civil service officer and a professional icon to Foreign Service officers who worked with him.

The opening to China also illustrates one important point Kissinger has in common with the diplomats who worked for him. Career diplomats believe in communication. They want to have diplomatic relations with others; they want to understand those with whom they share the world. They tend to dislike sanctions, precisely because they so often cut off communication.

Forty years on: US–China relations

The 'new normal' that the US and China developed in the 1970s and '80s reflected their experience of the opening of relations. It also reflected the changing power relationships within the 'balance of power triangle'. The Soviet Union broke apart and Russia's economy stagnated, while China became an economic powerhouse. At the turn of the century, the main issues between Moscow and Washington remained security and military ones. After Vladimir Putin came to power, his determination to recreate Russia's old sphere of influence led to troubled relations with Washington and somewhat warmer ones with Beijing. The geometry of Kissinger's triangle was under strain.

Meanwhile, the events at Tiananmen Square in 1989 delivered a shock to US–China relations. But it soon became apparent that many of the most active issues on the US–China agenda were economic. The Chinese economy surged ahead, especially after 2000.[13] China joined the World Bank and the International Monetary Fund in 1980, a decade before Russia. China's export-led growth made it the largest trade partner for the US and also an important one for Japan and the countries of Western Europe. China's accession to the WTO in 2001 was greeted at that time with the hope that its integration into global supply chains and trade rules would encourage China to become a 'responsible stakeholder'.

Two decades later, there is a darker assessment. After four decades of astonishing growth and twenty years of membership in the WTO, China had become increasingly willing to bend global trade rules to its own benefit. Despite an economic slowdown, China now has the second-largest GDP in the world. As the world discovered during the COVID-19 pandemic, China is at the heart of many global supply chains, and countries around the globe are struggling to diversify their sources of inputs for a variety of manufactured goods, notably those connected with dealing with pandemic illness. The Trump administration launched a trade war with China. Few considered it unwarranted. Rather, those who objected to this move complained about the in-your-face style and the absence of any US effort to make common cause with other countries affected by Chinese competition. It is not clear that this move has resolved the problems facing the US economy.

Whither the world order?

Where does this leave the global order to which Kissinger's opening to China gave birth? The basic model is still the triangular balance of power that Kissinger envisaged. Russia and China were always asymmetrical, but today, China's economic power greatly exceeds Russia's. The US and China are both economic and, potentially, military rivals; at the same time, they are major trade partners, with complex links tying them together through global supply chains. This remains true despite the Trump administration's trade war.

Another arena in the US–China rivalry is the regional politics in the Indo-Pacific area. Both countries are stepping up their activities—not only military, but also their commercial presence—in Southeast Asia. The US policy prioritizing its economic and security relations throughout the Indo-Pacific started during the Obama administration and continued into President Trump's presidency. China has made cartographic claims in the South China Sea, has displayed its unhappiness with Australia by cutting off certain exports and imports, and has ramped up its presence in the Indian Ocean. In August 2020, a faceoff in a previously peaceful part of the disputed India–China border left some twenty Indian soldiers dead. Talks are taking place, but the Indians are seriously concerned by what they believe is a Chinese effort to 'create new facts'. And the tone of Chinese public statements seems to have become more strident, in what some are calling 'wolf warrior diplomacy'.

Kissinger's 1970s-vintage triangular diplomacy had played out against the background of a military build-up at the Soviet–Chinese border, and involved the US enticing China to distance itself further from the Soviet Union. So far, although Russo–Chinese relations have improved, there is little evidence of the two countries making common cause against the US. What is clearly going on, however, is Sino–American competition for close ties with the countries of Southeast Asia. None of those countries wants to be the object of competition, but neither do they wish to alienate either China or the US. The maintenance of the standing the US has enjoyed in the Indo-Pacific since the end of World War II is more vulnerable now than it has been for years. Either a Russo–Chinese alliance against the US or a determined Chinese move to cut the US down to size in Southeast Asia would call to mind the statement attributed to Mark Twain: 'History doesn't repeat itself, but it often rhymes.'

Did Kissinger bring about the rise of China?

Kissinger will probably be remembered more for his opening to China than for any of his other diplomatic exploits. Does this mean that Kissinger caused the rise of China? His overture to China created circumstances that made China's rise more likely. But I would look inside China for the factors that so fundamentally changed the country's course.

When Kissinger first began his correspondence with the Chinese government, it had extraordinary leadership, big ambitions, and a long-term time horizon. China made the fundamental decisions that turned an opportunity into a change in the country's trajectory. The Chinese gave priority to economic growth. In another historical irony, they used the institutions that represented the 'liberal international order' to create internal incentives for growth. This changed the behaviour of economic actors in China and of the Chinese government, building the Chinese economic machine into a juggernaut. Contrary to what the stewards of US policy had hoped, however, it did not lead the Chinese government to give up the control they had of the population and economic activity. Those more steeped in Chinese history can assess better than me whether the government had made an implicit deal that China's people would accept subjugation if they could count on being more prosperous, or whether there was some other logic at work. The expanding economy also made it easier for China to expand its military, to develop a larger footprint in international organizations, and otherwise to expand its power.

Kissinger did, however, complete the work on the world order that he started as a PhD student. He brought about a new balance of power. But like other world orders before it, it did not last forever.

2

Evil Liberalism versus Moral Pragmatism

KISHORE MAHBUBANI

MAX WEBER MADE MANY WISE and profound statements. One of his most important ones was: 'It is not true that good can only follow from good and evil only from evil, but that often the opposite is true. Anyone who says this is, indeed, a political infant.'[1] He said this in 1919. Yet the remarkable prescience of his statement was confirmed by what happened when American liberalism dominated US foreign policy after the end of the Cold War.

The year 2021 marks the fiftieth anniversary of Kissinger's famous visit to China in July 1971. It also marks, more or less, the thirtieth anniversary of the end of the Cold War. With some risk of being accused of over-simplification, one can say in the twenty years after Kissinger's visit to China, US foreign policy was guided by the philosophy of realist pragmatism. By contrast, in the thirty years after the end of the Cold War, it was guided by the philosophy of liberal idealism. And the results are clear. Realist pragmatism delivered the greatest victory of American foreign policy: a victory over the mighty Soviet Union without the US firing a shot at Soviet armed forces. By contrast, the past thirty years have generated a lot of evil. Anyone who doubts this claim should consider the following facts: the US has wasted $5.1 trillion fighting post-9/11 wars.

In the fifteen years between 2004 and 2019, the US Air Force dropped 175,842 bombs on several countries, according to US Air Forces Central Command![2] Bombs dropped from the air are often not accurate. Hence, many innocent people were killed. The Brown University Watsons Institute's Cost of War Project estimates total casualties from all post-9/11 wars at 770,000 to 801,000 casualties.[3] The results are clear: when ethical do-gooders take over the US foreign policy, evil is generated: $5.1 trillion wasted; almost 800,000 lives lost.

Yet, the biggest damage done by the abandonment of Kissingerian realist pragmatism is that the US has become severely weakened both domestically and externally. Internally, the thirty-year period of liberal-idealist domination of the US foreign policy has coincided with a thirty-year period of stagnation of working-class incomes. Externally, the US literally fell asleep at the wheel while China rose dramatically. In 1980, in purchasing power parity (PPP) terms, China's gross national product (GNP) was 10 per cent of that of the US. By 2014, it had become bigger. Now there is no doubt that the biggest foreign policy challenge the US faces in the next three decades is China.

So, how should the US manage China? The main argument of this essay is that the US needs to engage in deep reflection on what went drastically wrong in the past thirty years. After reflection, the answer will become clear. The US made a major mistake in abandoning realist pragmatism and switching to liberal idealism. A return to Kissingerian realist pragmatism would be the best way to manage a rising China, as I document in *Has China Won?*

This essay will make this argument in five parts. In part 1, it will briefly try to elucidate the key concepts of realist pragmatism and liberal idealism, while emphasizing that they represent two ends of a spectrum, with no sharp divide between them in practice. Part 2 will discuss how realist pragmatism led to the eventual victory of the Cold War. Part 3 will discuss the dismal record of the liberal-idealist era. Part 4 will briefly discuss the Trump administration, only to point out the fallacy of the claim that the one right thing Trump did was to stand up to China. He strengthened China, instead of weakening it. Part 5 will explain how, going forward, it would be wiser for the US to return to the policies of realist pragmatism to manage the rise of China and the new major challenges the US faces both domestically and externally.

1. Realist pragmatism versus liberal idealism

Kissinger's highly celebrated 'secret' visit to Beijing in July 1971 is widely and justifiably regarded as a major move that swung the 'correlation of forces' in America's favour and led to the ultimate victory over the Soviet Union. What was remarkable about the widespread applause that this visit received, including from *The New York Times* and *The Washington Post*, is that so few Americans mentioned that the US was embracing a regime in China led by Mao Zedong, which had only recently created havoc in the country, leading to enormous human pain and suffering through the disastrous policies of the Great Leap Forward (1958–61) and the Cultural Revolution (1966–76).

In short, human rights were a secondary consideration when realist pragmatism reigned. Indeed, at the International Conference on Kampuchea of 13–17 July 1981, the US delegation, led by Alexander Haig, actually supported China against the ASEAN countries, when China said that the Khmer Rouge should be allowed to return to power in Phnom Penh after the Vietnamese withdrawal. I was personally present and shocked when this happened. Yet the same Reagan administration, in a more 'liberal' move, supported the removal of the dictator Marcos from the Philippines. In short, even in the realist-pragmatic era, there were liberal elements.

Kissinger wasn't the only major figure advocating realist pragmatism. Other major thinkers of that era did so, including George Kennan and Zbigniew Brzezinski. While George Kennan is often associated with the harsh policy of 'containment' of the Soviet Union, John Mearshimer reminds us in his introduction of George Kennan's book on US diplomacy that Kennan was a shrewd and sophisticated thinker.[4] Here are some key pieces of advice Kennan offered. Firstly, he emphasized that the outcome of the Cold War would not be determined by the size of their respective armed forces. Instead, it would depend on the 'spiritual vitality' of their domestic societies. This is what he had said: 'It is rather a question of the degree to which the US can create among the peoples of the world generally the impression of a country which knows what it wants, which is coping successfully with the problems of its internal life and with the responsibilities of a World Power, and which has a spiritual vitality capable of holding its own among the major ideological currents of the time.' He also called for 'greater humility in our national outlook.' According to John Mearsheimer, his call for humility was in response to a strong claim made by then Secretary of State Madeleine Albright in February 1998, when she had said, 'If we have to use force, it is because we are America; we are the indispensable nation. We stand tall and we see further than other countries into the future, and we see the danger here to all of us.'[5]

George Kennan lived to the ripe old age of 101 and died in 2005. Hence, he lived through the first fifteen years of the post-Cold War era. Significantly, he also disapproved of the many key moves when the US switched from realist pragmatism to liberal idealism. He disapproved of the expansion of NATO into the former Soviet bloc. Kennan also disapproved of the invasion of Iraq.

Dick Cheney confidently asserted that US troops would be welcomed in Iraq. He said, 'I really do believe that we will be greeted as liberators.' John Mearsheimer observes that in contrast to such beliefs that the US was morally superior, Kennan did not believe that the US was more virtuous in any meaningful way. Indeed, Kennan observed that Americans were suffering from 'delusions of superiority'.[6] Kennan strongly argued against the US taking a 'paternalistic responsibility to anyone, be it even in the form of military occupation'.

Many of the points raised in this section will be disputed. Yet, there is no doubt that the policies of restraint and pragmatism, advocated by people like Kissinger and Kennan in the Cold War era, contrast significantly with the liberal idealism of the post-Cold War era, as demonstrated by the statement of Democrats like Secretary Madeleine Albright and Republicans like George W. Bush. These contrasting approaches also explain the success of the Cold War era and the failures of the post-Cold War era.

2. Cold War realist pragmatism

Why did the US win the Cold War against the Soviet Union? Hundreds of books have been written on this, with a lot of attention paid to America's technological prowess (by, for example, sending a man to the moon) and superior military capabilities. Yet, the most important statistic that explains America's success is a simple one: the per capita income of all Americans went up 2.25 per cent per year from 1950 to 1980.

As indicated in the famous remarks by George Kennan that the outcome of the Cold War would be determined by the relative 'spiritual vitality', not military prowess of the US and the USSR. The post-World War II presidents focused their attention on improving the livelihoods of the American people. Eisenhower was known as a war hero. Yet it was he who famously warned, 'Every gun that is made, every warship launched, every rocket fired signifies, in the final sense, a theft from those who hunger and are not fed, those who are cold and are not clothed.' Similarly, when Nixon and Krushchev had their famous 'kitchen debate' in 1959, they didn't debate about who would build better rockets or aircraft carriers. Instead, they debated over which society would do a better job at improving the living standards of its people. There is no doubt that the US won this race handsomely. The living standards of the American middle class were the envy of the world. In the 1970s, even though the Soviet Union was a closed society, a famous French academic, Emmanuel Todd, wrote a prescient book in 1976, *The Final Fall: An Essay on the Decomposition of the Soviet Sphere*, based on data about the fertility and infant mortality rates in the Soviet Union. Fertility rates were declining. Infant mortality rates rose. Alcoholism was rampant. More families were broken. (Note: please see part 3 below. Similar indicators of social deterioration emerged in the US after the end of the Cold War.)

While superior American economic productivity and rising living standards were the key reasons why the US won the Cold War, they were also accompanied by military restraint, especially after the US lost the Vietnam War in 1975. Indeed, with a few minor exceptions, like the invasion of Grenada in 1983 and the bombing of Gaddafi's home in Libya in 1986, the US military was rarely used in the period 1975 to 1990. Instead, the US equipped proxies in war theatres like Cambodia and Afghanistan. Here's one useful statistic to demonstrate relative US military restraint. From 1975 to 1990, the US Air Force hardly dropped any bombs on other countries. By contrast, as mentioned earlier, the US Air Force dropped over 175,000 bombs in the fifteen-year period from 2004 to 2019, proving again that realist pragmatism causes less harm since it kills fewer innocent people than liberal idealism.

One historical study worth carrying out would be to study the mindsets of key foreign policy figures in the Cold War era (of people like Henry Kissinger, Zbigniew Brzezinski, George Schultz and James Baker), with their successors in the post-Cold War era (of people like Madeleine Albright, Dick Cheney, Donald Rumsfeld and Condoleezza Rice). Partly because of its fears of the Soviet Union, the US acted with relative restraint. Hence, when democratic revolutions broke out in Hungary in 1956 and Czechoslovakia in 1968, no major US foreign policy figure recommended that the US should get involved. By contrast, when similar democratic revolutions emerged in Ukraine and Syria in 2014, the US felt an obligation and got involved. Sadly, as will be documented in the next section, these US involvements led to disasters.

Another interesting study worth carrying out is of the different approaches taken by President George H.W. Bush and his son, President George W. Bush, when it came to dealing with Iraq. The impulses and instincts of the Cold War era taught father Bush to be careful and restrained. Firstly, he obtained the almost universal support of the international community before removing Iraqi forces from Kuwait. Secondly, he stopped at the border of Iraq and didn't believe in regime change. By contrast, son Bush invaded Iraq illegally, without UNSC authorization and against the advice of key allies like France and Germany. He didn't hesitate to carry out regime change. These two contrasting approaches bring out clearly the different behaviours of the US government, when it is guided by realist-pragmatic philosophy or by liberal-idealist philosophy. In the same country, the former approach succeeded in delivering a major foreign-policy victory in 1991 and the latter approach delivered a major foreign-policy disaster in 2003. Indeed, when future Chinese historians write their history of this period, they will document how the US invasion of Iraq in 2003 was a major geopolitical gift to China. It distracted the US in the decade when China experienced an almost explosive period of growth. In 2000, in nominal market terms, the US economy was eight times the size of the Chinese economy. By 2015, it had become only 1.5 times larger. So, the big question here is: What went wrong in the post-Cold War era? The next section will try to answer this question.

3. Post-Cold War liberal idealism

Sometimes it takes only one word to explain what went wrong: hubris. There can be no doubt that the spectacular US victory over the Soviet Union, demonstrated by the collapse of the Berlin Wall in 1989, led to a tsunami of triumphalism engulfing key Western capitals, especially Washington, DC. This triumphalism was best expressed in the famous essay by Francis Fukuyama entitled 'The End of History?' As I document in great detail in *Has the West Lost It?*, this essay did a lot of brain damage in the West, including the US, because it put the West to sleep precisely at the moment when China and India decided to wake up after 200 years of relative slumber, around 1990.

Even though Fukuyama was trying to put across a sophisticated message, the only message that the Western elites, including American elites, heard was that the West could carry on in an autopilot mode, without making any strategic adjustments and adaptations to new challenges. Indeed, key Western minds stopped thinking strategically and started taking moralistic positions. This switch from realist pragmatism to liberal idealism led to three key strategic mistakes in the post-Cold War era.

The first strategic mistake by the US was to not pay attention to the living standards of its own population, especially those of the bottom 50 per cent. If the US defeated the USSR by delivering better middle-class living standards, it could well be on the way to losing the economic contest with China because it is the only major developed country where the average income of the bottom 50 per cent has stagnated or declined over a thirty-year period. All the data supporting this claim can be found in chapter seven of *Has China Won?*[7]

This stagnation of income didn't just have economic consequences. It caused significant human distress. Two Princeton University economists, Anne Case and Angus Deaton, have documented how all this generated a 'sea of despair' among the white working classes. They document how the condition of poor economic prospects 'compounds over time through family dysfunction, social isolation, addiction, obesity and other pathologies'.[8] It is therefore shocking that almost no one is pointing out that in this respect the US today is becoming like the USSR of yesterday.

In a related development, the US has become functionally a plutocracy, as confirmed by the late Paul Volcker,[9] Joseph Stiglitz[10] and Martin Wolf.[11] The emergence of plutocracy has enormous consequences for Sino–US relations. If the contest between the US and China is a contest between a healthy and flexible democracy and a rigid and inflexible communist-party system, then the US will prevail. However, if the contest is one between a rigid and inflexible plutocracy and a supple and flexible meritocratic political system, China will win.

The second strategic mistake was to thoughtlessly expand NATO without thinking through the long-term strategic consequences. Significantly, George Kennan warned against the NATO expansion. While Kissinger supported the expansion of NATO to former East European countries, he cautioned against the expansion of NATO into Ukraine. Indeed, even when he supported NATO expansion, he added that assurances should be given to Russia. He proposed 'a security treaty between the new NATO and Russia to make clear that the goal is cooperation'. This advice was ignored. Why did the US push for NATO expansion? The simple answer is that it did so only because it could do so. Since no force could stop the US, it proceeded. In short, the cautious pragmatic impulses that guided the US in the Cold War had been effectively replaced by bold idealistic impulses. And did anyone think through strategically the consequences of NATO expansion? The answer is no.

Europe was equally complicit in this reckless exercise of NATO expansion without thinking through strategically the consequences. Unlike the US, Europe will have to live beside Russia for the next 100 years or more. Was it wise to alienate Russia? The answer is clearly no. Many Americans and Europeans still revere Gorbachev for ending the Cold War peacefully. Yet despite this, they rejected Gorbachev's vision of a 'common European home'. By rejecting Gorbachev and expanding NATO, the US and EU are essentially responsible for creating Putin, who embodies well the natural resentment felt by many Russians who feel humiliated by the US in the post-Cold War era. If both the US and the EU had retained their realist-pragmatic impulses of the Cold War era, Putin might not have emerged.

The third strategic mistake was to recklessly continue fighting wars in the Middle East and beyond. Apart from the attack on the Al Qaeda forces in Afghanistan, which was legal and justified, all subsequent US military interventions in that region of the Islamic world have been illegal and unjustified. Even more fundamentally, they have generated disasters and actually gone against the national interests of the US. Anyone who doubts this should read *The Hell of Good Intentions* by Stephen M. Walt and *The Great Delusion* by John J. Mearsheimer. Here's a small sampling of what they say. Walt says: 'Instead of building an ever-expanding zone of peace united by a shared commitment to liberal ideals, America's pursuit of liberal hegemony poisoned relations with Russia, led to costly quagmires in Afghanistan, Iraq, and several other countries, squandered trillions of dollars and thousands of lives, and encouraged both states and non-state actors to resist US efforts or to exploit them for their own benefit.'[12] Mearsheimer is equally harsh in his verdict: 'Washington's performance in Afghanistan, Egypt, Iraq, Libya and Syria have been dismal. Not only has the US failed to protect human rights and promote liberal democracy in those countries, it has played a major role in spreading death and disorder across the greater Middle East.'[13]

What is truly sad here is that even though the liberal policymakers who launched many of these unwise interventions had good intentions, the practical results have been to cause much pain and suffering. As documented earlier, many innocent lives have been lost. Peter Ford, the former British Ambassador to Syria, has described vividly the suffering that the Syrian people suffered from the US intervention. In an interview with the *Grayzone*, he said, 'The US strategy has been to punish the Syrian people, hoping to get at Assad in that way … The policy has been effective in the sense that Syrian people are suffering every day. There are long queues for bread, long queues for gasoline. The policy of sanctions and denial of assistance for reconstruction has been effective, but what kind of policy is it that tries to immiserate a whole country?'

The key point to emphasize here is that these three key strategic mistakes made by the US in the post-Cold War era have harmed US interests and effectively helped China's interests. Intuitively, Donald Trump realized that the post-Cold War US interventions overseas were flawed and unnecessary. He focused his attention on China. So, did Trump get the China question right?

4. Trump and China

The short answer is no. There is no doubt that the Trump administration generated some grief for China, with its trade and technology wars against China. Indeed, the only bipartisan support that President Trump received for any of his policies was for his China policy. Leading Democrats supported him. Senator Chuck Schumer of New York said (or tweeted), 'Hang tough on China, President [Trump]. Don't back down. Strength is the only way to win with China.' Nancy Pelosi said, 'In terms of some of these issues like Huawei, we have bipartisan agreement on that. I always say to members: don't be against something because President Trump might be for it. If there happens to be collateral benefit so be it, and let's all share in the responsibility to do something and the credit when we get it done.' Equally importantly, the intellectual establishment, especially in Washington, DC, also supported Trump.

To find out whether Trump succeeded or failed in his China policy, one needs only ask one simple question: Was China stronger or weaker at the end of Trump's four-year term? The short answer is stronger. Indeed, China's steady rise as an economic power continued, despite Trump's erratic trade and technology war against China. One statistic makes it clear how Trump failed to stop China's rise. In 2009, the size of the retail goods market in China was $1.8 trillion, less than half that of the US, which was $4 trillion. Ten years later, in the third year of the Trump administration, in 2019, the Chinese market had more than tripled to $6 trillion, becoming bigger than that of the US, which had only increased 1.5 times to $5.5 trillion. By 2030, there is no question that China's market will be much bigger. In short, all the measures taken by the Trump administration to stop China's eventual emergence as the number one economic power have failed.

5. What is to be done?

All this leads to the final question, the question that Lenin famously posed: what is to be done? There are three simple but critical steps that the US needs to take if this analysis of the failures of the great liberal push in the US foreign policy in the post-Cold War era is correct.

The first and most obvious step is to make a massive U-turn away from this great liberal thrust. Here's one small practical step that will expedite this U-turn: Just stop bombing other countries. As Nike would famously say: 'Just do it'. The evidence is clear. There is now no doubt that the massive number of bombs dropped by the US on other countries has had no successes. It has only generated misery.

There is also a sound liberal ethical principle that supports the case for stopping the bombing. American liberals believe in accountability. None of them hesitated to excoriate President Trump for pardoning the four Blackwater executives who committed murder in Iraq on 16 September 2007. Michelle Goldberg, a famous columnist for *The New York Times*, said, 'The last days of Trump's reign have been an orgy of impunity.' Yet, she failed to mention that it was not Trump's isolationist tendencies that carried these four Blackwater executives to the shores of Iraq. Instead, it was the grand tsunami of American liberalism, which was unleashed when the Cold War ended, that delivered the US armed forces and Blackwater mercenaries to many countries, dropping bombs and firing guns that led to the killings of many innocent people in many countries.

Thanks to Trump, we know that fourteen innocent Iraqis were killed at a roundabout in Baghdad on 16 September 2007. Yet, since the end of the Cold War, especially after 9/11 unleashed American firepower to 'shock and awe' the world, hundreds of thousands of bombs have been dropped on several countries. From time to time tragic stories appear, such as the one about an Afghan wedding party on 6 July 2008.[14] Yet, no major liberal organization has either requested or carried an audit of the number of innocent lives lost through all the 'liberal interventions' unleashed after the end of the Cold War.

There's a key reason why this essay on Kissinger discusses this issue of the lack of accountability by American liberals for the innocent lives they have killed, directly or indirectly. While many liberals acknowledge that Kissinger made significant contributions to strengthen the US and its role in the world, they still view with some disdain the cold and cunning 'realpolitik' approaches he took, especially in dealing with communist China. By contrast, they believe that if any the US statesmen had adopted more moral approaches, guided by the values of American liberalism, both the US and the world would have been better off.

Thirty years after the actions born of American liberalism were unleashed upon the world, we now have enough empirical evidence to prove that it has been a massive failure. Worse still, it has generated a lot of evil by killing hundreds of thousands of innocent people. By contrast, if the US foreign policies had continued to be guided by the values of pragmatism, underpinning the approaches of Richard Nixon and Henry Kissinger to the rest of the world, both the US and the world would have been better off. Indeed, going forward, as America's number-one geopolitical challenge is going to come from China, the

US would be far better off if it made a massive U-turn away from its 'liberal' directions and became more 'cunning' and 'pragmatic' in dealing with the world.

The second logical step to take, after a massive U-turn away from this liberal thrust in the US foreign policy, is to work out a comprehensive long-term strategy to deal with the rise of China. Many Americans would challenge the claim that the US lacks a strategy. Yet, the man who alerted me to this was Henry Kissinger. I still remember vividly the one-on-one lunch I had with him in a private room in his club in midtown Manhattan in mid-March 2018. On the day of the lunch, I was afraid that it would be cancelled as a snowstorm was predicted. Despite the weather warning, he turned up. We had a wonderful conversation for over two hours. To be fair to him, he didn't exactly say that the US lacked a long-term strategy toward China, but that was the message he conveyed over lunch. This is also the big message of his own book, *On China*. Indeed, I received the explicit permission of Henry Kissinger to make this claim in my book.[15]

So, how should the US go about formulating a comprehensive long-term strategy towards China? When I served in the Singapore Foreign Service, I was assigned to write long-term strategy papers for the Singapore government. The big lesson I learned from Singapore's three exceptional geopolitical masters (Lee Kuan Yew, Goh Keng Swee, and S. Rajaratnam) was that the first step to formulate any long-term strategy is to frame the right questions. If one gets the questions wrong, the answers will be wrong. Most importantly, as Rajaratnam taught me, in formulating such questions, one must always 'think the unthinkable'.

In this spirit of 'thinking the unthinkable', in my book *Has China Won?* I have suggested ten areas that provoke questions which America's strategic planners should address. The full list of ten areas can be found in this book. Here's a brief summary of the list:

1. Could the US GDP become smaller than China's in the next thirty years? If so, what strategic changes will the US have to make when it no longer is the world's dominant economic power?

2. Should America's primary goal be to improve the livelihood of its 330 million citizens or to preserve its primacy in the international system? If there are contradictions between the goals of preserving primacy and improving well-being, which should take priority?
3. Is it wise for the US to continue investing heavily in its defence budget? Or should it cut down its defence expenses and instead invest more in improving social services and rejuvenating national infrastructure? Does China want the US to increase or reduce its defence expenditures?
4. Can the US build a solid global coalition to counterbalance China if it also alienates its key allies? Was America's decision to walk away from the Trans-Pacific Partnership (TPP) a geopolitical gift to China? Has China already mounted a preemptive strike against a containment policy by engaging in new economic partnerships with its neighbours through the Belt and Road Initiative (BRI)?
5. Under the Trump administration, the US switched from multilateral to unilateral sanctions and weaponized the dollar to use against its adversaries. Is it wise to weaponize a global public good and use it for unilateral ends? Right now, there are no practical alternatives to the US dollar. Will that always be the case? Is this the Achilles' heel of the US economy that China can pierce and weaken?
6. Since 9/11, the US has violated international law and international human rights conventions (and became the first Western country to reintroduce torture). The US soft power has declined considerably, especially under Trump. Are the American people ready to make the sacrifices needed to enhance the US soft power?
7. Of the world's three largest democracies, two are Asian: India and Indonesia. Neither the Indian nor Indonesian democracies feel threatened in any way by Chinese ideology, although they are concerned by China's increasing power. Unlike the Soviet Union, China is not trying to challenge or threaten the US ideology. By treating the new China challenge as akin to the old Soviet strategy, the US is making the classic strategic mistake of fighting

tomorrow's war with yesterday's strategies. Are the US strategic thinkers capable of developing new analytical frameworks to capture the essence of the competition with China?

8. Are America's responses to China driven by reason? Or by subconscious emotions? The Western psyche has long harboured a deep, unconscious fear of the 'yellow peril'. In the politically correct environment of Washington, DC, is it possible for any strategic thinker to discuss this 'yellow peril' dimension?
9. In the eyes of many objective Asian observers, the CCP actually functions as the 'Chinese Civilization Party'. Its soul is not rooted in the foreign ideology of Marxism-Leninism but in the Chinese civilization. So, here's a test: What percentage of a Chinese leader's mind is preoccupied with Marxist-Leninist ideology and what percentage with the rich history of Chinese civilization? The answer would probably surprise many Americans.
10. Henry Kissinger in his book *On China* emphasized that Chinese strategy was guided by the Chinese game of wei qi (围棋), not Western chess. The emphasis is on long-term strategy, not short-term gains. So, is China slowly and patiently acquiring assets that are progressively turning the strategic game in China's favour? Does American society have the inherent strength and stamina to match China's long-term game?

Thirdly, and finally, if clear and honest answers are given to these ten questions, the logical conclusion will become clear: the US needs to make a fundamental rethink of all its current policies. It will need to formulate a totally new strategy to deal with the China challenge. Heeding Kennan's advice, the US should first focus on the 'spiritual vitality' of its own people. Consequently, instead of making the US primacy as the key goal, the US should make the well-being of its own people a priority. Equally importantly, the US should once again start listening to the views of the six billion people who live outside China and the US. Almost none of them support the zero-sum policies of the Trump administration towards China. The US policymakers must also acknowledge that common global challenges such as COVID-19 and global warming are of greater interest to humanity than the question of whether the US or China has won the geopolitical contest.

This is why I conclude my book *Has China Won?* with the following observation: 'The challenge that climate change presents for the human species is a simple one: can it demonstrate that it remains the most intelligent species on planet earth and preserve it for future generations? Humans would look pityingly at two tribes of apes that continued fighting over territory while the forest around them was burning. But this is how the US and China will appear to future generations if they continue to focus on their differences while the earth is facing an extended moment of great peril.'

3

Kissinger's Secret Trip, China's Rise, and a New Bipolarity[1]

KANTI BAJPAI

THE US OPENING TO CHINA in the summer of 1971, heralded by Henry Kissinger's secret trip to Beijing in July 1971, has been romanticized and celebrated in American and Western annals. In India, the trip was vilified and demonized. With time, the triumphalism associated with it in the US and elsewhere has meliorated and the opprobrium attached to it in India has softened. Fifty years on, how shall we assess it? The China opening played a role in the ending of the Cold War, though the Soviet Union played the decisive part in its own destruction. The normalization of US–China relations also played a role in China's rise. However, Kissinger was hardly the main architect. Much of the credit on the US side should go to the presidents that succeeded Richard Nixon and the National Security Advisors (NSAs) that followed in Kissinger's wake. The US sowed the seeds of China's rise for forty years, and now it and others must deal with Chinese power as never before.

Having said that, the next century will not be a Chinese century. The future will be bipolar, with three bipolar possibilities—the most likely being one that Kissinger would have been familiar with, namely, regulated competition. As for India, it missed the signs of the sudden rapprochement in 1971. It must be attentive to the signs of the US once again possibly changing course with China. It is good to remember that the US has long had a fascination with China. Even in these times of Sino–US conflict, the American interest in, knowledge of, and linkages to China are far greater than with India.

Kissinger and the opening to China

Henry Kissinger is credited with the opening to China in 1971, but it would be more accurate to say that he was 'associated' with it. America's decision to normalize relations with China was already in process before Kissinger became Richard Nixon's National Security Advisor: the thought of a strategic opening to China can clearly be traced to the Kennedy and Johnson administrations in the period 1961 to 1965. In any case, it was Nixon more than Kissinger who conceptualized the move. And it was President Jimmy Carter and his NSA, Zbigniew Brzezinski, and then President Ronald Reagan and his team who laid the foundations for the lips-and-teeth relationship that was to develop for the rest of the Cold War. Kissinger's informal advice to US presidents and Chinese leaders, his voluminous writings and his consultancy work may have done more for US–China relations than his policy interventions in office.

As early as 1963, the US was already working on a degree of normalization with China. Washington was aware of the Sino–Soviet rift of the late 1950s and sensed an opportunity. In 1961, when he took office, President John Kennedy wanted to move beyond the diplomatic stalemate with China under his predecessor, Dwight Eisenhower, but given the narrowness of his victory in the presidential elections, he held off. Even so, a policy review was quietly begun. The slow churn on China might have led to some 'breakthrough' initiatives in December 1963. With Kennedy's assassination in November those moves petered out. Nevertheless, in December 1963, Assistant Secretary of State for Far Eastern Affairs Roger Hilsman gave a speech where, in Joanne Chang's words, he 'urged Americans to take a realistic view of the PRC, asserting that the Communist regime was here to stay and recognizing the possibility that the PRC would evolve into a more moderate state'.[2]

Kennedy's death slowed down but did not altogether stop the winds of change. By 1965, President Johnson was already easing the travel ban and the restrictions on Chinese journalists—if this had little effect, it was because Beijing was not ready for an opening. Indeed, under Johnson, relations worsened due to the full-blown US military intervention in Vietnam. The anti-war protests at home doomed Johnson's re-election hopes, and in November 1968, Nixon, defeated by Kennedy in 1960, won the presidency. As early as October 1967, he had penned an article in the US journal, *Foreign Affairs*. Titled 'Asia After Viet Nam', it argued for the necessity of engaging China. Nixon's clinching argument was that 'Any American policy toward Asia must come urgently to grips with the reality of China ... Taking the long view, we simply cannot afford to leave China forever outside the family of nations, there to nurture its fantasies, cherish its hates and threaten its neighbors.'[3]

Between March and September 1969, China and the Soviet Union fought a series of battles along the Ussuri River over their unsettled border claims. The fighting started after the People's Liberation Army (PLA) ambushed Soviet forces. The emerging strategic convergence between the US and China may well have emboldened Beijing to precipitate matters with Moscow. In the event, the Soviets, rather shaken by the Chinese attack, were stirred to contemplate radical action including a possible joint nuclear attack with the US on Chinese nuclear forces. The US refused. China meanwhile decided that it needed a tacit alliance with the US.[4] A complex process of signalling between the two sides ensued.

Looking back on it, quite a bit of the process leading up to Kissinger's trip in July 1971 was jejune if not comical. A Chinese media account describes some of the communication that went on in 1970. First, Chinese leader Mao Zedong invited American journalist and writer Edgar Snow to stand on top of the Tiananmen gate to watch the National Day celebrations, a privilege never granted to a foreigner before. Then, President Nixon announced rather mawkishly during an interview with *Time* magazine, that 'If there is anything I want to do before I die, it is to go to China. If I don't, I want my children to.'[5] This was followed by the comedy of the US table tennis team meeting their Chinese counterparts in a tournament in Japan and asking to be invited to a subsequent tournament in China. The request was turned down until an American and Chinese player descended together from the Chinese team bus grinning in front of reporters. When Mao saw the picture of the two players, he ordered the Chinese team to accept the American request. The US team finally played in China in April 1971, and no less than Zhou hosted a reception for them. The Chinese also ensured that some of their players lost to the outgunned Americans—mocking their rivals and befriending them at the same time![6]

These and other—more serious—signals led up to Kissinger's incognito trip to Beijing, with its near-farcical elements. The trip was hilariously codenamed 'Marco Polo'. Before he went to the airport, Kissinger suddenly feigned heat sickness and was taken to Pakistani President Yahya Khan's retreat outside Islamabad to 'recover'. Later, he was to go to the airport with his face covered in a scarf and sunglasses.[7] There is a hint of Peter Sellers' farcical Inspector Clouseau from the Pink Panther movies here—secrecy that was hardly warranted and a disguise that would not have fooled anyone who was even vaguely familiar with the Kissinger visage.

The convulsive laughter in Beijing must have been a sight to see. Here were hard-boiled revolutionaries, who had fought and survived a cruel civil war and a war against Japan, being asked to play amateur cloak-and-dagger with the naïfs, Nixon and Kissinger. Is it any wonder that the meetings with Kissinger were marked by a touch of condescension on the part of Mao and Zhou? While Nixon and Kissinger were full of vanity and desperate to leave their mark in history, Mao and Zhou were comfortable in their own skins and had already taken their places in history. The meetings were not of equals: the Americans kowtowed, and the Chinese knew it. Kissinger seems to have been overawed and so desperate to make the opening that he exceeded his brief. For instance, according to John Pomfret, 'He [Kissinger] assured Zhou that whether or not China pursued *peaceful* unification with Taiwan, "We [the US] will continue in the direction which I indicated"—which meant that the US would withdraw recognition of Taiwan and establish ties with China.'[8]

Nixon and Kissinger certainly made the breakthrough—and more—with Beijing that the Kennedy administration had hoped to curate. Yet, the roots of the China opening go back to the assassinated president and his team. Neither Nixon nor Kissinger were ever generous with their praise of others. With the benefit of hindsight, we can see that too much credit has been given to Nixon–Kissinger and particularly to Kissinger, given that Nixon had conceptualized the opening as early as 1967.

The world after the Kissinger visit

The choreography around Kissinger's trip may have been ludicrous, but the purpose was serious as were the consequences. It was correct to bring China out of the cold and into international order: one billion people had to be recognized and integrated. The alliance against the Soviets was less understandable. If Washington and Beijing had read US diplomat George Kennan's 'Sources of Soviet Conduct' more carefully or taken more seriously the young Russian dissident Andre Amalrik's *Will the Soviet Union Survive Until 1984?* (published in 1970), they would have seen that they were confronting an increasingly hollow empire that was not far from self-destruction.[9] Or perhaps the Chinese knew the extent of Soviet infirmities but played on the credulity and greed of the Americans to further their own project—which was more about accessing US investment/technology than it was about forging a common front against Moscow. After all, Beijing could have hardly failed to notice that only those countries that befriended the US and accessed its capital and knowhow achieved rapid, sustained economic growth: that was the story of East Asia from the 1950s onwards.

More than Nixon and Kissinger, it was Carter/Brzezinski, then Reagan/George W. Bush Sr., and finally Bill Clinton that helped China on its extraordinary economic journey from 1979 to the present—which is why the Chinese accusation that the Americans have always tried to contain China's rise is so laughably absurd. Beyond economic partners, the US and China became strategic partners. When the Soviets sent in their forces to save the Babrak Karmal government in Afghanistan in December 1979, the US and China with Pakistan deployed Islamic radicals to wear down the Red Army. Over the next decade, the US released high technology and weaponry to China to bolster the quasi-alliance.[10] It granted most-favoured-nation (MFN) status to China, relaxed Cold War rules so that the US and its allies could sell advanced technology to Beijing, provided credits so that the Chinese could import US technology and approved World Bank loans.

The US also helped modernize China's military equipment. Chinese students and tourists in the US and Americans visiting (and sometimes studying) in China grew dramatically. When Warren Christopher, Clinton's secretary of state, rather timorously tried to raise the issue of human rights, Premier Li Peng, 'the Butcher of Beijing' (so named for his role during the Tiananmen Square protests), responded aggressively and cancelled the American diplomat's meeting with Jiang Zemin, general secretary of the communist party. Predictably, China gave no ground, and yet in 2001 the Clinton administration went ahead to endorse China's membership in the WTO.[11] And the rest, as they say, is history—the history of China's astonishing rise.

In sum, it was not so much Nixon and Kissinger that helped China—it was every administration thereafter right up to Barack Obama that hoped engagement would gradually cause China to become more liberal and cooperative. And when that did not happen, Washington opted to stay engaged in the hope that liberalism and cooperation were around the corner. The US strategy was carrots for good behaviour, and when a handful of carrots did not work, it was more carrots.

The US had helped its European allies to rehabilitate their economies after 1945 through the Marshall Plan. It had helped the East Asian countries led by Japan through asymmetric economic interactions—allowing those countries to protect their markets against the US while more or less freely exporting their goods to the US. Since these countries were no match for the US in terms of population, land area or economic size, they were never potential geopolitical rivals: the strategy therefore was rational. China was different. It had a population many times that of the US, an equivalent land area, and an increasingly dynamic state-capitalist economy. If it were to become rich, it would be a massive rival, the only power that could dwarf the US. Yet the US stuck its head in the sand strategically, made money off the China trade and waited fecklessly for the day when the emerging behemoth would embrace liberalism.

A Chinese century or bipolarity?

China's astonishing rise is by no means altogether due to the US, any more than Western Europe's economic rebuilding after 1945 and East Asia's success can be attributed solely to American aid and indulgence. The Chinese government and people worked hard at making their country rich and powerful. Yet, the US played a key role in China's ascent. Napoleon probably never said, 'China is a sleeping lion. Let her sleep, for when she wakes, she will shake the world.' But whoever said it, the prediction and judgement are apposite. The US helped wake the sleeping lion, and China is shaking the world.

Marxists argue dialectically that capitalism creates the seeds of its own destruction. Did the US help create the seeds of its own relegation to second place in the global hierarchy? Are we heading into a Chinese century? Probably not. Estimates of demographic change, growing expenditures on pensions and health, slowing GDP growth, dwindling natural resources including water, the burgeoning of debt, dwindling export markets and weaknesses in cutting-edge technology suggest that China will be unable to catch up and surpass the US.[12] Add to this the US advantage in geography: uniquely, it is separated from its rivals by huge oceanic expanses. While it has bases and other military facilities abroad, as well as a freewheeling navy, China finds itself bottled up. The US has a massive bicoastal navy, while China has only one coastline. This means that the Chinese cannot bottle up the Americans, but the Americans can bottle up the Chinese.

If it is not a Chinese century ahead of us, what is the future? Indian analysts, including Foreign Minister S. Jaishankar, haplessly mouth the words 'multipolarity' in describing the coming era. This is la-la land, wishful thinking—though quite understandable in a country where it is the norm for politicians to avoid unpleasant realities. Everything points to the future being a bipolar world, as far as we can reasonably see. In bipolarity, middle powers such as India will matter up to a point if they play the game wisely, but it is useless pretending that the century ahead is going to have much space for anyone except the top two. The nominal GDP gap between India and China in 2020 was about $11 trillion. This is likely to grow in the next decade and could double to $22 trillion by 2030. Some multipolarity that will be, when the next set of economies after China are leagues behind it!

What kind of bipolar world will it be? One possibility is that the US and China will compete relentlessly everywhere, limited only by their economic and military reach and administrative-policy competence. This would be a dire world with the risk of growing frictions and crises, and perhaps even a shooting war. Regional and multilateral forums would become irrelevant, functioning only as diplomatic meeting grounds for the rest of the world. On the whole, a hyper-competitive bipolarity is unlikely just because the potential dangers of outright conflict are too high. Also, the global outcry would be cacophonic. Competing for domination while alienating those one seeks to dominate is a political irony that would not be lost even on the US and China who are not the most ironic-minded powers.

A second possibility is a US–China condominium or G-2. In this case, the two superpowers would be less competitive against each other, would eschew outright spheres of influence and would work together to set the rules of the game over the heads of the rest of the world, including putative allies. Zbigniew Brzezinski along with US economist Fred Bergsten had floated the idea of a G-2 in 2011 during the Obama administration. Neither the US nor China warmed to it, at least in part because it would have alienated most of the world, including their allies. The G-2 idea also smacked of an arrogance that not even Washington and Beijing were ready to embrace (which is saying something, given their arrogance). In any case, it is hard to imagine that the two powers have the capacity to bring everyone to heel and that they would agree sufficiently to operate a condominium.

A third possibility is that two alliance-like systems will face each other as was the case from 1945 to 1989. In the Cold War, the US and Soviets had their spheres of influence where they had more or less exclusive rights and responsibilities with the tacit approval of the other side. Beyond those spheres of influence, they competed in varying degrees including in supporting proxy wars in the global south. They also cooperated where they could, particularly in multilaterals. The US–China cold war could replicate this except that proxy wars seem rather old-fashioned when you can disrupt opponents directly through misinformation and cyber-hacking.

Kissinger would be most at home with the third possibility. In his book on *World Order: Reflections on the Character of Nations and the Course of History* in 2014, he wrote:

> To strike a balance between the two aspects of order—power and legitimacy—is the essence of statesmanship. Calculations of power without a moral dimension will turn every disagreement into a test of strength; ambition will know no resting place; countries will be propelled into the unsustainable tours de force of elusive calculations regarding the shifting contradictions of power. Moral prescriptions without concerns for equilibrium, on the other hand, tend towards either crusades or an impotent policy tempting challenges; either extreme risks endangering the coherence of the international order itself.[13]

Bipolarity number three probably has about the right mix of power and legitimacy that Kissinger would support. In 1971, he and Nixon sought to modify the bipolarity between the US and Soviet Union in respect of both power and legitimacy. They cultivated China to balance Soviet power; and they sought to end the illegitimacy of excluding communist China from the chancelleries of decision-making. Since 2001, the US has flirted with doing a China on China by committing itself to building India's power to alter the present power equilibrium. It is also seeking to address the illegitimacy of excluding India from global decision-making.

Whether an India that 'never misses an opportunity to miss an opportunity' can take advantage of the moment is another question. In all likelihood, probably not, largely due to its shambolic internal politics and governance. This is related to the historical fact that India has never known total war and has never had to think stringently about grand strategy. It is the only major power that has escaped the terrible tragedies of total war. The US in its civil war years came close to a total mobilization of resources and people for the purposes of winning a war. It has also been in two world wars and a global cold war. China experienced total war in its civil war and the war against Japan. Total warfare fuses state and society such that clarity in grand strategic thought and an ability to sacrifice for a larger goal become possible. India's muddled thinking and its inability to make long-term sacrifices do not augur well.

Which is not to say that India should go through total war. There are other ways of thinking coherently and responsibly about power and making the social changes necessary to build power. The Modi government likes to think it is the first hard-headed government in modern India dedicated to the cultivation and pursuit of power. Its foreign policy and domestic policy, on the other hand, suggest that it is as inept and confused as governments before it, indeed it may be even more inept and confused—but that is another discussion.

Conclusion

As NSA and secretary of state, Kissinger's contributions to US–China relations were quite limited. One reason for it is that by August 1974 Nixon had left the White House after the Watergate scandal. Under President Ford, for the next eighteen months, Kissinger faced serious difficulties within decision-making structures and was beset by leaks from within the administration. All in all, in the four years after July 1971, his handling of China is not an edifying legacy. He was obsequious to Mao and Zhou (even as Beijing continued to publicly criticize the US), badmouthed and belittled Japan, and had few compunctions in selling out the Taiwanese (agreeing that the US decision to recognize Taipei and not Beijing in 1949 was a mistake).[14]

This pattern of unrequited concessions continued beyond Nixon–Kissinger: the Americans showing eagerness for the China relationship and the Chinese being measured and stiff-necked in reciprocating. Along the way, the US did benefit. Almost immediately after the China opening, Moscow became more amenable to dealing with Washington. Seven years later, after the Soviet invasion of Afghanistan, the Chinese agreed to join the US–Pakistan coalition against Moscow. That led to the Soviet defeat and withdrawal from Afghanistan. It also helped in the unravelling of the Soviet Union and the ending of the Cold War. There was commercial gain from the China opening as well. In the nineteenth century, the US had protected China against various European powers and Japan who wanted to divide the country into exclusive enclaves. Washington's aim at the time was to ensure that American traders had access to the vast Chinese market. The opening to China after 1971 led to a massive American economic relationship with China that fattened US businesses. It is also fair to say that China's 'hide and bide' strategy after 1979 allowed Washington to have its way on multilateral and regional issues. That said, with China's rise, America's indulgences have come home to roost.

Geopolitical and material interests—and even the personal interest of Nixon and Kissinger in leaving a mark on history—played a role in the Nixon–Kissinger diplomacy of 1971–72. But beyond this there was something more cultural and psychological at work—an American fascination with China that has much older roots. A 1958 study of American elite attitudes towards China and India showed that US interlocutors admired the 'pragmatic, down-to-earth and hard-headed' nature of the Chinese. Of the 181 elite Americans interviewed, 102 of them subscribed to the following additional list of qualities: 'China's ancient and great culture; a beautiful, wonderful, cohesive culture; its great civilization; a bond of ancient traditions; a culture devoted to the arts and sciences; an aesthetic, artistic style of life, unaltered through the centuries; exquisite, stylized poetry, paintings; have great respect for Chinese art, Chinese thought, Chinese architecture, customs, mores ...

the wise old Chinese; a great and noble race; a people highly cultured for many centuries; the outstanding inhabitants of Asia …'[15]

By comparison, 137 respondents out of 181 had negative views of India, particularly of its religion and customs, and nowhere was the study able to produce the kind of approbatory list presented for China.[16] The conclusion is clear: Even at a time of war and conflict with China, elite Americans preferred China to India. The US fascination with China has a history. It could set limits to the incipient cold war between the two powers. Whether a new cold war, limited or unbridled, is good for India, is the question.

4

How Unique Was the Kissinger Moment?

RANA MITTER

ON 23 JULY 2020, AT the Richard M. Nixon Library in Yorba Linda, California, Secretary of State Michael R. Pompeo paid tribute to the Nixon–Kissinger mission for opening up relations with China in 1971–72. Then his tone darkened. 'The kind of engagement we have been pursuing has not brought the kind of change inside of China that President Nixon had hoped to induce,' he declared. Instead, in Pompeo's view, successive US administrations were far too accommodating to Chinese demands, allowing the PRC's power to grow unchecked—at least, until the arrival of President Trump. The implication is that the US should not have opened the door in the first place.

Pompeo's speech shared an assumption that is still found, in differing ways, in aspects of Western foreign policy more broadly. This is the idea that it is up to the West to decide whether or not China will be admitted to, or excluded from, the international community. In reality, as Nixon himself reflected, the Kissinger visits mirrored a wider reality: that 'taking the long view, we *simply cannot afford to leave* China forever outside the family of nations.' (Emphasis added.) China was always likely to be a major factor in global politics in the modern era. Kissinger's visit, while crucial, was one event in a much longer trajectory of China's relationship not just with the US, but with the world.

Kissinger's visit was ground-breaking because of a historical anomaly: the isolation of China from the US between 1949 and (in diplomatic terms) 1979, a diplomatic freeze unprecedented in modern history. The West learned one lesson from the League of Nations debacle in the interwar years: that it was important that the international order should find ways to incorporate ideologically dissimilar states; hence, the US and the USSR were both founder members of the United Nations. Yet that post-war order was lacking in another significant way: The only non-Western member of the Permanent Five on the United Nations Security Council until 1971 was the Republic of China, located after 1949 on the island of Taiwan. To understand how contingent and in some ways unnecessary the isolation of the People's Republic of China (PRC) was, and why it had long-lasting effects that are still powerful today, we have to examine the role of the different factors that shaped the hits and misses when it came to US–China relations in the Cold War years.

In this short essay, I argue that the Kissinger visit in 1971 was indeed vitally important, but that it benefited from taking place at a moment when China, as well as the US, was able to draw on factors that made a reset of relations likely to last. For, in the previous decades, there were at least two moments—in 1945 and 1950—that had a potential for a new trajectory for China's relationship with the world, and with the US in particular, but which particular circumstances prevented from coming to fruition.

1945, 1950, 1953 ... and 1971

In August 1945, China found itself in a historically unprecedented and anomalous position, simultaneously stronger and weaker than it had been for a century. China, the US and the British Empire had formed the Allies in the Asian theatre of World War II. During the last years of the war and the immediate post-war period, China's international position was greatly boosted, in particular because of American keenness to bolster

China's role in the world. There was personal animosity between the then Chinese leader, Chiang Kai-shek, and the administration of Franklin D. Roosevelt, but the Americans were also keen to make sure that the post-1945 settlement was not dominated by the European empires of Britain and France, and to encourage the end of those empires. Policies such as the installation of China as the only non-Western permanent member of the United Nations Security Council served this purpose.

However, China itself was not a passive recipient of these changes. Chiang, and the Chinese Nationalist Party's leaders more broadly, saw the end of the war against Japan as a moment for a major strategic reset in China's relations with the world; from being a country constrained by various treaties it had been coerced into signing by foreign powers to one which itself could control the geopolitical weather in its own region, and which would be an exemplar for a reconstructed Asia.

Geopolitical thinkers within Nationalist China proposed a range of important ideas about what a post-war China would look like, and how it would shape its region and the world. These included reconstruction of the economy at home to create a modernized industrial sector and revive the agricultural sector which had been destroyed by the war, allowing an export-driven economy to develop. They also indicated strong support for anti-imperialist movements in countries still under the British, French and Dutch rule, and development of political norms that would suit both Chinese circumstances and international demands, including limited multi-party democracy. They also provided some innovative thinking in the creation of new alliances; in particular, a bold proposal to forgive Japan for its invasion of China and instead turn their old enemy into an ally with regard to China's regional ambitions, and they took active and leading roles in international organizations including the international legal system (such as international war crimes trials in the post-war years).

These efforts bore some fruit as China swiftly rose in status in the non-Western world in the years immediately after 1945. Independence movements in countries that were still colonized sent petitions to Chinese ministers asking for their support (for instance, Sukarno in Indonesia). Its first ambassador to the United Nations, Jiang Tingfu, became a prominent figure in the organization, and was also heavily involved in emergent international organizations such as ECAFE (the Economic Commission for Asia and the Far East). China was still not taken very seriously by the Western world, including by an increasingly hostile Truman administration. But among emergent states and liberation movements in Asia, China's new status was regarded as an important turning point for the non-Western world much of which was still colonized.

Yet the ability of the Nationalist government to control its circumstances was heavily shaped by a phenomenon over which it had little control: the emergent Cold War. On the international front, Chiang tried at first to balance between the great powers. He received considerable attention from the US, which naturally considered that a post-war China would provide support for the new US-defined global order. However, Chiang also moved in summer 1945 to sign a Soviet–Chinese Treaty, which would ensure that the USSR would not intervene on behalf of the Chinese Communists in exchange for the Soviets gaining certain rights of control in the crucial region of Manchuria. This seemingly astute national-level balancing, however, proved fragile. The Soviets started to violate the agreement within a few months, giving arms and strategic support to the Chinese Communists in breach of the agreement, while the US made it clear that their support for Nationalist China would be limited and increasingly reluctant. The domestic situation worsened. The war had destroyed China's economy and created a massive domestic refugee crisis, which even $600 million of United Nations relief could not solve. Chiang had had hopes that if Thomas E. Dewey won the White House for the Republicans in 1948, it might mean greater leverage for the Nationalists in China, though this would surely not have been guaranteed. However, domestic problems meant that Chiang's international status also weakened, ultimately irrecoverably, as the Nationalists lost the civil war and were forced to flee to Taiwan in 1949.

Could this have been the moment for a serious reset of the relationship between China and the US? Certainly, there was little remaining affection between the Nationalist Chinese and the Truman administration. Truman disliked the regime, and his secretary of state, George C. Marshall, believed that his own year-long mission to bring peace to China in 1946 had failed in large part because of Nationalist intransigence and had little regard for them. By 1950, the Truman administration was getting ready to abandon the Nationalist government to its fate on Taiwan, essentially allowing unification with the mainland. The factor that turned the tide was the outbreak of the Korean War in 1950, which historians such as Chen Jian show that Mao entered half-reluctantly, but convinced that his ideological reputation rested on showing loyalty to his fellow-communist Kim Il-Sung and the Boss, Joseph V. Stalin. If the PRC under Mao had not entered the Korean War, then there is a chance that it might have been left free to retake Taiwan; as it was, Chiang was transformed from nuisance to Washington into an ally of the US. Beijing miscalculated overall by entering the Korean War. Had it not done so, not only it might have taken Taiwan but it might also have been able to establish a wary diplomatic relationship with the US, albeit certainly not a friendship.

The Korean War came to a stalemate and armistice in 1953, yet on this occasion, it was the US that made the misstep in terms of the relationship. A new, more hard-line secretary of state in the Republican Eisenhower administration, John Foster Dulles, argued against opening up relations with Mao's China. From that decision came an isolation which shaped many disastrous decisions within China, exacerbated by the worsening relationship with Moscow from the mid-1950s. The Great Leap Forward, which eventually caused over twenty million deaths from starvation, was driven by an urgent, manic need for China to find self-sufficiency, something that might have been averted had it been part of either global trade bloc by that stage. The inward-looking destructiveness of the Cultural Revolution was both a cause and effect of China's isolation.

The Kissinger mission came after a decade and a half, in which both China and the US failed to find a way to talk to each other openly (though there were undercover talks in Warsaw), and both sides had made missteps. The opening to the US allowed the recommencement of what ultimately became the most turbulent and crucial bilateral relationship in the world—that between the US and China. In February 1972, US President Richard Nixon met Mao Zedong in Beijing, marking the beginning of the end of the diplomatic freeze between the two countries, which had lasted since the Communists' rise to power in 1949. This event marked one of the most important strategic resets of the post-1945 era, and there is a direct line of connection to the present-day US-China relationship. The encounter has become one of the most famous diplomatic realignments in history, even being commemorated musically in John Adams's opera *Nixon in China*.

However, at the time, it was significantly contested within the Chinese leadership itself. A lack of historical sources makes the precise details murky, but there is evidence that significant figures within the leadership, such as Defence Minister Lin Biao, did not want to open up to the US, whereas Premier Zhou Enlai was enthusiastic. (Lin later died in a mysterious plane accident while fleeing Beijing in 1971 after a leadership struggle.) The debate centred on the ideological significance of the meeting: Would compromise with the old enemy, the US, mean ideological contamination of a pure, radical socialism as expressed in the Cultural Revolution, which was raging at the time?

For both the US and China, there were significant advantages in choosing to meet at that moment. In both cases, they were under severe domestic and international pressure. For the US, an oil crisis and high inflation were on the way, and the Vietnam War showed no signs of ending. For China, the Cultural Revolution had plunged the country into chaos, and it had alienated all its overseas partners including the USSR, leaving only Albania as an ally. Each side could see that the talks might provide a genuine opportunity for their counterparts.

Yet it mattered also that in 1972, despite the Cultural Revolution, China was not in a state of near-collapse as it was in 1945; in that way, the moment when Kissinger visited Mao was different from the one when Chiang sought to give China a global role at the end of World War II. Mao, Zhou and others saw that a significant shift in international policy could be implemented because domestic politics was (just) stable enough to allow a new arrangement to stick. They could see many advantages to such an agreement. It would provide a tacit partnership with the US, protecting China against the USSR, which they considered a much greater threat to them than the Americans. It might open the way for economic assistance for the incipient economic reforms (which in contrast with conventional wisdom did not begin in 1978, but were already under way under Zhou Enlai in the early 1970s). Overall, it would provide a startling new narrative about China's engagement with the world; indeed, it is still discussed, half a century on, as a major moment in the global history of the twentieth century.

Yet, in retrospect, one key lesson from the Kissinger visit and the subsequent Mao–Nixon encounter was that strategic resets do not proceed in a smooth, linear fashion. Having been national security advisor when he first visited China, Kissinger continued to visit Beijing during his time as secretary of state (1973–77), yet he found his Chinese interlocutors grudging on occasion and unwilling to move forward at pace with diplomatic recognition. It was another seven years (and under a different US president, Jimmy Carter) that China and the US finally established full diplomatic relations.

What did it mean?

How important, then, was Kissinger's visit? The answer is still immensely important. By the early 1970s, the importance of bringing China back into the family of nations was clear. Pompeo's 2020 speech implies that continued refusal to engage with China seriously in the 1970s might have been an option; it was not. The death of Mao and the end of the Cultural Revolution would surely have brought China back into contact with the West anyway; better that an active, positive move should have been made ahead of time to engage with China.

To describe the Kissinger mission as hugely important, however, is not to claim that it was the only opportunity for better US–China relations in the post-war decades. For many years, the 1945 moment has been interpreted purely as a lost opportunity. Despite the fact that the Chiang regime did indeed seek a new settlement between itself and the world, as well as the US. At that time the civil war devoured almost all the attention of the Nationalist government, and any attempts to focus on other aspects of the government's performance seemed almost irrelevant. However, the view of this post-war 1945–49 period has changed within China itself. In the early twenty-first century, surprisingly, China's actions in 1945 have become a source of enormous rhetorical power in contemporary China, particularly as the PRC seeks to portray itself as a citizen of—rather than a challenger to—the dominant order. Today, considerable attention is paid within the PRC to the attempts in the 1945–49 period by the Nationalist government to redraw maritime boundaries, establish a firm Chinese position in international organizations, in particular the United Nations, and to portray itself as a leader in the Global South, all of which have clear parallels today. The post-1945 foreign policy reset is being selectively, and powerfully used by today's regime. This means that 1971–72 was not the very first moment when China sought to take a prime spot in a world where the US would be an ally of sorts, rather than an enemy.

In some ways, that 1945 moment echoes some of China's dilemmas today. China's plans were rooted in an ideological vision that was in many ways very suited to the time. The growth in anti-colonial sentiment in 1945 meant that there was room for a powerful non-Western actor to take a leadership role in international society. However, China's regional and global aspirations were near-impossible when the country's economy was in dire straits and the Nationalists had insufficient understanding of the profound divisions within their own society. There is an intriguing counterfactual as to whether a reset might have been possible with Mao's fledgling state in 1950, if China had not chosen to join in the Korean War. The US, already worried about Stalin's intentions, would surely have been keen to maintain at least diplomatic relations with the new China, which would have brought it closer to the global community earlier on.

In contrast, 1971–72 seems like much more of a moment when the circumstances were right for a propitious reorientation of China–US relations. The general consensus over half a century has been that the re-establishment of links between China and the US was a long-overdue step that created a more stable and globalized world. Between the 1970s and the late 1980s, China was, in essence, a tacit ally of the US, allowing the Reagan administration more space to confront the USSR in the final phase of the Cold War. Meanwhile, China's move to a market economy, combined with the US willingness to become a debtor nation, fuelled a global economic boom. None of this would have been possible without the opening to China in 1972.

Still, the China of 1972 was the right state at the right time for the Kissinger mission to succeed. Grand strategy is important, but it needs economic and political strength and stability to operate. China in 1945 was a wartime victor, with the standing accrued to that position, but it was, by a wide margin, the most impoverished and internally riven Allied power. Thus, when the Roosevelt administration charged it to take a globally leading role, China chose to take up the role of a strategic power at a time when it could not guarantee stability in its cities or sufficient food supplies for its population. Its aspirations and responsibilities heavily outweighed its capacity. Domestic stability and support were also crucial. In 1945, the Nationalists' genuinely ambitious and innovative plans in many areas—most notably a new role for China in international organizations—were destroyed in part by domestic instability and a lack of popular support. In contrast, in the early 1970s, the prospect of the Communist Party being destroyed either from within or outside was relatively low, and this gave more heft to the new policy of closeness with the US with all its geopolitical implications.

Credibility was also important, and China's credibility was lower in 1945 than in 1971–72. Nationalist China in 1945 had more credibility among its Asian peers than is sometimes realized, because it was seen as an Asian power that had fought essentially alone against an imperialist invader (Japan). Yet the domestic crisis in China prevented it building on that genuine goodwill. The PRC in 1972 had actually destroyed much of the credibility it had built up in the 1960s as a Third World leader. Yet it had also understood that successive US administrations were trying to reach out to it, and was aware that a deal with China was of sufficient value to Nixon that it was worth taking the trouble to create a credible, if fractious, relationship between the two.

The fact that it is half a century since Kissinger's momentous journey reminds us that long-term verdicts are sometimes different from short-term ones; but the 'short' term can last decades. It is possible that the 1972 meeting, regarded for half a century as a great diplomatic triumph, may instead be criticized as a diplomatic failure in the future in the terms implied in the 2020 Pompeo speech. Of course, it is a fool's errand to try to predict opinions decades into the future. But it is worth remembering that long-term effects do matter and it is best to avoid projecting wishful thinking about what might happen. Much of the disappointment over contemporary China, at least in the Western world, is based on the idea that China failed to become a democracy after its rapprochement with the US. Since a democratic system was never the Communist Party's intention, it might have made more sense for Western governments to understand what *China* thought it was doing in having Mao meet Kissinger and Nixon, rather than concentrating on the West's assumptions about the meeting. For despite what may have been implied by Mike Pompeo, the ultimate goal of Mao, followed by all his successors since, was to create in China a confident, rich and powerful nation, but not a liberal one.

5

China's Rise and Asia's New Security Dilemma

CHUNG MIN LEE

HALF A CENTURY AFTER RICHARD Nixon and Henry Kissinger's historical opening toward China, and right after the end of Donald Trump's presidency defined by the slogan 'Make the US Great Again', revisiting Kissinger's legacy is most timely. This is because China today is America's most prominent challenger and US supremacy in Asia is no longer assured. In the five decades since Nixon's groundbreaking meetings with Chinese Premier Zhou Enlai and Chairman Mao Zedong, China has been totally transformed. So, too, has Asia and, equally important, America's role and place in Asia's balance of power. Fifty years after the normalization of relations between the US and China, the US is no longer the world's preponderant power. It is still the only superpower, but China is on the cusp of overtaking the US as the world's largest economy. And the PRC wants to reclaim its imperial glory, power and influence.

Return of the celestial empire

That China is back to its imperial impulses is anathema to many in the US. It already sees China as the only power that can catch up with the

US economically, militarily and technologically. Even with the setbacks in Vietnam and the long-drawn-out wars in Afghanistan and Iraq, the US never felt that its military preeminence was under serious threat. Today, China is no longer perceived as a mere theatre peer. Although China doesn't need to project power globally like the US, China seeks A2/AD (anti-access, area-denial) capabilities that will enable it, hopefully, to become the undisputed military power in the Western Pacific.

These concerns are very real and will remain as the central driving force of American defence and foreign policies well into mid-century. Both the US and China, however, exhibit cognitive dissonance even as they continue to practise their own versions of realpolitik. For the US, it is the overriding assumption that China should not act like an imperial power because that goes against the grain of the established world order. For China, it is the overriding disbelief as to why the US, its allies and even partners are contemplating various counterbalancing strategies. The US is upset that China is acting like a great power or even an over-the-horizon superpower and China is upset that the US and key American allies are contesting China's rightful place in the pantheon of great powers. Beijing also wants the US and the world to see China with respect and awe that it feels is long overdue. Unpacking this dichotomy lies at the heart of understanding Nixon's and Kissinger's China legacy and the earnest beginning of the struggle for mastery in Asia.

Although Nixon and Kissinger were both uber realists, neither of them really imagined the strategic consequences of unleashing China into the world. China opened its doors to the US not because it aspired to become an Asian version of the US but because it was weak, isolated and backward. Above all, China needed to buy time: to counterbalance the military preponderance of the Soviet Union; to nurse itself out of two cataclysmic failures—the Great Leap Forward and the Great Cultural Revolution; and to navigate the treacherous waters of post-Mao power politics. Nixon and Kissinger enabled China to buy ample time *and* credibility on the world stage to ultimately emerge as the one world power that had the capability and political will to directly contest the US supremacy.

Asia in the 2020s confronts unparalleled opportunities and challenges but the one common denominator is the preponderance of the China factor on every single issue affecting Asian security, stability and prosperity. Without exception, all crucial security hotspots, be it the Korean Peninsula, the East China Sea, the Taiwan Strait, the South China Sea or the burgeoning Sino-Indian contest in the Indian subcontinent, have a China dimension. If the US played an indispensable role in the shaping of Asia throughout the Cold War, China, at the very least, is going to co-share the stage with the US into mid-century and beyond. Since the US has never ceded de facto control of the Western Pacific to any other power since World War II, it is going to become extremely difficult to accept competing spheres of influence in the South China Sea. China isn't satisfied with the status quo and it will do everything in its power to push the US back to the so-called second island chain.

The delayed emergence of Asia's new Pandora's box

Henry Kissinger holds a unique place in the annals of post-1945 American foreign policy. No other appointed US official played such an outsized role in the making of the US foreign policy, instanced by his dominance over it from 1969 to 1977. Kissinger's colossal legacy also stems from the fact that no American was so successful in merging academia with foreign policy, not unlike the renown literati of Chinese dynasties. His closest rival was Kissinger's one-time Harvard colleague, Zbigniew Brzezinski—President Jimmy Carter's NSC advisor who left equally notable treatises on American grand strategy. However, Kissinger not only served in office longer than Brzezinski, the magnitude of the issues he dealt with were more consequential.

There is no doubt that Kissinger was at the epicentre of Nixon's foreign policy. But it is important to note that it was Nixon who provided Kissinger the room with a view—of the world, America's place in it and how he wanted to tweak the liberal international order in the depth of the Cold War. In post-World War II American foreign policy, two presidents played monumental roles. Other than Nixon, President George H.W. Bush led the US at a time of groundbreaking developments, including the downfall of communism in Eastern Europe, the unification of Germany and the dissolution of the Soviet Union. And, of course, Bush defeated Saddam Hussein in the first Gulf War and reaffirmed—for a time—US supremacy in the Middle East.

Most recently, Mike Pompeo's ties with Donald Trump come to mind but the Trump-Pompeo relationship wasn't a geo-strategic partnership. Trump's transactional foreign policy and highly personalized initiatives such as his meetings with North Korean leader Kim Jong Un in 2018 and 2019 had very little to do with grand strategy. Pompeo was arguably one of the most loyal secretaries of state and according to a *New Yorker* article, a former official noted that 'there will never be any daylight publicly between him and Trump' and that even in private Pompeo was 'among the most sycophantic and obsequious people around Trump'.[1]

Nixon and Kissinger dealt with the Soviets at the *height of their power* and with the Chinese at the *height of their isolation*. While Kissinger (and Nixon) were heavily criticized for their realpolitik, and paid little attention to domestic determinants or ethics in foreign affairs, the longer consequences were especially crucial for Asia. Nixon and Kissinger strengthened the status quo in Europe—enshrined in the 1975 Helsinki Accords signed by Ford and Brezhnev—but neither could have imagined the cumulative impact of opening up China. Other issues mattered. The breakout of the 1973 Yom Kippur War and the subsequent creation of the Organization of the Petroleum Exporting Countries (OPEC) illustrated the fragility of security and the increasingly complex economics of oil in the Middle East. The US-sponsored Chilean coup in September 1973, for example, was a reminder that when it came to matters in the western hemisphere or America's near-abroad, the US had no compunction in behaving like an imperial power. For Nixon, however, it was Asia and especially China that captured his political imagination.

A little under two years after Ford left office in December 1978, Deng Xiaoping unleashed China's economic reforms. Without US–China rapprochement, it would have been extremely difficult, if not virtually impossible, for Deng to pursue economic reforms at home. Attracting foreign capital, knowledge and technology were instrumental to China's economic U-turn. And normalization of relations with the US provided China with international respect and acceptance. China really entered the world during this period; Nixon provided the impetus.

Kissinger played a central role in opening relations with China and has remained deeply engaged on China since he left the government in 1977. Writing on the eve of Xi Jinping and Barack Obama's rise to power in 2011, Kissinger noted in his book *On China* that 'A country facing such large domestic tasks is not going to throw itself easily, much less automatically, into strategic confrontation or a quest for world domination' and stressed that nuclear weapons, for instance, would be a critical deterrent since contemporary leaders are fully aware of thc enormous destruction such weapons would unleash.[2] He concluded on a positive note by stressing that:

> The appropriate label for the Sino–American relationship is less partnership than 'co-evolution'. It means that both countries pursue their domestic imperatives, cooperating where possible, and adjust their relations to minimize conflict. Neither side endorses all the aims of the other or presumes a total identity of interests, but both sides seek to identify and develop complementary interests.[3]

Kissinger's relative optimism was premised on the view that containing China on an 'explicit American project to reorganize Asia' based on a coalition of democracies, was unlikely to succeed, given the growing and arguably irreversible economic ties between China and its neighbours.[4] He also argued that 'a Chinese attempt to exclude the US from Asian economic and security affairs will similarly meet serious resistance from almost all other Asian states, which fear the consequences of a region dominated by a single power'.[5]

Nine years into Xi Jinping's reign and right after the end of Trump's single term, it seems increasingly unlikely whether Xi and his cohorts in the Chinese Communist Party (CCP) and the People's Liberation Army

(PLA) share Kissinger's thoughts on 'co-evolution'. For Joe Biden, 'adroit constraining' seems to be the preferred approach in the very early days of his administration, although he has called on the need for the region's democracies to jointly address China's accelerated rise. Quite apart from whether such a strategy is likely to succeed, America's Asian allies and partners aren't going to line up automatically to join a broad anti-China coalition. The Quad, an informal grouping of the US, Japan, India and Australia, has emerged as a stepping stone towards the creation of a more durable anti-China coalition. But the verdict is very mixed. Many in Washington assert that while the Quad is a work in progress, 'a sizable group of countries will find value in working with the Quad if China continues alienating its neighbors and peers, including in the South China Sea'.[6] As one American analyst noted:

> The point of the Quad is not to launch a Soviet-era containment policy. It is to present a more united front of well-armed, highly capable, largely aligned democracies that can have a deterrent effect on Chinese adventurism and efforts to upset the status quo. The more the Quad and like-minded partners speak with a united voice, and the more clearly they articulate their core interests, the costlier it becomes for China to test or cross them. The goal is to win without fighting. The success of the Quad makes that more likely.[7]

The Quad gained increasing attention during the Trump administration when the Pentagon began to earnestly emphasize the return of great-power competition. Trump's Pentagon supercharged the China threat and his administration launched a highly politicized trade war with China. Biden's temperament compared to Trump's couldn't be more different. But given the growing consensus in Washington on addressing the expanding menu of challenges stemming from an increasingly powerful and confident China, Biden isn't likely to jettison the Quad or a firmer stance against China. Yet it remains to be seen if the Biden administration will succeed in transforming the Quad into some type of a cohesive military partnership given the groupings divergent security, economic, and political interests and impulses, even though they agree on the need to maintain American strategic supremacy in the Indo-Pacific.

Asianization of Asian security

Nixon was the first post-1945 president who set his sights on readjusting the global balance of power when the US was still the most powerful country in the world. He knew that Vietnam was draining American strength and credibility. And, as Kissinger noted in December 1969, less than a year after the Nixon administration came into office, the days when 'the country [US] without whose leadership and physical contribution nothing was possible' were over.[8] As difficult as it was to imagine, Nixon began to think seriously about a new modus vivendi with the PRC. If successful, Nixon and Kissinger thought that it would be possible to provide incentives to the two communist giants to forge new ties with the US.[9] Or, as Kissinger told Nixon in 1972, 'With conscientious attention to both capitals, we should be able to continue to have our mao tai and drink our vodka too'.[10] Nixon also wanted Asians to assume primarily responsibility for defending Asia.

In July 1969, during his first Asia tour, Nixon outlined what was initially referred to as the Guam Doctrine but subsequently known as the Nixon Doctrine. Nixon stressed the need to think about the longer-term view, in Asia and other areas where the US had key strategic interests, such as Europe and the Middle East. With growing Asian nationalism, Nixon noted that Asian leaders reminded him that they 'do not want to be dictated to from outside. *Asia for the Asians. And that is what we want, and that is the role we should play.*'[11] (Emphasis added.)

He emphasized that while the US will retain its treaty commitments, 'we must avoid that kind of policy that will make countries in Asia so dependent upon us that we are dragged into conflicts such as the one we have in Vietnam'.[12] Nixon amplified his thinking on a more self-reliant Asia. When asked how the US could continue to play a significant role in Asia if the US pulled out of Vietnam, Nixon answered that '[a]s far as the problems of internal security are concerned, as far as the problems of military defense, *except for the threat of a major power involving nuclear weapons, that the US is going to encourage and has a right to expect that this problem will be increasingly handled by, and the responsibility for it taken by, the Asian nations themselves*'.[13] (Emphasis added.) In thinking about whether a collective security system could take hold in Asia, Nixon was realistic but hopeful that it could be possible.

I should add to that, also, that when we talk about collective security for Asia, I realize that at this time it looks like a weak reed. It actually is. But looking down the road, five or ten years from now, collective security—insofar as it deals with internal threats to any one of the countries or a threat other than that posed by a nuclear power—is an objective which free, independent Asian nations can seek and which the US should support.[14]

Nixon and Kissinger began their rapprochement towards China in 1971 at the height of the Vietnam War. Nixon, however, emphasized a new approach to Asia and China as early as 1967 when no one expected him to make one of the greatest comebacks in American politics. Writing in *Foreign Affairs* in October 1967, Nixon famously noted that '[t]here is no place on this small planet for a billion people of its potentially most able people to live in angry isolation'.[15] He stressed that to the degree possible, the US should encourage China to change in order to pay attention to domestic issues and to rejoin the family of nations. But Nixon argued against containing China by a coalition of great powers or European powers. Instead, he emphasized the need for Asian countries to carry the bulk of the responsibilities in constraining China:

> For the US to go it alone in containing China would not only place an unconscionable burden on our own country, but also would heighten the chances of nuclear war while undercutting the independent development of the nations of Asia. *The primary restraint on China's Asian ambitions should be exercised by the Asian nations in the path of those ambitions, backed by the ultimate power of the US*. This is sound strategically, sound psychologically and sound in terms of the dynamics of Asian development.[16] (Emphasis added.)

For Nixon, sustaining US supremacy after Vietnam was only really possible if the US didn't have to continue to fend off both the Soviet Union and the PRC. Through Kissinger, Nixon's China gamble paid handsome dividends. Beijing appreciated Washington's willingness to share vital intelligence and assessments on the Soviet armed forces and Kissinger's assurance that Taiwan would never support Nationalist adventurism against China. As Kissinger told Zhou on 10 July 1971 in their last meeting during his first secret trip to China, '[i]t is the policy of this Administration [Nixon's] to give no support whatsoever to any nationalist attempt to invade the People's Republic of China from Taiwan, and without our support they are technically unable to invade the mainland'.[17] And Washington appreciated Beijing's understanding not to escalate China's support for North Vietnam and agreeing to disagree on the US military footprints in East Asia.

Contrary to what Washington was telling its allies in Tokyo and Seoul, Kissinger was very frank with Zhou on America's posture towards Japan and South Korea. When Zhou remarked that North Korean opposition would increase to mixed US and South Korean forces, Kissinger noted that '*[t]hee joint command is not a new policy; its purpose is to make our withdrawal easier [from South Korea] and not to increase our commitment*'.[18] (Emphasis added). Kissinger, however, also noted that 'we oppose military aggression by South Korea against North Korea. But I also must tell you that sometimes North Korea has been very harsh in its military measures both against South Korea and against the US. We believe that it would help maintain Asian peace if you could use your influence with North Korea to not use force against US and against South Korea.'[19] On Japan, Zhou expressed concern about 'Japanese militarism' but stressed that '[y] ou know we are not afraid of that … No matter how large Japan grows it has had experience with us. If they want to create great trouble, let them come. Changes have also occurred among the Japanese people over the last 25 years.'[20]

Half a century after Nixon's historic trip to China and reaching out his hand to Zhou Enlai, two contradictory forces were unleashed. First, Nixon was correct in sensing that if China looked to economic success stories in her neighborhood, she would have seen that all of them were American allies or close partners—Japan, South Korea, Taiwan and Singapore. China was not only poor compared to its Asian geopolitical rivals; it was even significantly behind the Soviet Union. Zhou Enlai and his protégé Deng Xiaoping understood that if China had any chance of breaking out of endemic poverty and its status as a second-rate power, it had little choice but to fundamentally alter its economic model. In a little over four decades since Deng introduced economic reforms, China has emerged as a global economic superpower.

Second, what Nixon and Kissinger unwittingly also helped trigger was China's rise as an increasingly technologically savvy military power. Enmeshed for decades under Mao's People's War strategy, the PLA was stifled by the convulsions wrought by the Great Leap Forward and the Great Cultural Revolution. China became a nuclear power in 1964, but it was woefully behind the Soviet Union's Red Army in virtually all categories of military technology. Today, the PLA is not only modernizing at a very fast rate, it is on the verge of attaining across-the-board power projection capabilities that hitherto was primarily the purview of the US armed forces. To be sure, America's key Asian allies including Japan, South Korea and Australia have followed Meiji Japan's mantra of *fukoku kyohei* or 'rich country, strong army'.

Asia into the 2020s and beyond will face increasingly vexing security dilemmas. Driven primarily by China's military rise and also partially by North Korea's growing nuclear weapons capabilities, all of the region's strategically consequential states are planning their longer-term military modernization programmes and strategies predicated on at least some dimension of the growing China threat. This overarching trend is unlikely to be curtailed. Given the immense costs and global repercussions of any major Asian conflict, conflict mitigation and war-avoidance must receive the highest of security priorities across the region. Nevertheless, it is also true that as the US–China strategic rivalry intensifies and China (and partially Russia) continues to increase the tempo and magnitude of military probes, America's Asian allies won't just watch from the sidelines.

In more ways than one, Nixon's admonition of Asian security being led and managed by Asian powers has come true with profound consequences for regional stability.

Living with an assertive China

Throughout this century, China is going to have the biggest influence in shaping Asian security. This does not mean that China will be successful in decoupling US's key allies—Japan, South Korea and Australia—from it anytime in the near future. But it does mean that every major security issue from the Korean Peninsula to strategic stability on the Indian subcontinent will have a Chinese dimension. By 2049, when the People's Republic of China celebrates its 100th anniversary—just a little less than three decades away—the PRC will have the requisite capabilities to counterbalance, if not override, America's strategic presence in the Western Pacific.

Of course, history never proceeds along linear highways. China and the Chinese Communist Party (CCP) faces immense challenges: endemic corruption, uneven economic development, widening income gaps, stifling censorship, suppression of the Uyghurs and atrophied political leadership. The US won't sit still and evacuate to Hawaii. But nor will America's allies jump on the bandwagon automatically on an anti-China coalition. Increasingly, China's rulers are convinced that time is on their side. Asia's American allies all share virtually irreversible economic ties with China. South Korea's dilemma between the US and China, for example, is going to get progressively worse even as Seoul touts the values of maintaining its alliance with Washington.

Beijing's imposition of a harsh National Security Law (NSL) in Hong Kong in July 2020 killed Hong Kong as Asia's most vibrant and free financial hub.[21] Although the US and the European Union condemned China's actions, Beijing didn't bat an eyelid. Moreover, Hong Kong's NSL has global implications. According to Article 38 of Hong Kong's National Security Law, any act can be deemed a crime against any person regardless of citizenship or residency outside of Hong Kong so that the law 'is asserting extraterritorial jurisdiction over every person on the planet'.[22] Given China's enormous economic leverage throughout the world and increasing self-assurance, China has the barest of minimum incentives in being attentive to world opinion.

Chinese authorities are increasingly convinced that the Trump administration's dismal handling of the COVID-19 pandemic and more poignantly, pro-Trump mobs who ransacked the US Capitol on 6 January 2021, point to America's inevitable decline. In the short time he has been in office, President Joe Biden has provided a dramatically different leadership style. His national security and foreign policy team is made up of veterans with decades of experiences. However, even if the US restores some of its lost global leadership and influence, Biden won't be able to stall or dent China's accelerated rise as an emergent superpower. Moreover, while Chinese President Xi Jinping is hoping for more normal relations with the Biden administration, Beijing is equally like to prepare for what one of its key security officials called a protracted battle with the US. Chen Yixin, secretary general of the Central Political and Legal Affairs Commission of the CCP—China's top law enforcement agency—stated in January 2021 that China's rise was inevitable and that the upcoming struggle with the US will be a 'long protracted battle'.[23] He also noted that America's suppression of China was a major threat and that the struggle with the US was a long war.[24]

China's growing hubris is built upon a draconian security apparatus that has gained greater traction under President Xi Jinping. Leader since 2012, Xi has amassed more power than any other Chinese leader since Mao Zedong. Many argue that he is even more powerful than the Great Helmsman. Just four years after succeeding President Hu Jintao as secretary general of the CCP, president and head of the Central Military Commission, the Party accorded Xi the title of 'core leader' in October 2016 during the 19th National Congress of the CCP. This Congress also added 'Xi Jinping thought on Socialism with Chinese characteristics for a new era', signalling his status as China's paramount leader.[25]

Xi's consolidation of power has brought the PLA and security forces under stronger party supervision and '[d]espite the fact that senior PLA generals have been targeted and the autonomy of the PLA threatened to a far higher extent than in the past, the party has reduced the risks through a relentless anticorruption drive and intrusive organizational and administrative reforms led by Xi'.[26] The Party's relentless anti-corruption drive under Xi has yielded dividends. Still, '[t]he party's centralization of political power in pursuit of its reform agenda has elevated the importance of security forces in domestic politics in a manner not seen since perhaps the 1989 Tiananmen Square massacre'.[27]

Biden appointed seasoned Asia hand Kurt Campbell as the NSC's Asia czar in charge of coordinating the Biden administration's Asia policy. Campbell is likely to look carefully into the possibility of redistributing the US forces that are currently heavily concentrated in Japan, South Korea and Guam, and stressed the need to spread them out across Southeast Asia and the Indian Ocean.[28] There will be enhanced cooperation and coordination with US allies but the fundamental dilemma confronting Asian states, that is, the spectre of an increasingly powerful and assertive, if not aggressive, China, won't be diluted by the actions and policies of the Biden administration. If much of Europe's security dilemma was resolved after the collapse of the Soviet Union and the dissolution of the Warsaw Pact Treaty, Asia's is just beginning in earnest. This is, arguably, the lasting unintended legacy of Nixon and Kissinger's normalization of relations with China and the Asianization of Asian security.

6

Kissinger and the Selling of America

SANJAYA BARU

IN HIS BOOK *WORLD ORDER*, Henry Kissinger wrote eloquently about the role of power and legitimacy in defining the status of nations. He defined these concepts, at a global and regional level, as 'a set of commonly accepted rules that define the limits of permissible action and a balance of power that enforces restraint where rules break down'. The 'world order', suggested Kissinger, reflects 'the nature of just arrangements and the distribution of power'.[1] In summing up his enquiry Kissinger concluded, 'In our time—in part for technological reasons … power is in unprecedented flux, while claims of legitimacy every decade multiply their scope in hitherto-inconceivable ways.'[2]

Nowhere in the book, published as recently as 2014, does Kissinger consider the question of the role played by the US, and indeed of the administration of which he was a key functionary, in granting both legitimacy and power to one of its principal adversaries, the People's Republic of China (PRC). It was President Richard Nixon's outreach to China in 1971, facilitated by his then National Security Advisor Henry Kissinger; the decision of the US to not veto a resolution to replace Taiwan with mainland China in the United Nations Security Council and other multilateral organizations; and a new trade and investment relationship that followed in subsequent decades, which not just enhanced the legitimacy of Mao Zedong's regime within the international comity of nations, but over time also facilitated the accumulation of power by communist China. Even as the US and China find themselves in the midst of a new cold war, the fact remains that more than any other country it was the US that enabled the meteoric rise of China in the post-Cold War era.

Political legitimacy and economic power

The political legitimacy acquired by communist China in 1971 with its membership of the United Nations Security Council and the recognition afforded by the US, created an international political environment conducive to China's rise as an economic superpower. In purely diplomatic terms, the US was among the last of the major countries to recognize the Maoist government in Beijing. India was among the first. Yet, the belated recognition accorded by President Nixon, and the manner of US outreach, gave Beijing the legitimacy it longed for. Power, on the other hand, was not an inevitable consequence of legitimacy. Many legitimate regimes have little power and some powerful regimes, like the apartheid regime of South Africa, have crumbled due to the lack of international legitimacy. While the Soviet Union enjoyed considerable legitimacy as a communist state, it finally imploded due to inadequate economic power.

China was neither a geopolitical nor an economic power in 1970–71, when the US decided to imbue the communist regime with international political legitimacy. China's rulers were successful in using the political legitimacy their government acquired in 1971 to build China into an economic power. That power, in turn, has reinforced the regime's legitimacy. Ironically enough, this granting of political legitimacy to Mao's communist regime occurred at the very time when the US continued to mount a worldwide 'anti-communist' campaign aimed at questioning the legitimacy of the communist Soviet Union. The US outreach to China has for long been justified in the name of realpolitik and balance of power politics. It was ostensibly aimed at balancing the Soviet Union. However, with time, an equally if not a more important objective seemed to define the US policy. This was the desire of American capital to secure access not just to China's continental market, but to its non-unionized and trained working class. While China's market was still in the making, what it offered to the US was cheap labour power and the infrastructure required to make China the manufacturing hub for US multinationals targeting the growing Asia–Pacific market. China mimicked the East Asian export-oriented growth model by offering its trained yet docile labour power to western multinationals that exported worldwide. The economic rise of communist China was facilitated by this new equation with the capitalist West, in particular the US.

To be sure, China acquired economic power through the hard work and creativity of its own people and the investment it made in its own capacities and capabilities. However, it benefited considerably from the supportive global environment that it secured thanks to US diplomatic recognition in 1971, the political legitimacy bestowed by Western powers on China's communist regime and the opening to the global market it secured through admittance into the WTO and multilateral financial institutions.

While the West remained hostile to the communist Soviet Union till its eventual implosion, it invested in the resurgence of China through the last quarter of the twentieth century. In this process, the US played an important role in China's rise—as a source of investment, as a market and as a knowledge provider. As China's most important bilateral economic partner, the US has played a key role in enhancing China's geo-economic and, consequently, geopolitical power and influence. The opening to China greatly benefited US companies. Kissinger was an important architect of and an intermediary in this process.

The politics of normal trade

In the 565-page treatise *On China* that begins with what strategic affairs scholar Edward Luttwak dubbed as a 'fawning dithyramb to the farsighted strategic wisdom of the Han',[3] Kissinger makes but a passing reference to the normalization of trade relations between the US and the People's Republic of China and a cursory one to US support for its membership of the WTO.[4] Yet, China's rise as a major power in the first two decades of the twenty-first century has been contingent upon its emergence as a trading superpower, aided by US investments in China and the US–China trade relations.

The rapid escalation of the US–China economic and business relations in the 1970s and '80s was rudely interrupted by the events at Tiananmen Square in 1989. The US administration had no option but to link its annual extension of the 'most favoured nation' (MFN) trade status to China to the latter's record on human rights. As Kissinger notes, the 'core' of President Clinton's China policy in the early 1990s was a 'resolute insistence upon significant progress on human rights in China'.[5] Through the first two years of his first term, President Clinton adhered to this principle, while China resolutely opposed it. Kissinger notes:

> These tensions, which seemed to undo two decades of creative China policy, led to a split in the administration between the economic departments and the political departments charged with pressing the human rights issues. Faced with Chinese resistance and American domestic pressures from companies doing business in China, the administration began to find itself in the demeaning position of pleading with Beijing in the final weeks before the MFN deadline to make enough modest concessions to justify extending MFN.[6]

The 'intertwining' of the two economies, as Kissinger puts it, through the '90s, of the US trade with China overtaking its trade with Taiwan, resulted in a sevenfold increase in Chinese exports to the US. 'American multinationals viewed China as an essential component of their business strategies, both as a locus of production and as an increasingly monetary market in its own right.'[7] Kissinger viewed increased Chinese exports to the US as contributing to an American leverage on China, increasing China's 'dependence' on the US. What he failed to draw attention to was the equally important leverage China had acquired vis-a-vis the US by becoming a vital component of the business strategy of every Fortune 500 company in the US.

Commenting on the complaints of US economists about China undervaluing its currency to push its products into the US market, Kissinger argued, 'Were China to adopt the American conventional wisdom, it might reduce its incentives for ties with the US because it would be less dependent on exports and foster the development of an Asian bloc because it would imply enhanced economic ties with neighbouring countries.'[8] In what sounds like a defence of China's exchange-rate policy—a deliberate undervaluation of the Yuan aimed at export-promotion—Kissinger was mouthing an argument of the left-wing Latin American dependency theory that viewed exports as creating a dependence that was beneficial to the importing country and not the exporting economy.

'The underlying issue is therefore political not economic,' concluded Kissinger. 'A concept of mutual benefit rather than recriminations over alleged misconduct must emerge. This makes it important to evolve the concept of co-evolution and of Pacific Community.'[9] Kissinger's idea of 'co-evolution' and the suggestion of an *entente cordiale* within a 'Pacific Community', generously dubbing human rights abuses in China as 'alleged misconduct', helped communist China consolidate its gains and seek great power status as a 'civilizational power'.

While Kissinger does not offer any discussion of China's entry into the WTO in his book *On China*, apart from noting the fact that like the staging of the 2008 Beijing Olympics, this too was a positive achievement for China, the fact is the US treatment of China as an economic partner rather than a political adversary, readily willing to ignore its 'alleged misconduct', defined the bilateral relationship through the period of China's rise from 1980 to 2010.

Publishing his book on China in 2011, three years after the trans-Atlantic financial crisis and China's emergence as a trading superpower, Kissinger found no reason to revisit his argument about co-evolution of the two trading giants. Kissinger's support for China's entry into the WTO was not just academic. He used his considerable influence to actively lobby on behalf of American corporations with financial and commercial interests in China.[10] Kissinger Associates, Inc. became an influential money-spinner in Washington, DC's policy world, with many of its associates walking in and out of key government jobs as senior members of successive administrations.[11] In 'buying' Chinese friendship during the Cold War, Kissinger had essentially invested in the 'selling' of American business to China and Chinese interests to US policymakers. The bilateral business and political relationship has since defined the US–China equation through the post-Cold War era.[12]

US acquiescence in China's mercantilism

In an address to the Shanghai Fortune Global Forum in September 1999, to an audience that included top Chinese officials and top Chinese and American business leaders, Kissinger spoke eloquently in favour of US treating China as a 'normal trading' nation and backed its entry into the WTO. The US and China were in the midst of negotiations on the terms of that entry. Kissinger lent his weight, stating that China's membership of the WTO 'should be in the interest of China, of the US and of the world community'. Kissinger told his Shanghai audience, clearly with an eye to Washington, DC, that maintaining a cooperative relationship between China and the US will be in the interest of both nations and indeed the entire world. Urging both countries to come to an early understanding on the issue, Kissinger concluded, 'I cannot consider that we can have stability and progress in Asia if China and the US are in a cold war with each other.'[13] Kissinger was responding to a view gaining currency in the US that it should not concede to China the status of a 'normal trading' nation, nor support its membership of the WTO.

It was as early as in 1974 that US President Gerald Ford, whose secretary of state was Kissinger, secured from the US Congress the right to negotiate trade deals with other countries without prior approval of the Congress. The US Trade Act 1974 had, however, designated the Soviet Union and China as 'non-market' economies. This restricted the scope of normal trade with China. In 1980, under pressure from US business and commercial interests, the US Congress modified the provisions of the Trade Act by extending what was termed as 'most favoured nation' (MFN) status to China that facilitated normal trade. This was done on the condition that the administration had to secure annual renewal of this provision from the Congress. This opened the floodgates to corporate lobbying, with the annual Congressional review becoming a battleground between corporate interests that eyed the growing Chinese market and the China business opportunity, and conscientious political objectors concerned about human rights and democratic freedoms in communist China. Every year the wielders of money power prevailed over the voices of freedom and human rights.

An early, conscientious objector to the ongoing US–China trade negotiations was Robert Lighthizer, who rose to become the US trade representative in the Donald Trump administration. As early as in February 1997, Lighthizer drew attention to the growing influence of Chinese money power in US politics. Writing in *The New York Times*, he accused the Democratic Party, and Bill Clinton in particular, of soliciting funds from Thai business persons of Chinese origin who had business links with China.[14] Naming names and specifying amounts donated, Lighthizer charged the Chinese with buying up political support in the US to secure China's membership of the WTO: 'The money was meant to influence the decision on whether China should be permitted to join the World Trade Organization and, if so, on what terms. This is far and away the most important trade issue between the two countries.'

Lighthizer believed the Chinese had already succeeded in dividing the West by securing European support for WTO membership. The Europeans were also eyeing investment and market opportunities in China and paid little attention to larger geopolitical issues. The US alone could make political demands on China and it ought to. Hence, the corruption of US politicians by Chinese business interests worried Lighthizer greatly. He believed China viewed WTO membership as being 'critically important' not only to 'enhance its prestige but also because membership would offer assurance to investors that China is part of the trading community and give it protection from countries taking unilateral action against it.'[15]

Lighthizer's worries were not ill-founded. Influenced by the combined lobbying efforts of both US and Chinese business interests, and encouraged by Republican strategists like Kissinger, Clinton went ahead to not only grant permanent normal trade relations (PNTR) status to China but also support its WTO membership. Writing again in *The New York Times* in April 1999, Lighthizer pointed to all the risks associated with this misadventure. Continuing his criticism of President Clinton, his advisors and US business lobbies, Lighthizer dismissed the possibility that the US could draw on the national security clauses in WTO rules to punish China for actions it might take with regard to either human rights or Taiwan. 'The Clinton administration may not see the link between China's actions in various areas, but you can be sure that the Chinese do. After all, China is neither a free market nor a democratic country,' wrote Lighthizer.

The US economists too played their part by ignoring for years mounting evidence of Chinese mercantilism. Harvard economist Larry Summers used his influential position as treasury secretary to reject charges of currency manipulation by China and his successor Hank Paulson became a passionate advocate of financial and commercial links with China.[16] Surjit Bhalla pointed out as early as in 1998 how many American economists and analysts at the International Monetary Fund did not just ignore but in fact actively rejected the hypothesis that China's mercantilist exchange rate policy not only gave it trade benefits, but also contributed to the Asian financial crisis of 1997–98.[17]

Of all the strategic decisions the US took with respect to its relations with China, the two most important ones were its acquiescence in China's status within the United Nations Security Council and its support for China's membership of the WTO.[18] It was entirely understandable that the US sought to establish 'normal trade relations' with China in the 1990s since most major economies, including the European Union and Japan, had already done so. However, the decision to graduate out of annual Congressional approvals of 'normal trade relations' and confer permanent normal trade relations (PNTR) status in 2000 and deliberately ignore China's mercantilist trade and exchange rate policy laid the foundation for China's rise as a global trading superpower.

It is China's rise as a trading superpower, accumulating foreign currency reserves of over a trillion US dollars that has, in turn, enabled China to undertake geo-economic initiatives such as the creation of the Asian Infrastructure Investment Bank, the China–Pakistan Economic Corridor and other projects in Africa, Asia and the Indian Ocean region, and the Eurasian and maritime Belt and Road Initiative. China's geopolitical reach has been bank-rolled by its cash reserves accumulated through the instrumentality of a mercantilist trade policy.

Alliance of business and diplomacy

It was not surprising that the Nixon–Kissinger diplomatic outreach triggered US business interest in securing not just a trade deal with China but also improved political relations.[19] Dong Wang quotes a 1978 report that captures the sentiment:

> Within weeks of diplomatic recognition, seminars and conferences on trade with China proliferated throughout the country (U.S.), playing to packed houses of several hundred business executives at a time. U.S. Department of Commerce officials reported an average 350 calls a day and a flood of inquiries in the mail. Teng Hsiao-ping's [Deng Xiaoping] pointed interest in automobiles, petroleum equipment, and aircraft manufacturing plants gave an additional impetus to the snowballing interest in Chinese markets.[20]

The semantic transition to PNTR signalled a more enduring shift in attitudes. As Reihan Salam, President of the Manhattan Institute puts it, 'One could argue that the final defeat for China trade hawks came not in 2000, when Congress actually passed PNTR for China, but in 1998, when lawmakers decreed that most-favored-nation status would henceforth be known as "normal trade relations".'[21]

Writing again in 1999, Lighthizer offered a perceptive assessment of China's geo-economic strategy stating: 'China's leaders view economics the same way they view defense, foreign policy or human rights. It is a means of expanding the power of the state and maintaining control of its population. Since the Administration made clear its intention to separate economic from other issues, China's behaviour has taken an alarming turn for the worse, virtually across the board.'[22] This argument reflects an early geo-economic formulation that has since been developed in the writings of Luttwak, Blackwill and Harris.[23]

Foreign affairs analyst Robert Kagan also argued at the time that the grant of PNTR in 2000 made little strategic sense given the absence of any political change in China in the preceding three decades since the restoration of diplomatic relations. He stated:

> President Clinton was right when he said last Wednesday that the decision to grant China permanent most-favored-nation trading status will have a historic significance equal to Richard Nixon's opening to China and Jimmy Carter's normalization of relations. But if that's true, why is the president rushing Congress to make a hasty decision, with almost no time to consider the merits and consequences of this momentous step?[24]

Kagan went on to conclude that: 'big corporations want to use their big money to frighten members of Congress into supporting permanent MFN before those members have a chance to hear from their constituents. Polls show that a large majority of Americans oppose China's entry into the World Trade Organization and oppose granting China permanent trade relations.'

Robert Cassidy, who in 1999 was an assistant US trade representative and lead negotiator for China's Market Access Agreement that facilitated China's membership of WTO, is categorical in his assessment as to who was behind Clinton's hasty decision of 2000:

> The beneficiaries of the agreement with China fall into two groups: multinational companies that moved to China and the financial institutions that financed those investments, trade flows, and deficits. Foreign direct investment (FDI) in China accelerated at a time when

> such investment to other parts of Asia was declining and, in 2001, even matched FDI to the US. Sourcing from China, whether from direct investment or through licensing arrangements, has allowed companies to cut costs and increase profits, as reflected in increased corporate profits and the surge in the U.S. stock market.[25]

Ignoring all such warnings, US business and political leadership signed off on China's WTO entry. As Blackwill and Harris observe: '… the largest beneficiary of current practices may well be China. By 2011, ten years after joining the WTO, Chinese imports from other WTO members had grown substantially, with an average annual net increase of more than $100 billion. China also saw its dollar GDP quadruple and its exports almost quadruple over this decade.'[26]

Lighthizer sums up the three arguments that were proffered in favour of US granting PNTR and admitting China into the WTO as follows: (a) trade with China would benefit US companies and workers; (b) trade with the US would encourage China to abide by international norms, including with respect for human rights and the rule of law; (c) the US would gain more than China out of increased bilateral trade and economic relations.[27] Deposing before the US–China Economic and Security Review Commission, Lighthizer argued that none of these objectives were truly met.[28] First, the bilateral trade deficit with China tripled in the period 2000 to 2009 and millions of US jobs were transferred to China; second, there has been no visible adherence to the 'rule of law' and increased respect for human rights over that decade; third, Chinese mercantilism, best exemplified by its exchange rate policy, skewed the balance of trade in favour of China.

Summing up his sharp and exhaustive critique of the US trade policy towards China, Lighthizer pointed out that it had:[29]

(a) failed to adequately account for many unique facts about China, including its political system and its adherence to mercantilism;
(b) misjudged the influence that WTO membership would have on China's domestic policies;

(c) ignored the incentivization to off-shore production by US companies into China;

(d) gave up critical policy tools that could have provided leverage to push China toward market liberalization and failed to adequately use available tools;

(e) and, finally, demonstrated 'hubris' about the 'inevitable' triumph of democracy and capitalism, and therefore overlooked the strengths that would enable China's economy to outperform the US.

In the two decades that followed trade normalization, China has emerged as a trading superpower, overtaking Japan and subsequently the US. China's share of world merchandise trade doubled from 2 per cent in 1990 to 4 per cent by 2000 and more than doubled to 10.7 per cent by 2010 (Table 1). Between 2001 and 2009, US exports to the rest of the world increased by 45 per cent, while China's exports increased by 351 per cent.[30] While China's trade increased with all major economies, the US itself became an increasingly important destination for Chinese exports with America's share in China's exports increasing from 6 per cent in 1979 to 14 per cent in 1985 and to 26 per cent by 1991. A large part of this was in fact imports into the US of products manufactured in China by US firms.

Table 1: China's share in world merchandise trade

Year	Percentage
1990	2.0
1995	3.1
2000	4.0
2005	7.5
2010	10.7
2015	14.1
2019	13.0

Source: World Trade Organization

The provisions of the US Trade Act 1974, as well as such US laws as Special and Super 301, created uncertainty in the minds of corporate boardrooms when it came to taking investment decisions in China. There was an element of political risk involved in making investments in China given the possibility that the US government would take trade limiting action in response to events like the Tiananmen Square protests. PNTR and WTO membership removed, or at least certainly reduced, that risk, encouraging US companies to relocate manufacturing capacities into lower-cost China. This produce could then be exported back home and to the rest of the world at competitive prices. As *Forbes* magazine reported in 2007, 'A large portion of the frighteningly lopsided US–China trade deficit can be traced to goods made by Western companies in China, then shipped home for sale. In practice, "Made in China" often really means ""Made by the US in China".'[31]

Not surprisingly, American firms, aided by influential lobbyists like Kissinger Associates, Inc., became the most influential advocates of 'permanent normal trade relations' with mercantilist China. As Davis and Wei note: 'In the mid-1990s, Boeing formed what it called "the Rump Group" of ten major US exporters, including AT&T, AIG, Chrysler and General Electric, to push a "normalization initiative" for improved economic relations between the US and China. Boeing put up $2 million in seed money for a lobbying campaign that would spend far more in the years ahead.'[32]

Conclusion

Half a century after the Nixon–Kissinger outreach to Mao's China, it is worth asking whether this historic geopolitical rapprochement was authored in the White House, the State Department and the Pentagon, or in the boardrooms of US corporations and by members of Kissinger Associates, Inc. Geopolitical analysts have long argued that Nixon's China outreach was aimed at checkmating the Soviet Union and that the US–China entente helped the US emerge as the victor in the Cold War. This is a debatable proposition. The 'old' Cold War may well have come to an end because the Soviet Union imploded under the weight of its own internal contradictions and the inability of the Soviet economy to keep the political system afloat. An increasingly decrepit order in the Soviet Union simply imploded.

What the US–China entente did was to facilitate the rise of China even as the Soviet Union was imploding and this, in turn, laid the foundations of the 'new' cold war. Dazzled by the potential of China's market and, more importantly, the possibility of retaining its global economic dominance by relocating US manufacturing to China with its low labour costs and efficient infrastructure, US multinationals bankrolled American diplomatic outreach, encouraging the political leadership to grant normal trade status to an authoritarian regime in the hope that economic openness and integration into the world economy would eventually make China a liberal democracy.

Kissinger and his associates coaxed the American power elite into legitimizing China politically and diplomatically so that they could invest in it economically and derive financial and business benefits. China's rise as an economic and trading superpower was built not just on the basis of its own capabilities, which are impressive, but equally on the foundations of the political legitimacy and financial power transferred to it by the American power elite. Paraphrasing Karl Marx one could say that the American bourgeoisie sowed the seeds of their own destruction by creating a relationship of interdependence between the US and Chinese economies that in time enabled China to emerge as a geo-economic, if not a geopolitical, challenge to the US.

7

Secrets, Subterfuge, Subordination

The Key to China's Rise

RAHUL SHARMA

Let me put it in the context of the secrecy problem: Without secrecy, there would have been no invitation or acceptance to visit China. Without secrecy, there is no chance of success in it.

—Former US President RICHARD NIXON[1]

SECRECY IS A DEFINITIVE AND a useful tool of diplomacy, but sometimes nations need to act in other strange ways for necessary results.

So, as it happened, it took US diplomats—pushed by Henry Kissinger, who recounts the incident in his book *On China*—a good chase of their Chinese counterparts on the streets of Warsaw after a Yugoslav fashion show in the Polish capital five decades ago to break a deadlock and open the door for historic secret negotiations between the two countries. Several months after the once-in-a-lifetime chase, Kissinger's secret visit to what was then Peking to break bread with Chinese Premier Zhou Enlai would set in motion events that changed the world forever.

Over two days in the July of 1971, President Richard Nixon's National Security Advisor spent long hours with Zhou, walked around the

Forbidden City in the heart of Beijing and put in place a bilateral order that he influenced in so many different ways for much longer even after he moved out of the government.

Nixon, who was keen to reach out to the Chinese even before he became president, fully supported Kissinger's secret mission that took months to put together through several world capitals. Others in his administration, however, had little clue about what was happening and wouldn't know about it for several days later after the visit.

The marquee diplomatic event triggered developments that had a long-term impact not only on what are today the world's two biggest economies, but the overall geopolitical grid of the world, bang in the middle of the Cold War. More importantly, it set up the rules of engagement between the two nations that continued for decades beyond Nixon, Kissinger and Zhou. Secrecy and personal networks became the cornerstones of bilateral ties.

While diplomatic relations between the two nations would still take some years to formalize, Kissinger's visit also heralded the start of a long period during which successive US administrations would play second fiddle to China's ambitions and allow the djinn to escape the bottle and ultimately become the challenger it is today.

In the last fifty years, the two countries, which could never really become friends, have travelled a rough road of competing ideologies amid a Washington fallacy that Beijing would adopt democratic values and eventually become a society very different than the one that Mao Zedong had constructed. However, while Peking became Beijing and China dumped its socialist economy to run a comfortable marathon to become the world's second-biggest economy, what never changed was the complete control of the Communist Party over the country, its politics, economy and people. Mao's long shadow still looms over everything in China even though from a status quo nation it has become a muscle-flexing, money-flexing revisionist power.

On a merry ride

There are many who believe that China took the US for a merry ride and most administrations had no well-thought-out policies around China except the secretive course set by Nixon and Kissinger—the first cheerleaders—that became the base model for their successors. 'Obsessed with secrecy, Nixon and Kissinger were so awed by the historical significance of their visits to Beijing that they confused Mao's banalities for words of great wisdom. George Bush foolishly sought to revive secret meetings in the wake of the Tiananmen tragedy. Both Ronald Reagan and Bill Clinton had to make total about-faces from their positions as candidates to their official China policies.'[2]

Tensions began simmering at the turn of the century, though, as China grew economically and militarily and seemed to fast become a direct threat to the US. However, George W. Bush had his own battles to fight in Afghanistan and Iraq, while the huge global financial crisis that welcomed him to presidency kept Barack Obama occupied for most of his first term. The 2008 financial crisis substantially weakened the West. China not only came out stronger, ably traversing the difficult times through large-scale spending that boosted its economy as the rest of the world struggled, but also convinced that its own political and economic model was better than what the West had to offer.

By the time Obama began his second term, his desire to push democracy in China was replaced by one to work closely with Beijing. China had become too big, too overtly ambitious and a clear challenger to US supremacy. It had to be managed. Moreover, Xi Jinping had arrived on the scene and had gradually begun pushing hard for domination, throwing money around to buy out nations, offering them railways, highways, stadiums and power plants as part of his One Belt One Road initiative. The Americans, given Beijing's rising influence and the world at large, have a lot to complain about China, as it 'implemented a grand strategy designed to undermine US–Asian alliances, which has accelerated under Xi Jinping'.[3]

What has China done since Xi became the head of the party, military and the government? According to Blackwill, it has coerced its neighbours; violated international commercial practices; manipulated its currency for trade benefits; threatened Taiwan; built up its military forces to push the US beyond Japan and the Philippines; constructed and militarized artificial islands in the South China Sea; violated the human rights of its own people; and patiently and incrementally built its power and influence with the strategic goal of replacing the US as the primary power in Asia.[4]

A 2020 report on the US intelligence community's capabilities and competencies with respect to China to the House Permanent Select Committee on Intelligence was succinct in its conclusions when it said 'while the US was busy engaging al Qaeda, ISIS, and their affiliates, offshoots, and acolytes, Washington's unchallenged dominance over the global system slipped away.'[5]

In late 2019, the emergence of a novel coronavirus in Wuhan, China, demonstrated to the world the profound danger associated with transnational crises originating within China's borders. China's enduring interest in preserving its own domestic political stability and international image in lieu of fostering a transparent and effective approach to public health, placed the US, our allies, and the world at risk.[6] The intelligence report worried over the fact that China had used the past two decades to transform itself into a nation potentially capable of supplanting the US as the leading power in the world, which is a scary thought not only in Washington but in many parts of the world.

It is now evident that while China had a long-term strategy to deal with the US, successive administrations in Washington didn't. It wasn't until an outlier Donald Trump called a spade a spade and took on China in his efforts to hurt Beijing where it hurt the most—trade and technology—that Beijing began to get really worried. But truth be told, if the US finds itself being challenged by China today it is not so much because of Beijing's ability to outsmart Washington, but because of the inability of the US to read the tea leaves.

There is a past that haunts the present. And, for that, many still blame Kissinger because the processes he set in place became a habit for his successors as much as the man himself became a habit for the Chinese, a permanent go-to for advice, because for them he could be trusted given the decades-long familiarity. But it is important to understand that China under Xi, unlike under Deng Xiaoping, Jiang Zemin and Hu Jintao, is no longer a status quo power. It has become a revisionist power. For the US, its allies and the US-led liberal international order, this represents a fundamental shift in the strategic environment. Ignoring this profound change is to court peril. Xi is no longer just a problem for US primacy. He now presents a serious problem for the whole of the democratic world.[7]

On the other side of the Pacific Ocean, Trump's gone. Joe Biden is at the helm of a deeply divided country battling a pandemic that many blame China for, but few know when it might end. The old dispensation is back in Washington, but this time with a clearer bipartisan realization that China, not Russia, is the new enemy. This then brings us to the big question: What from here? Before we get to answer that, it is necessary to understand how China got to where it did.

Clandestine diplomacy

Five decades ago, secrecy was important in building relations with China after the US had spent two decades questioning the legitimacy of the Communist Party rule, but few would have imagined that it would become a cornerstone of bilateral ties initiated and shepherded first by Kissinger and then by many of his followers.

The anti-communist ideology was strong within its domestic politics and Soviet Union was enemy number one. China couldn't be seen through any other prism until Kissinger's realism ordained that an enemy's enemy is a friend. Nixon was pragmatic. He knew the US would have to one day deal with China, which would eventually become a major power in Asia. Border altercations between China and the Soviet Union that led to tensions between the two neighbours gave Washington the golden opportunity to 'play one communist government against the other for American interests'.[8]

China was wary, too. Why would the US want to reach out, it wondered, as both Zhou and Mao Zedong looked for strategies to make the sun shine over the Middle Kingdom once again? The two found a midwife in Pakistan, as President Yahya Khan became a key, trusted interlocuter in setting up Kissinger's secret mission.

Nixon was in fact candid about both the need for secrecy and Pakistan's role in one of his letters to Zhou. 'It is proposed that the precise details of Dr Kissinger's trip including location, duration of stay, communication and similar matters be discussed through the good offices of President Yahya Khan. For secrecy, it is essential that no other channel be used. It is also understood that this first meeting between Dr Kissinger and high officials of the People's Republic of China be strictly secret,' he wrote.[9]

Kissinger eventually landed in Islamabad on an official visit to Pakistan, called off his engagements on grounds of an upset tummy and instead jumped on a plane that took him to Beijing. Such was the secrecy that the visit was concealed even from part of the US delegation that travelled to Pakistan with Kissinger. 'The person running Kissinger's diary had to keep three different diaries designed for three different groups of individuals accompanying Kissinger on his trip to Pakistan. It was an outstanding organizational feat as well as a major diplomatic achievement.'[10]

In Beijing, Kissinger was feted and fed. He returned to Washington deeply impressed with Zhou and Mao and China in general, badly hit by the ancient civilization bug that continues to be part of his China narrative even today. What followed was pure theatre. Nixon's famous visit to Beijing in February 1972—set up by Kissinger—stunned the world, providing the US with a renewed image of power in Asia and new leverage over regional events. The two scored a big victory for US interests by self-consciously compromising on longstanding anti-communist principles.

However, they were also laying grounds for what James Mann in his book *About Face* calls multifaceted, often clandestine diplomacy with Beijing.[11] 'The opening to China was accompanied by a series of bargains, negotiations and what Nixon privately referred to as a trade-off,' Mann writes, adding that the leaders of the two countries were joining hands to decide the future of Asia—Japan, the two Koreas, India and Pakistan. They did so amid extraordinary secrecy, pledging that what China and the US said to one another would not be disclosed to anyone else.[12]

The secrecy worked well for the Chinese; they could play around with officials in Washington, throwing favours at them and stunning them with rich civilizational banalities that Americans were in awe of. 'Sometimes, not even the secretary of state knew what was happening . . . leaders in Beijing were often able to exploit or manipulate the differences in Washington, rewarding and flattering China's friends, instilling a sense of obligation, freezing out those US officials who were considered less sympathetic.'[13]

Thus, in the earliest days of the Nixon era, was established the pattern that China would follow for decades in dealing with US leaders. US politicians regularly sought permission to visit China. The Beijing leadership could either grant the invitations or hold them in abeyance, depending on which option would be better for China. The handling and scheduling of presidential candidates, ex-presidents, opposition party leaders and out-of-office politicians was to become an important component of China's handling of the US, says Mann.

Many squarely blame Nixon and Kissinger for the rise of a 'dictatorial' China, accusing them of contributing to the threat as 'one of the major creators and advocates of the decades-long US strategy towards China emphasizing cooperation so that Beijing could be brought into the international order and become a responsible stakeholder.'[14] The general expectation was that China would play the game honestly and cooperate with the West to preserve the liberal global political order. But that was not to happen and it took some time for the US to realize its approach was a mistake, for which it would eventually have to pay a far bigger price than it ever expected.

According to Thayer and Han, 'China hid behind a false promise to abide by Western rules and norms to forestall balancing against it, while it rapidly developed economically and militarily—and was creating a new international order to replace the one that is so rightly valued in the West.'[15] A recent long report in *The Wall Street Journal* called US officials getting China's Xi Jinping completely wrong 'one of the biggest strategic miscalculations of the post-Cold War era'.[16]

The Kissinger school of thought pushed the belief that China was mostly a status quo power, one that was not expansionist, that needed to become part of the world order for everyone's benefit. The result was that the West actively worked with the Communist Party of China to support its growth. According to Thayer and Han, there were three reasons why the West played along. First, large corporations got profitable access to the vast Chinese market in return for providing technology and processes, which in turn gave Beijing the ability to access and influence Western governments. All that helped China's economic growth.[17] Second, what the Chinese government could not get from economic cooperation they might steal through the development and employment of advanced cyber capabilities. And thirdly, most importantly, China's rise was seen as benign that led to a lowering of its threat perception in Western capitals. After all, here was a developing country that was ready to embrace the liberal internal order rather than create a new one as the Soviet Union did.

Wilful Ignorance

The wilful ignorance of the China threat was the greatest US strategic blunder certainly since the Cold War, and likely the most significant in US history. Countless academics, think thank denizens, Silicon Valley and Wall Street gurus, and policymakers contributed to this. Yet, curiously, Kissinger, who was famous early in his career as an advocate of realpolitik and the balance of power, missed it too.[18]

The reality, as it struck Western officialdom somewhere through their customary regulated walks in the Forbidden City, was that China was indeed a 'revolutionary great power that seeks fundamental and permanent changes to the contemporary order in international politics. If it achieves its objectives, it will be the death of the existing liberal order. That indeed will be a new epoch in global politics.'

Very few nations know and understand China's subterfuge better than India. Since much before the West got enamoured with China and began pouring in billions in factories and technology across the vast swathes of that land and helped create a monster it now simultaneously hates and fears, India has faced the threat from across the mighty Himalayas. India, its leaders, its military and security experts have watched China use its new-found economic might and trillions of dollars in its banks to expand its arc of influence across Asia, and beyond into Africa and South America, before convincing the Europeans that their future would look better if they joined hands with Beijing.

Embroiled in a long, tough border dispute, which in many ways is unwinnable for India without the help of the US and other Western powers, a new world order dictated and helmed by China is as unacceptable to it as it is to the US. However, China's growing influence in South Asia—for long seen as India's backyard—is difficult for it to counter for the very reasons that the US finds itself in a bind—Beijing's rising economic and financial heft.

China's global order—as it is being shaped—is completely different from the one the world got used to in the aftermath of the collapse of the Soviet Union. It is not collaborative, but hierarchal. It is not about geographic status quo, but expansionism. It is about building competing economic institutions and taking over existing global organizations to expand its influence. And it is about aggressive military and technology muscle flexing, not partnerships. Kissinger's argument is that given the current world order was built largely without Chinese participation, China sometimes feels less bound than others by its rules. Where the order does not suit Chinese preferences, Beijing has set up alternative arrangements, he said.[19]

Indeed, China doesn't seem to be bound by the old rules, because it wants to set its own. In his eight years at the helm of Chinese affairs, 'Xi has pursued an expansive, hyper-nationalistic vision of China's future, displaying a desire for control and a talent for political manoeuvring'.[20] He has crushed critics and potential rivals, revitalized the Communist Party and changed laws, which could allow him to rule for life if he wants.[21] Given Xi is now the paramount leader—controlling the party, the government and the military—he is 'promoting his self-styled, tech-enhanced update of Marxism as a superior alternative to free-market democracy—a "China solution" to global problems'.[22]

China under Xi, unlike under Deng Xiaoping, Jiang Zemin, and Hu Jintao, is no longer a status quo power. It has become a revisionist power. For the US, its allies and the US-led liberal international order, this represents a fundamental shift in the strategic environment. Ignoring this profound change courts peril. Xi is no longer just a problem for US primacy. He now presents a serious problem for the whole of the democratic world.

His ambitious One Belt, One Road initiative that threatens to expand China's influence deep into Europe, Africa, the Pacific and South Asia is the new cornerstone of China's economic and foreign policy. Everything that China stands for runs counter to principles shared by the US and many like-minded countries, of representative government, free enterprise and the inherent dignity and worth of every individual.[23]

Xi probably had compelling political reasons to take actions that risked antagonizing the US, Denny Roy wrote in *The National Interest*.[24] According to him, Xi faced difficult domestic tasks that included restructuring the Chinese economy for long-term growth, restoring the authority of the Party over Chinese society, making the military more efficient and more tightly controlled, subjugating the powerful vested interests that would oppose his efforts, and strengthening the Chinese political system against threatening foreign ideologies. Xi needed to simultaneously consolidate his own personal power and authority, which in turn required him to satiate a nationalistic mass public's demand that the government demonstrate Chinese strength in response to foreign challenges to China's honour and interests.[25] With Xi's ascent, China's longstanding worldview changed sharply. Paramount leader Deng Xiaoping's advice that China keep a low profile and the plan for a peaceful rise slowly disappeared from the public narrative as a new China under Xi began flexing its muscles.

The Kissingerian approach is that the rise of China is more a result of America's own deficiencies—its declining competitive position, driven by factors such as obsolescent infrastructure, inadequate attention to research and development, and a seemingly dysfunctional governmental process.

Conclusion

If there was one factor that has accounted for the longevity of the Kissingerian approach to China, it is the people under or around the man. He was, in effect, a godfather, the leader of a small cadre of men serving under him who were to guide US policy towards China for a quarter-century after he left the government. Among those working under Kissinger at the National Security Council and the State Department were two future secretaries of state (Alexander Haig and Lawrence Eagleburger); three national security advisors (Brent Scowcroft, Robert McFarlane and Anthony Lake); and one ambassador to China (Winston Lord).

Many, after them, were in awe of him and others sought his advice, allowing him to seed his thoughts and approach into policy while at the same time also advising the Chinese. However, much has changed since the early part of this century and the battle lines drawn slowly over the past decade have solidified into a global understanding that the Chinese world order may not be the best for most. At the same time, China's growing economic and military might makes it difficult for many nations to directly challenge Beijing's ambitions and its ascension as a global power.

It is, therefore, up to the US to take the lead in again aggressively projecting the alternative the world has been used to for long, but lost out on when Trump decided to forego the unipolar global leadership that Washington provided since the end of the Cold War. But to project power and protect and preserve the liberal world order that China is challenging, the US—and all other nations—need a long-term China strategy—a thorough appreciation of what China is attempting to achieve and what needs to be done to counter it on a sustained basis.

Some will argue that the US already has one, pointing to the Trump administration's declaration of 'strategic competition' as the 'central challenge' of US foreign and national security policy. However, while the Trump administration did well to sound the alarm on

China and its annunciation of strategic competition with Beijing was important, its episodic efforts at implementation were chaotic and at times contradictory.[26]

China's biggest advantage has been and is its ability to look beyond a normal timeframe allowed to nations that have to choose new leaders every few years. The Chinese Communist Party, which will be celebrating its centenary this year, has the ability to see the world through a civilizational prism and plan five decades ahead. And Xi is likely to be around for longer than the usual ten years as some of the past Chinese leaders have, controlling a country that has successfully bullied neighbours to expand its geographical boundaries in the past four decades without actually fighting a war. Hit hard by a pandemic, economic downslide and geopolitical uncertainties, the world has only become more wary of China's intentions.

Former Singaporean Prime Minster Lee Kuan Yew once said that the size of China's displacement of the world balance was such that the world must find a new balance. 'It is not possible to pretend that this is just another big player. This is the biggest player in the history of the world.'[27] With the 'China is changing' narrative finally buried, it is time for the US to use Biden's long years of foreign policy experience to take along traditional allies and new friends to jointly create a compelling economic, technological and diplomatic alternative that can be quickly and successfully made available to nations gathering under the Chinese umbrella. A new balance needs to be found—one that will be in favour of the world, not just China.

8

A Future beyond the Past

SUJAN CHINOY

HENRY ALFRED KISSINGER IS PERHAPS the only titan among all the strategic thinkers and practitioners of national security and foreign policy to have stridden like a colossus during the Cold War, shaped its direction, and to now have the burden of reflecting on his own role as chief architect of former President Richard Nixon's outreach to China against the backdrop of a New Cold War in the twenty-first century. The contemporary shifts in Sino–US relations afford the nonagenarian a chance to review the underlying assumptions of the past. It also affords the international community an opportunity to challenge his thesis in his presence. The Cold War that followed World War II had involved the Soviet Union. The substantive stakes for the US had revolved around trans-Atlantic European security. The New Cold War of the twenty-first century involves an Asian power, the People's Republic of China, which threatens peace and security in the Indo-Pacific.

The US–China historical engagement

The US, the world's oldest democracy, is also among its youngest nations. Historically, the US had itself demonstrated a streak for isolationism, perhaps drawn out of it only by the realism of its participation in the two great wars, its emphatic use of the enormous power of the atom bomb and the finality of the end of Pax Britannica after 1945. As a great power drawn into a global role, the US had no real experience of China, situated in Asia, far away from continental US. This is unlike India, which has coexisted with China cheek-by-jowl for millennia, or even the European colonialists who had obtained trading rights and territorial concessions in enclaves along China's southern and eastern seaboard.

After US independence, over the next half century, American merchants were also lured by the prospects of trade with Canton, plying, among other things, quantities of lower quality Turkish opium. It was in 1844 that the US first entered into an official treaty with the Qing regime through the Treaty of Peace, Amity and Commerce, between the US and the Chinese Empire, which remained in effect till 1943 until it was replaced by the Sino–American Treaty for the Relinquishment of Extraterritorial Rights in China.[1] However, the access to the Old China Trade under the 'Canton System' as it was known, also paved the way for the controversial influx of thousands of Chinese émigrés for the California Gold Rush, and later as a labour force for building railroads, leading to legislation and bilateral treaties in the 1880s to prohibit immigration from China.[2]

Yet, through all this, there was a certain fascination for the esoteric land of the Middle Kingdom, distant, mysterious, yet beckoning. Missionaries and Southern Baptists were drawn in sizeable numbers by the prospects of proselytization among the teeming millions in China.[3]

The Boxer Uprising of 1900, in which foreigners and European missionaries were massacred, resulted in a punitive mission; what is noteworthy is that US Marines were part of the Eight-Nation Alliance that sacked Beijing in 1901 and forced China to pay huge indemnities.[4] This was the first instance of US armed action against the Chinese people, bracketing the US alongside the European colonial powers that had long engaged in depredations in China against an enfeebled Qing regime.[5]

Broadly speaking, there was also a fascination among Americans for all things Chinese, bordering on romantic notions of deciphering a forbiddingly remote agrarian Asian society. American author Pearl S. Buck epitomized such writing.[6] Later, Edgar Snow romanticized the life of Mao Zedong and his band of survivors of the Long March in his book *Red Star Over China.*[7] Spending some time in the hard-scrabble mountains and barren loess plateaux of Yan'an in Shaanxi Province in China with Mao, he introduced Mao's thoughts to Americans flirting with Marxist ideology in the aftermath of the Great Depression.[8]

The McCarthyism of the post-World War II period that shaped US policy towards communism, most notably under Secretary of State Dulles in 1953–59, had its roots in the First and Second Red Scare; US apprehension about the implications for the US of the emerging world of communism had an even track record going back to the Bolshevik Revolution in Russia and the rise of leftist political thought in advanced liberal societies as the very antithesis of capitalism.[9]

Kissinger's intellectual moorings

Professor Kissinger made his debut in a government position in a world in which he explored strategic thought, international relations and foreign policy with his books such as *Nuclear Weapons and Foreign Policy* (1957) and *The Necessity for Choice: Prospects of American Foreign Policy* (1961). He had no known training as a China specialist, nor did he speak any Mandarin. In 1957, China had no nuclear weapons and could not have figured centrally in his book as it might today with long-range missiles that can threaten every part of continental US and even erode its superiority at sea and in space through asymmetrical means.

In many ways, Henry Kissinger's thoughts on China have displayed the lack of the familiarity and historical perspective that might come naturally to peoples and nations with a longer history. As a brilliant polemicist, his thoughts about China were bereft of the baggage of the past. They had the freshness of purpose, the hope and excitement and even dispassionate objectivity in dealing with the contemporary. His own life experience, as a young German immigrant fleeing persecution for a better future in the US, no doubt honed a certain neuroplasticity to spot, interpret and seize strategic opportunities.

As a European immigrant, it would have come naturally to Kissinger to be steeped in the statecraft of Klemens von Metternich and Carl von Clausewitz and the Westphalian balance-of-power politics of three centuries. His doctoral dissertation, understandably, was on 'Peace, Legitimacy and the Equilibrium' (A Study of the Statesmanship of Castlereagh and Metternich)[10], an early deep dive into the world of realpolitik that would define him as a preeminent national security advisor and secretary of state under two administrations and an informal advisor to several others.

Kissinger would undoubtedly have known, better than most while still at Harvard in the 1950s, how Wilhelmine Germany had picked up the mantle of a German Empire united by Otto Von Bismarck to upset the balance of power through imperialism, ultra-nationalism, naval expansionism and competition with England, and a scramble to seek colonial privileges in Africa.[11]

Many of these traits, Kissinger would not fail to notice now, are evident a hundred years on, in China's unilateralism and aggressive policies. As the world rapidly cleaves itself into two camps led by the US and China, a New Cold War looms ahead. China under President Xi Jinping is actively seeking to replace the US as the world's largest economy and most powerful nation. It promises to be a titanic struggle between a wealthy single-party autocracy founded on extreme notions of ideology and nationalism against an inclusive rules-based order favoured by liberal democracies.

Kissinger's understanding of Asia

Kissinger looked at the issue through the lens of classic European balance of power. It is one of the greatest shortcomings of US strategic thought, including Kissinger's own, that it could never quite clearly reticulate the various parts of the Asian power equation. The big pieces in the jigsaw puzzle in Asia, such as the question of Taiwan, peace in the Korean peninsula, Indochina, and the rise of communism, were apparent.

However, Kissinger's appreciation lacked a proper understanding of other dynamics such as relations between China and neighbours such as Japan and India.[12]

For a post-World War II US, flushed with victory, the priority in East Asia was to keep Japan from re-militarizing, and to leverage its considerable trade and investment ties, alliance partnerships, and bases, to maintain equilibrium in the Asia–Pacific.[13] The US opened up its market across the Pacific to resurrect Japan's economy and extended similar access to other Asian economies such as the Republic of Korea, Taiwan, Singapore and Hong Kong.[14] In incrementally providing China the same advantages after the great reset in relations following the Nixon visit in 1972, the US failed to fully foresee the longer-term implications of such a policy, including the flow of high-end technologies in the defence sector, leading to the economic and military rise of China.

From all that he has written about China, particularly in his seminal book *On China* (2011), it is clear that Kissinger was fascinated by the possibility of creating history. His record of meetings with Chinese leaders reveals the constant awe in which he held them, especially during one-on-one meetings with Mao Zedong and Zhou Enlai, both hardened veterans of the Long March and masters of guile.[15] Even President Nixon, during his historic visit in 1972, was summoned by Mao for a meeting without any advance notice, as if that were the most natural thing to happen to a person occupying the world's most powerful public office, to be ushered into the presence of a 'philosopher-king' and subjected to his musings for an indeterminate period of time.[16]

US opening to China

By the end of the 1960s, it had become apparent that Sino–Soviet relations had fundamentally deteriorated.[17] The breakthrough in ties with China came within two years of Nixon's inauguration as president in 1969. China dreaded the possibility of a full-fledged Soviet attack after the armed border clashes of 1969, the most serious of which was at Damansky/

Zhenbao Island on the Ussuri River.[18] The US spotted an opportunity to provide strategic reassurance to an erstwhile inveterate foe.[19] A triangular relationship was established over the next few years. An implicit strategic partnership between two ideological adversaries was forged to overcome a common challenge they faced from the Soviet Union.

In opening up to China, diplomatically and through economic ties, the US set into motion a process over which it later lost control, leading to vested political and commercial interests driving US policy towards China. A China, which regarded any US presence on its periphery ever since the formation of the People's Republic of China in 1949 to be 'encirclement' that thwarted its rise,[20] was unhesitatingly supported by the US. A policy, once implemented, has its own logic, and in this case, it rested on the premise that if the US opened up its markets, investments and technologies for China to access, it might lead one day to a more prosperous and democratic China.[21] The US entrepreneurs dreamt of big profits if the billion-plus Chinese people drank Coca-Cola, imbibed Starbucks coffee or ate McDonald's hamburgers. The naivety lay in the expectation that once the Chinese wore jeans and adopted some of the American lifestyle, an ineluctable process of political change would be set off in China. A 'peaceful evolution' implied, for a generation of policymakers that followed Kissinger, a possible change in the system of governance by the Communist Party of China.[22]

Over the last seventy years, the US has repeatedly misread China's true intentions or chosen to sacrifice reality on the altar of political expediency and commercial interests. Numerous examples of the strategic misreading of China by the US, resulting in outcomes being diametrically opposite to those envisaged in the original calculus, can be gauged from James Mann's trenchant book *The China Fantasy: Why Capitalism Will Not Bring Democracy to China*, published in 2008.[23] The book lays bare the weaknesses of all the premises of the Nixon–Kissinger duo that continued to guide US policy towards China well into the present times.[24]

The Nixon–Kissinger legacy

When one assesses US motivation in seeking a rapprochement with China, it is clear that the seeds of such policy reorientation were visible soon after Nixon took oath in 1969. The threat of an expansionist Soviet Union with conventional superiority in Europe, fast closing the gap with the US in strategic missiles, was a primary consideration. The US obviously had an eye to achieving an honourable retreat from the quagmire of an unending war in Vietnam. There was the unprecedented public reaction to the body bags coming in and the rampant drug abuse among the American soldiers, apart from the astronomical economic and political costs.[25] Alongside a reset in triangular relations, things began to look up somewhat between the two superpowers in 1972, with progress on Strategic Arms Limitation Talks (SALT) and better economic and trade arrangements.[26] Of course, this was only superficial progress as some might aver, perhaps a limited corollary of the forward movement in Sino–US relations. The decade of the 1970s no doubt continued to demonstrate that genuine détente was all but buried, Soviet interference in Angola and Ethiopia showed no sign of abeyance[27] and the arms race reached its acme. The decade ended with the Soviet occupation of Afghanistan in 1979, further fuelling the rise of neo-conservatism in the US.[28]

The Nixon–Kissinger move at the start of the 1970s had the effect of ensuring that China would emerge, as surely as would a butterfly from a chrysalis, from the limitations of the self-imposed isolation of the Cultural Revolution. By the end of the decade, China under Deng Xiaoping had created the right framework[29] in support of the open-door policy and the Four Modernizations, to make the fullest use of propinquity in a new-found partnership with the US.

By the end of the decade, the Soviet threat was already receding, having reached its zenith. Unlike the brutal military interference during the Hungarian Revolution in 1956 and the Prague Spring in 1968, the Communist Party of the Soviet Union, under an ailing Leonid Brezhnev, did not intervene in the Solidarity Movement which started at the Gdańsk

Shipyard in Poland in 1980, leaving it to General Wojciech Jaruzelski to deal with local opposition through martial law.[30]

In November 1983, the Reagan administration publicly announced new regulations for the transfer of technology to China.[31] The new regulations were designed 'to reflect a more liberal export control policy' by raising dramatically the volume and sophistication of technologically advanced goods developed in the US available for licensing and export to China.[32] To facilitate the policy, the administration even reassigned China to the country grouping under the Export Administration Regulations placing it alongside the NATO countries and other friendly non-aligned nations.[33] The immediate effect of this re-categorization was that the export of most goods and technology to China began to be fast-tracked rather than be subjected to the old policy of case-by-case reviews.

Ironically, with the path paved by the Nixon–Kissinger opening to China in the course of the previous decade, it was under a neoconservative president, Ronald Reagan, that the US transferred several military technologies to the People's Republic of China in 1983–87, although the momentum in such cooperation was disrupted by the Tiananmen massacre, and never quite regained subsequently. Reagan's military cooperation had a precedent in the Carter administration's erroneous assessment, as Kissinger himself asserts, that an increase in China's technological and military capacities enhanced global equilibrium and American national security![34]

Looking beyond Tiananmen

In fact, after the Tiananmen events of June 1989, President George H.W. Bush almost competed with Nixon in sending secret outreach missions to China. Within weeks of the crackdown which led to global outrage, Bush sent his National Security Advisor Brent Scowcroft, accompanied by Deputy Secretary of State Lawrence Eagleburger, to Beijing on a secret trip in July, followed by another trip later.[35] The Soviet Union disintegrated in 1991, and for reasons that were no longer related to the original motivations of the early 1970s, the US resumed full cooperation with China after only a short interregnum.

The dissolution of the Soviet Union in 1991, in a way, had removed the fundamental underpinning of the triangular logic of US policy towards China, in which it sought better ties with both China and the Soviet Union as compared to what the other two had with one another. The CCP's harsh crackdown on peaceful demonstrators at Tiananmen in 1989 and its reaction to the end of the Soviet Union[36] should logically have alerted the US to the real nature of China's political system. The US failed to be mindful of the ominous implications of the rise of communist China as a global power. Following a brief interregnum, ties were normalized and China resumed its growth trajectory.

By the time President William Jefferson Clinton took office in 1992, levelling the charge that his predecessor Bush had been 'coddling the butchers of Beijing',[37] other interests had taken over. The US entrepreneurs viewed China as an opportunity to lower manufacturing costs, access the growing Chinese domestic market and to expand markets globally.[38] After initial friction over trade and human rights, followed by tensions sparked off by Chinese missile tests across the Taiwan Strait, Clinton ordered two US carrier battle groups to steam through the narrow waterway.[39] After that, things moved quickly to reveal contradictions in the US's China policy. On the one hand, a US warplane 'mistakenly' bombed the Chinese embassy in Belgrade in 1999, leading to unprecedented mass demonstrations against US diplomatic compounds in China.[40] On the other hand, Clinton moved from annual trade certifications for China to grant permanent normal trade relations (NTR), previously known as most favoured nation (MFN) status, through the US–China Relations Act of 2000.[41]

From then on, there was no looking back for China. Unimpeded and guaranteed access to the US market paved the way, under the subsequent Republican administration of President George Bush, for China's entry into the WTO. Since then, the entire world has been China's oyster. Its 'state capitalism', backed by hidden subsidies, has helped it notch up huge trade surpluses, especially with the US. In the two decades since, China has hollowed out many a manufacturing capability in the world's most advanced economy.

Today, after decades of unbridled growth, China can claim satisfaction from the fact that it outwitted the US, thanks to the fundamentally flawed premises of the US policy, the groundwork for which was laid by Henry Kissinger under Nixon. China's state-led economy emerged relatively unscathed from the Asian financial crisis of 1997 and succeeded in locking many Asian countries in its embrace through currency swap agreements under the Chiang Mai Initiative.[42] Its endurance during the global economic and financial crises a decade later left it in an advantageous position vis-à-vis the US and other large liberal democratic capitalist economies. Both before and following the outbreak of the COVID-19 pandemic, China's 'socialism with Chinese characteristics' and 'state capitalism' have demonstrated greater capacity than others for economic growth and recovery, thoroughly disproving Kissinger's view of the 1970s that wherever market economies and communist economies have competed in roughly comparable circumstances, the communist economies have been left far behind.[43]

Departure from policy reticence of the past

The US traditionally had no interest in challenging China's territorial integrity, with the proviso that force would not be used in resolving the question of Taiwan. When Japan occupied Manchuria in the 1930s and expanded its conquests across much of East China, it was ironically the colonialists and the US which sought to preserve China's independence. In fact, Secretary of State Dean Acheson had stated as early as in January 1950 that China's integrity was in American national interest regardless of communist China's ideology.[44] Though the Taiwan Relations Act of 1979 kept Taiwan within the US Security perimeter,[45] it is only recently that the US passed the Taiwan Allies International Protection and Enhancement Initiative (TAIPEI) to encourage countries to maintain ties with Taiwan and back its participation in international organizations such the World Health Organization (WHO).[46]

The US had little interest in Tibet's independence or even autonomy in the years leading to the formation of China and its military takeover of Tibet in 1950. It took no heed of Tibet's pleas to the United Nations for assistance in 1950, or later, when the Dalai Lama fled to India in 1959.[47] For a brief while during World War II, President Roosevelt had reached out to the Dalai Lama's administration in Lhasa for access to Tibet's territory to aid the war effort.[48] Even the low-intensity covert operations by the CIA ended with the Sino–US rapprochement in 1971. President Trump filled in the vacant post of special coordinator for Tibetan issues in the Department of State, building on the Tibet Policy Act of 2002, the Reciprocal Access to Tibet Act of 2018 and the Tibet Policy and Support Act of 2019.[49]

Hong Kong's future has figured on the list of US interests only recently, sparked off by the trampling of democracy and human rights. A subject long outsourced to the British, the US was happy to make use of the territory to monitor China and to avail its use for rest and recreation by US vessels in the region. Growing Chinese sensitivity to US military activity on its periphery, including the Taiwan Strait, has put an end to this. The US recognized Hong Kong's autonomy through the Hong Kong Policy Act of 1992 and adjusted policies to give the territory trade and other benefits even after its handover to China in 1997.[50] Since then, China has systemically eroded the territory's special status guaranteed under the 'One Country Two Systems' formula. The brutal repression of pro-democracy protests followed by the passing of a new draconian National Security Law 2020 by Beijing[51] led to the US president signing the Hong Kong Human Rights and Democracy Act of 2019.[52]

Of the many examples of China's heavy-handed actions, none is perhaps as egregious as Xinjiang. The US has boldly criticized China for human rights violations, forced detentions, desecrations of mosques, and restrictions on religious symbols and practices.[53] The US has passed the Uyghur Human Rights Policy Act 2020 authorizing periodic reviews, freezing of assets and sanctioning of Chinese entities and officials involved in surveillance and human rights violations.[54]

In the South China Sea (SCS), the US has not done enough to prevent China's territorial grab or restore status quo ante. Under President Obama, the pivot to Asia was little more than lip service. President Xi executed his own pivot after coming to power in 2012, defying the United Nations Convention for the Law of the Sea (UNCLOS). Attempts to reticulate the region through the Belt and Road Initiative and predatory finance have further complicated the situation in Southeast Asia. The Trump administration finally realigned its official position on the SCS with the 2016 tribunal ruling of the Permanent Court of Arbitration which deemed Chinese claims unlawful.[55]

The more things change the more they remain the same

Some aspects, especially in China's character, transcend both its ancient civilization and modern ideology, and remain unmuted over the past half century. The concept of 'strategic encirclement' remains ingrained in Chinese strategic thought. As was once the case in dealing with the Xiongnu[56]—barbarians on its northern borders—China continues to employ ancient stratagems to pit one nation against another on its periphery to weaken and subjugate contending forces through guile and inducement.

There are both similarities and dissimilarities that can be observed through the lens of half a century. Mao, nearing his end when Nixon visited him, had no real successor. He had identified and banished several over time and Hua Guofeng, the anointed one at the time of his death, was a nondescript provincial lightweight who was quickly removed by Deng Xiaoping. Today, Xi Jinping, like Mao, has arrogated extraordinary powers to himself. Xi too has no successor in place. Xi, like Mao, appears to have anointed himself leader in perpetuity. If Mao said in the 1970s to Kissinger that China would not foreclose its option to use force over Taiwan,[57] and indeed expected to have to use it someday, Xi Jinping's China has taken the same line.

There are subtle differences too: Xi Jinping's resurrection of Confucius,[58] who had been denigrated by Mao, to justify imposition of his own version of harmony and order under the heavens. Having explored the limits of China's 'socialism with Chinese characteristics' in reconciling China's economic development and the growing aspirations of its people, Xi Jinping is now using China's ancient civilization, as embodied by Confucius, to demand complete order and loyalty of citizens to the authoritarian CCP. In his keynote speech on 24 September 2014, commemorating the 2565th anniversary of Confucius' birth, Xi Jinping held up the CCP as the 'successor to and promoter of fine traditional Chinese culture'.[59]

From the outset, as Kissinger writes, Mao had no intention to accept an international system in the design of which China had no role.[60] Today, under President Xi Jinping, China is following a subtler policy. It has greatly benefited from the post-World War II financial and political structures in the creation of which communist China had no role, such as the United Nations Security Council or the WTO. It has spearheaded new ones such as the Asian Infrastructure Investment Bank (AIIB) and the New Development Bank (NDB) of the BRICS (Brazil, Russia, India, China and South Africa) grouping. The US pull-out from the Paris climate change accord and Trans-Pacific Partnership (TPP) negotiations under President Trump, as well as withdrawal from UNESCO and UNHRC in 2017 and 2018 respectively, created new opportunities for China. Trump imposed cuts in financial contributions to UN agencies such as the United Nations Population Fund (UNFPA) as early as in 2017, and later, in the midst of the COVID-19 pandemic, announced a decision to cut funding to the WHO.[61] In the meanwhile, China has championed free trade and emerged as the largest economy in the RCEP, besides offering to ramp up its funding of UN agencies.

A common Chinese assessment that runs through the 1950s to the time of Kissinger's visit to China and up to now, is the belief in the superiority of China's systems and the conviction that the US is on the decline. More than the actual decline of the US, it is the perceived relative decline in US power that has often led China to believe that it is in a stronger position. Mao had labelled Hitler, the tsar of Russia, General Chiang Kai-Shek, Imperial Japan, and the US as 'paper tigers'. The others had met their end, and so would the US one day, he averred.[62] This unrealistic assessment of US power did not prevent Mao from bringing China closer to the US to ward off the Soviet threat.

New Cold War

So much has changed in the last fifty years. Already the world's second-largest economy today,[63] China hopes to overtake the US around 2027, the year in which the PLA will celebrate its centenary.

Over the decades, the US has not only run up a colossal annual trade deficit of about US $450 billion, but also allowed itself to walk into a blind alley of dependence on China in biotechnology, pharmaceuticals, rare earths, and even micro-electronics such as integrated circuits and transistors, which are used in critical platforms such as satellites, cruise missiles and drones, not just cell phones.[64]

More than in trade, it is in technology that the New Cold War is manifesting itself. The extreme dependence of Chinese tech giants such as Huawei, ZTE and SMIC on US exports of chips and semi-conductors does not diminish the fact that its research and development budget was US $321.3 billion in 2019, dwarfing the US outlay of US $156.8 billion.[65]

The New Cold War is playing out in myriad ways—competing lending mechanisms and programmes for regional economic development, capacity building and connectivity. For many, Pax Sinica is emerging as an alternative to Pax Americana.

Today, slogans such as the 'China Dream', 'New Type of Great Power Relations', 'Community of Shared Future of Mankind', backed by 'wolf-warrior diplomacy' are a means of enforcing a China-centric unipolarity in Asia.

Conclusion

To borrow a phrase from Kissinger's own writings, he has remained the 'perennial counsellor' to presidents and secretaries of state.[66] Recently, in an interview to Bloomberg,[67] Kissinger warned the incoming Biden administration to move quickly to restore lines of communication with China frayed during the Trump presidency in order to avoid drifting towards a catastrophe comparable to World War I.

Communication at this stage should mean firmly conveying US rejection of China's unilateralism and assertive policies. Now firmly in place, the Biden administration can ill afford to be lulled into the same sense of complacency that afflicted previous administrations. It should not allow China to get away with egregious violations of international law and blatant disruption of the regional balance of power.

A softer conciliatory approach by Biden will embolden China to continue to question the existing rules-based order. It will not prevent China from working on an old objective, a priority since 1949, of seeking the complete eviction of the US from Asia. Kissinger would understand this better in light of the US's historical experience of the 'Monroe Doctrine' in the nineteenth century, which sought to keep the Americas as a US preserve.

A Biden administration that eases pressure on China to conform to a rules-based order would sow the seeds of doubt in the capitals of all its alliance partners about the emergence of a potential US–China condominium, much like the 'Super-Yalta' feared by Europe in the 1960s.[68] So far, all indications point to the Biden administration sharing its predecessor's misgivings about China.

Fifty years after Kissinger's trip to China, a new relationship similar to the one that he helped forge between the US and China is now taking shape between India and the US. As between the US and China at the time, the new partners today seek to coordinate their actions without creating a formal obligation to do so. China's avowed goal to enlist the US as a counterweight to the 'polar bear' (Soviet Union) is similar to the way the US and India view one another in an attempt to deal with the dragon (China).[69]

Kissinger suggests in his book *On China* that an aspect of strategic tension in the current world situation stems from the fact that China fears that the US is seeking to contain China, and that this is paralleled by the US concern that China is seeking to expel the US from a region to which it has long contributed to through trade, investment, and security.[70] This is an assessment which was valid in the 1950s and '70s, and rings true even today.

The difficulty with superpowers, or perhaps great powers would be a more apt description today, is that they seek exceptionalism as a matter of right. Today both the US and China seek exceptionalism in their own ways. The difference is that the systems created by a US-led world order have proven themselves over the past seventy-five years, and succeeded in keeping peace through the Cold War and beyond. But the alternative order that China seeks to shape, and to lead into the twenty-first century through its slogan of 'community with a shared future for mankind' and 'wolf-warrior diplomacy', is unlikely to promote regional peace and stability. For that to happen, China will have to change. China's purposes withal will need to change.

9

Did Kissinger Wake the Dragon Up?

FRÉDÉRIC GRARE

FIFTY YEARS AFTER HENRY KISSINGER'S historic visit and the subsequent opening up to China by the US, how should the episode be assessed? For decades, successive US administrations and, with them, most of the world, chose to look at China as a source of economic opportunities and dismissed warnings about Beijing's potential strategic challenge in Asia. But today the world is in the midst of a painful reconsideration of its relations with China. What was then seen as the major achievement of the Nixon administration, with Kissinger as its centrepiece, is now criticized as being the source of US illusions vis-à-vis China or, to use the terms of US academic Michael Auslin, of 'America's China dream'.[1] Except for the notable exception of Pakistan, China is perceived as a threat by all countries on its periphery. It is also widely seen as the main challenge to the existing international order, and therefore to the US, as the existing liberal order is itself a reflection of US global dominance since the end of the Second World War.

Looking at the world today, it is indeed tempting to ask whether Kissinger and his associates did underestimate China's potential; if they, in effect, laid the foundation for another Cold War. Moreover, with Russia reduced to the status of junior partner to China, questions arise sometimes about the true importance of the Russian factor and its possible exaggeration at the time by successive US administrations, not only out of self-interest but also as a consequence of some supposed cultural bias on behalf of a national security advisor of German origin.

But questioning the wisdom of Nixon/Kissinger's China policy also raises issues which go beyond history. Questions about history are not just intellectual exercises. They almost always express insecurities, concerns about the present when it becomes unreadable or anxieties about the future when it seems too threatening. They can be a search for scapegoats and often reflect also the ideological beliefs of the moment.

This essay argues the idea that Kissinger and Nixon's visit to China in 1970 and '71 unleashed China's phenomenal rise and its perceived emergence as a threat to the existing world order is a historical shortcut which does not stand up to the test of history. It is based on an underlying belief in some cultural and/or historical determinism that is questionable at best. True, China was already seen as a potential threat by some of its neighbours at the time of the US–China reconciliation. Korea and India had fought wars with China only a few years earlier. In 1967, the creation of ASEAN was the outcome of the regional fears of Chinese subversion. True also, some academics had somehow envisaged the possibility of China's rise. When it did exist, mostly in radical left-wing intellectual circles, the prescience of China's rise was based on ideological considerations and the conviction of the moral superiority of the Maoist system. It would have occurred to very few that China would one day become a superpower by converting to the tenets of the capitalist economy. The idea that China, still largely an agricultural economy, absorbed moreover in its Cultural Revolution, would become a superpower, capable of challenging the US and the liberal world order, would have been surprising to many in the 1970s.

But even the possibility of predicting China's rise and intentions would not mean that the Nixon–Kissinger diplomacy could be held responsible for it. China shifted from a highly ideological course of action to a more pragmatic one on its own, not at US instigation. At the time of Kissinger's visit, Deng Xiaoping, who was to become the father of Chinese reforms, was in exile in Nanchang (Jiangxi province) to be re-educated in Mao's

Zedong thought.[2] The revolution he would initiate a decade later was simply unthinkable. The US initiative did change the relationship between Beijing and Washington but China, not the US, changed the course of Chinese history. The significance of the opening should not be overstated with regard to other developments which expanded China's influence.

What is at stake here is also the notion of 'long term' as a driver of foreign policy decision-making. History, more than the will of the decision-makers, confers on a given sequence of events a meaning and a logical articulation, which does not necessarily express the will of their authors at the time of the decision. Above all, it incorporates new events which at each stage of a process enrich the field of possibilities and lead to a result that is sometimes very different from that envisaged.

The ambitious yet limited objectives of 'triangular politics'

The rapprochement with China initiated by Kissinger in 1970 and the 1972 reconciliation between the US and China are often presented not just as the first step toward the normalization, which took place in 1979, during the Carter administration, but also as an essential piece in a sort of master plan that was to lead later on to the collapse of the Soviet Union. Yet, according to Kissinger himself, its objectives were, if ambitious, more limited in scope.

By taking advantage of the Sino–Soviet split, and the likelihood that Moscow might launch a broader attack on China, Kissinger and Nixon intended to open relations with Beijing in order to bring the latter into the realm of great-power relations as an instrument to pressure the Soviet Union. Kissinger envisioned 'a subtle triangle of relations between Washington, Beijing and Moscow, [in which] we improve the possibilities of accommodations with each as we increase our options with both'.[3] Establishing relations with China, while dealing with the Soviet Union, had an immediate objective. It was meant to convince both of them to slow down the provision of aid to North Vietnam and was supposed to give Hanoi a sense of isolation,[4] thus facilitating the quest for an agreement.

The move was also meant to shape a global equilibrium by dividing the communist world. China being the weaker of the two protagonists, it made sense for the US to provide it with some diplomatic support. China had, of course, objectives of its own and intended to use its new relationship with the US to achieve balance with the Soviet Union. But, in a triangular relationship, the 'Soviet card' was also played by the US toward China, while in all likelihood a 'US card' was also being played within the Sino–Soviet relationship.[5]

The effectiveness of the policy with regard to its objectives for Vietnam can be debated, but the outcome of the Nixon–Mao summit of 1972, which paved the way for the 1979 normalization, did not contain the seeds of the spectacular economic development that turned China into a superpower half a century later. The 'Shanghai Communiqué' was a political document which pledged that it was in the interest of all nations for the US and China to work towards the normalization of their relations and agreed that neither they, nor any power, should seek hegemony in the Asia–Pacific. It also recognized the 'One China policy', although without withdrawing US troops from Taiwan, but it did not contain any economic clause. It took, moreover, seven additional years and a completely different administration for relations to fully normalize.[6] By then Mao had passed away, the Gang of Four had been arrested, and ideology relegated to second-rank priority. China was about to enter a new era.

Deng Xiaoping and China's second 'cultural revolution'

Mao's China was unable to challenge the US in any significant way. It took another 'cultural revolution' of China's own making, one that Mao would have never allowed, for the 'middle of empires' to thrive, modernize and, ultimately, challenge the international status quo.

The China that Kissinger visited in 1970 was weak and poor. Famines had been the consequence of the Great Leap Forward. Moreover, China was still in the throes of a self-destructive Cultural Revolution, for which capitalism was the ultimate horror. China's pre-reform economy was informed by a constant quest for 'self-reliance'. It did allow for some

Chinese exports according to the political needs of the moment but kept imports to a bare minimum, and limited foreign economic contacts as much as possible. Under Mao, the private sector had been entirely taken over by the state. The flaws of the system had been moreover exacerbated by the Cultural Revolution, by Mao's ideological fantasies as much as by the limits of the centrally planned system leading to shortage of food and basic consumer goods. If China possessed some of the factors of power traditionally defined by political scientists (space, population, national spirit, ethnic homogeneity), it lacked others, (resources, technology, industrial organization and, to some extent, political stability).[7]

Today's China is characterized on the contrary by trade surpluses, double-digit growth, huge hard-currency reserves and a growing middle class whose quality of life has generally improved. But it took more than just technical improvements to turn an essentially agricultural economy into the world factory. This second 'cultural revolution' was led by a victim of the previous one. Acknowledging China's backwardness, Deng Xiaoping embarked on a series of economic reforms, developed in several stages over three decades, which made China the second economy in the world over half a century. A gradual de-collectivization of agriculture was followed by industry reforms, including price and wage liberalization, and promotion and decentralization of trading activities. Then, came the formation of special economic zones and the creation of joint ventures to facilitate technology transfers and attract foreign direct investments. The role of the market economy and the right to private property were officially recognized in 1992. Since 1998, and even more so since China's accession to the WTO in 2001, the Chinese economy has been characterized by growing openness, while the regional economic integration dynamic initiated by China at the time contributed to the substantial increase of its regional and international leverages. The rapprochement Kissinger and Nixon initiated with Beijing provided none of these. It was political and had no bearing on China's economic situation and its capacity to modernize.

The reforms introduced by Deng Xiaoping required more than the pragmatism of a man known for his famous statement that 'it does not matter if the cat is black or white as long as it catches mice'. It required a fundamental change of the political circumstances that prevailed at the time of Kissinger's 1971 visit and the 1972 Nixon–Mao summit. Mao was unquestionably a mortal and therefore bound to die one day, but had the 'Gang of Four' prevailed, China would have likely continued on a radical ideological path, which may or may not have altered over time, but which certainly challenges the idea of China's rise as the unintended consequence of the Nixon administration opening up to China. Kissinger's later positions on China, whether he condoned later developments in US policy vis-à-vis China, such as its entry in the WTO or calls for a new way of thinking vis-à-vis China, does not contradict the fact that its policies could not and did not propel China into being the superpower it has now become.

Economics versus politics: 'It's [not quite just] the economy, stupid'

The pertinence of American decisions for the evolution of China should be examined from the point of view of their understanding of the political dynamics at the time of their respective decisions. The implicit accusation of naivety, or lack of prescience, does not stand up to a careful examination of the facts and does apply to other periods of US–China relations. For that matter, US support to China's accession to the WTO, which considerably boosted China's trade and integration in the world economy, constitutes an interesting case study.

Bill Clinton's views on the potential risks and benefits for the US of China's accession was anything but naïve. The US President believed that China's accession to the WTO would, for the first time, open the Chinese markets to American products and ensure that US companies would be able 'to sell and distribute products in China made by workers [...] in the US without being forced to relocate manufacturing to China, sell through the Chinese government, or transfer valuable technology'.[8] Bill Clinton knew that the US margin of action was limited and that if it could, at best, influence China, the path that Beijing would take for the future was its own choice. He also understood the nature of the Chinese regime and had no illusion that membership in the WTO would turn China overnight into a free society or guarantee that it would play by global rules. The question for him was not whether to approve or disapprove of China's practices, either. He did consider, however, that China's accession to the WTO would constitute a step in the right direction. Beijing would, for the first time, subject some of its most important decisions 'to the review of international bodies with rules and binding dispute settlements'.[9]

By contrast, opposing the accession would not 'free a single prisoner or create a single job in the US or reassure a single American ally in Asia. It [would] simply empower the most rigid anti-democratic elements in the Chinese government'.[10] He therefore considered that the US would 'have a far greater chance of having a positive influence on China's action if [it did] welcome China into the world community instead of shutting it out'.[11]

The years following China's accession to the WTO seemed to vindicate US beliefs. China accepted significant tariff reduction, the gradual elimination of all quotas and licenses, and a large increase in availability of trading rights. It did agree also to abide by international standards in the protection of international property and accepted the use by its trading partners of mechanisms that could be used to reduce the flow of Chinese goods in their domestic markets.[12]

True, China has since been accused of violating its own international commitments. But it is also fair to note that China, too, was taking a gamble. Accession to the WTO came with heavy costs in the short run, in the form of unemployment. Moreover, economic growth had been impressive since the beginning of the reforms without WTO accession. By the time it entered the trade organization, it was already the most open developing economy. But China's economy was not creating jobs fast enough to meet the demands of a still-growing population and needed to expand further and faster. The US decisions were, therefore, driven by both a sense of self interest and an acute understanding of the vulnerabilities of China.

More questionable, perhaps, has been the US belief that with the market economy, China would over time move towards greater political freedom because 'when individuals have the power to dream, not just to dream but to realize their dreams, they [...] demand greater say'.[13] In the post-Cold War years, such beliefs reflected US optimism. But China's political evolution, too, seemed to vindicate the idea. Deng Xiaoping never questioned the primacy of the Chinese Communist Party, but he promoted inner-party democracy and tried to overcome excessive bureaucracy in order to improve the efficiency of the system.

The US factor in comparative perspective: China and India's economic trajectories

The comparison between the trajectories of China and India provides useful parameters to assess the importance of the US factor in China's rise. The two countries have been partners against Western imperialism, fellow non-aligned countries, before becoming enemies—for India, China has been an existential threat ever since the 1962 War. Both countries entertained difficult relations with the US. Prior to China's reforms in the early 1980s, their economies were highly comparable. In 1978, the ratio of exports of goods and services to GDP was quite similar in the two countries. Both were amongst the most closed economies in the world. But they have since differed considerably in terms of regional economic integration as well as technological development, setting the countries on radically different paths.

But the US factor hardly explains the dramatic asymmetry between the two economies and, therefore, between their potential power. Political choices and strategy, not diplomatic support, explain the difference of economic development and power. Indian decision-makers decided to focus on domestic consumption when their Chinese counterparts turned their country into an export-oriented economy. By international standards, India remains today a very protectionist economy. The point here is not to demonstrate the supposed superiority of the Chinese model of development, but simply to highlight that relations with the US—which for India are at a historical high—do not suffice to explain the difference in the trajectories of the two countries.

Indian views on the role of the US in China's rise, after the Nixon administration's opening up, are likely to be negative, since the early 1970s marked a historic low in the US–India relationship. Today, however, the US factor plays in favour of India. Despite both the two countries being large democracies, relations between Washington and New Delhi have always been complicated and started warming up only in the late 1990s and early 2000s. But ever since Bill Clinton's historic visit to New Delhi in 2000, the US has consistently tried to help India, including with transfers of sensitive technology—as exemplified by the 2008 civil nuclear agreement. This was a result of its willingness to create a balance with China.

Conclusion

China's rise since the early 1980s has unquestionably been spectacular, but our reading of history reflects our concerns about the present. Questions about the wisdom of the US opening up to China reflect primarily the sense of vulnerability or, on the contrary, of self-confidence which characterizes each of the periods considered. The Nixon administration's opening up to China took place during the Vietnam years, a period of self-doubt for the US, but its ability to take advantage of the Sino–Soviet split and to further divide the communist world was perceived as a major diplomatic achievement and generated confidence in the US. The Clinton administration, whatever its actual understanding of China's evolution, could support China's accession to the WTO because the self-confident US believed that its national interest lay in a strong China, not a weak one beset by internal chaos. Today, Beijing's assertiveness is a reality—at least since Xi Jinping's ascent to power—but it is perceived as particularly threatening because US self-confidence has been dented by a series of events for which China bore no responsibility.

Beijing was not responsible for 9/11 and the following war against terrorism, in Afghanistan and elsewhere. Nor was China the cause of the Iraq War or the 2008 financial crisis. But these prompted some introspection in the US, which generated, in turn, in some quarters, a desire to withdraw—at least temporarily—from international affairs, a temptation that generated an uncertainty that China exploited to its own benefit, filling up the political space thus created. It is, therefore, not surprising if articles reassessing the Nixon administration's policy or later developments of US policy vis-à-vis China, like the Clinton administration's support to Beijing's WTO accession, appeared after 2010.

In India, the same question reflects primarily the concerns arising within it from the border clashes of the summer of 2020, as well as the deep anxiety about its own ability to reform and maintain the asymmetry of power between the two countries at a manageable level. In spite of persisting tensions with China since 1962, Indian decision-makers handled their relations with Beijing quite adroitly. But with the growing asymmetry of power between the two countries, their diplomatic agility may face some limits. India is constrained by its own underperforming economy and, for the time being, its incapacity to reform it, and its subsequent fear of being unable to catch up.

Moreover, for the first time, the global narrative is no longer on the side of the democracies. China generates envy and admiration. Its main contribution to political innovation may have been market authoritarianism, but it is certainly powerful enough to have democracies doubt themselves. Related, but not limited, to this socio-psychological dimension is the question about how history relates to the configuration of the international system and its dynamic at a specific moment of history while questioning the role of 'anticipation' in foreign policy decision-making.

In 1973, two years after Kissinger's historic visit to Beijing, a French author, Alain Peyrefitte, published a book titled *Quand la Chine s'éveillera . . . le monde tremblera* (*When China wakes up, the world will tremble*),[14] in which he predicted that China would inexorably end up imposing itself on the rest of the world as soon as it had mastered sufficient technology. Peyrefitte was no stranger to geopolitics or diplomacy. A minister in De Gaulle's cabinet, he had served a president who had actively encouraged Nixon and his national security advisor to open up to China and never questioned the wisdom of the decision. He was, on the contrary, criticized for his fascination for Mao's China. And when, starting in the early 1980s, China actually did turn its economy around, it was another illusion—the idea that a capitalist China would inevitably, over time, turn into a liberal democracy—which partly led the US, followed by many in Europe, to facilitate its accession to the WTO, leading to its vast increase in economic (and subsequently military) might.

It is, therefore, not a surprise that the question of the political and strategic wisdom of Kissinger and Nixon opening to China comes at a time when the US fears the potential loss of its primacy, or when India notes that strategic deference can no longer suffice to guarantee peaceful relations with Beijing, and when the rest of the world still hesitates on the posture to adopt vis-à-vis Beijing. But they all tend to forget that the current uncertainty comes after a period of historical optimism. It was not until Barack Obama's 'pivot to Asia' that China transitioned from the status of potential long-term problem into actual threat, generating policies to counter it.

In India, China had been seen as an existential threat ever since the 1962 border conflict. But it was only in the 2010s, after a long period of spectacular economic growth accompanied by growing self-confidence, that it started questioning its own capacity to manage its power asymmetry with Beijing. It took even longer for the powers situated beyond China's immediate periphery to understand the reality of China's rise and the reality of the power shift. By then the rationale and impact of the Kissinger–Nixon policies had long vanished.

Ultimately, Kissinger's legacy should be considered for what it is: not a lesson in futurology, but in statecraft and diplomacy. Central to the latter was the notion of national interest, which he pursued indefatigably for the US, although not always with the desired success.

Through the reconciliation with China, he established a Sino–American entente against Soviet ambitions in Asia and a lasting détente with the latter. Following administrations no longer had to face a two-pronged communist threat. But he never obtained a promise from China to stop support to North Vietnam. The war ended in confusion for the US. But Kissinger understood that the pursuit of national interest was the goal of every nation. That China did and would continue to pursue the same objective, even if by different ways and means, certainly came as no surprise to him—not out of indifference, but because it was something he could not stop.

10

The Kissinger Paradox

A 20th Century Investment for a 21st Century Threat

SAMIR SARAN AND KALPIT A. MANKIKAR

Everywhere under the vast Heaven
There is no land that is not the king's
To the borders of those lands
There are none who are not the king's servants.

—*The Book of Odes*, Zhou dynasty (1046–256 BCE)

The skilful strategist
Defeats the enemy
Without doing battle,
Captures the city
Without laying siege,
Overthrows the enemy state
Without protracted war.[1]

—Sun Tzu

Introduction: Historical overview

On 9 July 1971, a limousine, blinds drawn, rolled into a state guesthouse in Beijing, carrying American visitors. Breaking diplomatic protocol, the second-most powerful man in China, Premier Zhou Enlai, received his portly and professorial-looking guest, Henry Kissinger—national security advisor to US President Richard Nixon. China had been a pariah in the eyes of the US and its allies since the Communist takeover in 1949, with the then Secretary of State John Foster Dulles refusing to shake Zhou's hand when they met in 1954. This time, Zhou and Kissinger would shake hands with gusto—this moment was to be one of three key realignments of the twentieth century, the other two being Adolf Hitler's pact with Joseph Stalin, and Stalin joining the Allies in World War II.

Zhou and Kissinger's talks paved the way for rapprochement between the US and the People's Republic of China, and the formation of a new strategic anti-Soviet Sino–American partnership. There have been intense debates since then, on why Kissinger facilitated US alignment with authoritarian China. Clearly, Cold War-era geopolitical concerns did guide America's decisions as subsequent events would soon establish.[2] The lure of a huge market may also have been a motivation, as some analysts have argued.[3] Or, perhaps, Kissinger was merely restoring America's historic ties with China after Mao's anti-American aberration.

The long arc of US–China relations has been shaped by many leaders in both countries across centuries. Kissinger—national security advisor to Nixon from 1969 to August 1974, when Nixon resigned following Watergate—was amongst the most influential in this regard. He was responsible for introducing his brand of realpolitik in this most important contemporary relationship of the US with China.

In the nineteenth century, Protestant missionaries came to China and founded institutions like Nanking University and Yenching University. Children of some of these missionaries, such as Henry Luce (founder of *Time* magazine) would later become opinion-makers in the US. Pulitzer Prize-winning historian Barbara Tuchman has written that such 'influencers' had an 'accompanying sense of obligation towards the subject of one's beneficence'.[4]

However, it is also true that these missionaries invited the ire of conservative elements, eventually leading to the Boxer Rebellion. In 1900, members of a secret society murdered Chinese Christian converts and missionaries, wrecked churches in Beijing and cordoned off the area that housed foreign envoys. Eight nations, including the US, later sent an expeditionary force of nearly 20,000 soldiers to rescue their citizens after Qing Empress Dowager Cixi declared war. China was told to pay more than $330 million in reparations.[5]

The anti-Western sentiments that had culminated in the Boxer Rebellion, and the subsequent deployment of US soldiers to crush the insurrection, threatened to damage US's moral posture that was distinct from the colonial powers of that day. This discord—between power and values—would surface on occasion. In 1905, stories of mistreatment of Chinese in the US sparked off a boycott of US goods in China.[6] In a bid to temper hostility, the US decided to use the Boxer Rebellion reparations to fund scholarships and bursaries for Chinese youngsters to study in the US.[7] In 1924, the US Congress allotted a sum of nearly $12.5 million for these education ventures, and mandated the formation of a Sino–American panel to oversee the fund's utilization.[8] In what was perhaps a tribute to such contribution, the US started to be popularly referred to in China as 'měiguó (美国)', which means 'beautiful country' in Mandarin.

In the first half of the twentieth century, the US was concerned by the growing influence of the Communist International in China, and decided to support Nationalist leader Chiang Kai-shek.[9] Chiang's marriage to Soong Mei-ling, the daughter of Harvard University-educated T.V. Soong who had strong ties with the US establishment, led to his reputation growing in the eyes of the US administration.[10] Chiang's baptism in 1930s as a Christian, and his close personal ties to missionaries, burnished his credentials.[11] the US thought it was prudent to influence China through this power couple. After all, Soong Mei-ling alone was formidable: she led the Chinese air force during the war with Japan, and had extensive contacts in the Congress.[12]

The US's demonstration of friendship and compassion for China turned into antagonism after the Communist takeover in 1949. The early years of the People's Republic of China (PRC) coincided with the Korean War (1950–1953), in which the People's Liberation Army fought against US forces. The US leaders started to perceive the Middle Kingdom differently—as a 'realm of fanatical revolutionaries'.[13] In turn, Mao Zedong derisively referred to the US government as a 'paper tiger'.[14] This was to change in less than two decades and by the late 1960s, there was renewal of mutual interest due to geopolitical and market considerations. When Kissinger received an invitation from Chairman Mao to visit China, he told Nixon that it was 'the most important communication received by the President since the World War II ended'.[15] Arguably, this assessment was to lay the foundations for the emerging bilateral relationship, the American investments that would fuel the rise of China, and perhaps the romanticization of the oriental giant that would pose the single biggest challenge to the US in the twenty-first century.

American exceptionalism: The 'Godfather syndrome'

> '*A nation's foreign policy must be rooted in an assessment of strength, not sentiment.*'
>
> —Henry Kissinger

Prince Otto von Bismarck was a statesman who amalgamated Germany in the seventeenth century. For Kissinger, Bismarck's talent lay in his ability to manage contending forces by manipulating their antagonisms—this perhaps gives us an important insight into Kissinger's view of the world of politics and power.[16] It was certainly a pillar of his realpolitik outreach to China.

In the 1940s, the conflict escalated between the communist North Vietnam and the South, which had America's support. Kissinger viewed the conflict as a result of Soviet expansionism, and not an anti-colonial struggle.[17] He supported US President Lyndon Johnson's move to dispatch combat units to Vietnam.[18] The North's Ho Chi Minh and his army engaged the US military in a long-drawn-out war, buoyed by China, the Soviet Union and sheer grit. American involvement in Indochina was the glue that brought the Vietnamese, Chinese and Soviets together.[19] Kissinger realized this quicker than many of his peers and began to rethink US battle strategy.[20]

Meanwhile, French President Charles de Gaulle was among the first world leaders to consider making overtures to China; in February 1969, he broached the idea with Nixon, suggesting that the latter exploit Moscow's exasperation with Mao.[21] It was becoming apparent that tensions were brewing between the communist titans. Since its formation, the Soviet Union had been showering its munificence on Beijing, helping build its physical and human capital. Soviet leader Nikita Khrushchev assisted China's industrialisation,[22] specifically in the setting up of factories and the dispatch of technocrats to build capacities in fields as diverse as mechanical engineering and atomic energy. Thousands of Chinese students received vocational and technical training—including Jiang Zemin, who trained at an automobile factory in Moscow in the 1950s and would later be the president of China.

The year 1956 witnessed a watershed moment when Khrushchev denounced Stalin and began seeking rapprochement with the West.[23] For Mao, it was a blow to the communist bloc and weakened his own persona modelled on Russia's 'Man of Steel'.[24] China froze its ties with the Soviets, recalling their technicians and personnel—a jolt, paradoxically, to China's nascent economy. Matters came to a head in March 1969, after Chinese and Russian forces engaged along the frozen Ussuri River, and in Xinjiang; scores died. The clashes inspired Russian poet Yevgeny Yevtushenko, who had once been censured by the authorities, to caution China that they could meet the same fate as the Mongols, whom Russia vanquished earlier.[25] There were fears that the skirmishes could grow into a full-scale war.

Mao decided to use the US card to keep the Soviets at bay.[26] For its part, the US deemed it crucial to have an influence on China in order to check the Soviet Union on the geopolitical chessboard of that period.

Kissinger was the one who threaded these coincident yet individual assessments together through a new US outreach to Beijing. Theodore Roosevelt may have been prescient when, during his presidency as the twentieth century opened, he said: 'America's future history will be more determined by our position in the Pacific facing China than our position in the Atlantic facing Europe.'[27] Kissinger was more pragmatic and decided to alter the course of the future with his new plan for ties with Beijing.

Realpolitik: An eye-opener to friends and foes

The strategic bond of the US with the communist China altered the balance of power in Asia. Zhou gauged that this shift had 'shaken the world'.[28] As the US normalized its relations with China, new security arrangements between the US and its allies in Asia emerged. The reverberations were felt, in particular, in Japan and Taiwan that were under the US's protective umbrella. Japan gave its steadfast support to the US during the Vietnam War and eschewed a resumption of official relations with China. It had been assured that any opening to Beijing would happen with its knowledge and tacit consent.[29] Japanese were, hence, taken by surprise with the unilateral announcement of Nixon's visit to China in 1972. The 1970s saw the ascent of the 'land of the rising sun' literally from the ashes of Hiroshima and Nagasaki bombings, and increasing US–Japanese economic competition. In overtures to Mao, Kissinger schemed to also pit China against Japan for the benefit of the US. As a collateral benefit, the US achieved its objective to get Japan to double its expenditure on self-defence forces in line with the spending by key allies like UK, Germany and France, and cut the then $3.5 billion trade deficit by acquiring US planes.[30] Many in Japan began questioning the rationale of refraining from establishing relations with China.[31] Following Nixon's visit to the Middle Kingdom, Japanese Prime Minister Tanaka Kakuei visited China to offer regrets about his nation's mistreatment of the Chinese before 1945 after which the two nations established diplomatic relations. In this way, a 'recalcitrant' ally had been cut to size.

Taiwan, too, began to feel the heat as Sino–American relations thawed and the US recognized the People's Republic of China as the sole legal government. Taiwan terminated its relations with the US, it lost its seat in the United Nations, the US–Taiwan mutual defence treaty was scrapped and US military personnel withdrew from Taiwan. The Guomindang regime had been undermined.[32] However, back-channel efforts by its diplomatic corps led to the US Congress approving the Taiwan Relations Act, which pledged to provide the island with arms and help resist any aggression or coercion.[33]

These developments caused sufficient worry for Moscow. Kremlin immediately tasked its US envoy Anatoly Dobrynin to propose a US–Soviet summit in Moscow, before Nixon's meeting with Mao. The conference in Moscow would ultimately be held in May 1972, after the China conference. President Nixon and Soviet President Leonid Brezhnev concluded treaties on anti-ballistic missiles and strategic arms limitation, followed a year later by the Agreement on the Prevention of Nuclear War. This partly fulfilled the US establishment's aim, as articulated by businessman and politician Nelson Rockefeller thus: 'In a triangle with China and Soviet Union, [the US] would ultimately improve relations with each of them as their eagerness for peace would be tested.'[34] Moscow saw this as containment and moved to rebalance, signing a cooperation pact with India.

Over the decades, America's aim of containing Russian influence has not waned even with the demise of the Soviet Union. Since the 1990s, NATO has expanded to include the Eastern bloc and former Soviet nations. Georgia and Ukraine,[35] which already have an understanding with the US-led military pact, may be added soon; this would take the military alliance to Russia's doorstep.

The plan to construct a missile defence shield in Eastern Europe in 2007 to protect Europe from an Iranian nuclear attack proved to be another trigger. Realizing that it could neutralize Russia's nuclear deterrent,

President Vladimir Putin proposed a joint radar warning mechanism in Azerbaijan. The US ignored the proposal.[36] Putin subsequently categorized NATO as a threat.[37] Russia has also hit back by annexing Crimea from Ukraine, and supporting separatist groups fighting the Ukrainian government. The resultant sanctions by the US and EU, ironically enough, have forced Russia into China's willing arms. The expansion of NATO stems from Kissinger's rationale that the US building up regional powers would engender a 'sense of local responsibility', reducing America's burden.[38] In recent years, Kissinger has spoken about the need for NATO to be revamped 'beyond a military alliance', and the US to provide stability.[39] The high priest of US strategic thought warned that the West abjuring from its responsibilities would open the space for Russia, and that engaging in conflict without 'strategic concept' would result in chaos.[40] He has also made a case for keeping Russia away from NATO, saying admitting it to the alliance would take the geopolitical games to China's door.[41] Hence, in Russia's post-Cold War encirclement, Kissinger's legacy has lived on, contributing to a source of instability in the old continent and may have paved the way for unchecked growth of China's power and clout.

Kissinger's legacy: China as America's greatest challenge

In Kissinger's calculation, the Nixon administration's initiative had 'transformed the structure of international politics'.[42] The camaraderie also was to have an impact on the economic relationship. Mao's policies had resulted in a slower pace of industrialization and sluggish economic growth. Nixon, for his part, had to contend with the country's coffers being drained by the war in Vietnam, its economic dominance being eroded due to the rise of Western Europe and Japan, a rising trade deficit, and diminishing confidence in the dollar.[43]

Walt Rostow, National Security Advisor to US President Lyndon Johnson, argued in the 1960s that rampant poverty in developing nations was driving people towards communism. This could be rectified, he said in his book *The Stages of Economic Growth: A Non-Communist Manifesto* by promoting modernization supported by US economic aid. His theory gained traction in the US effort to counter increasing influence of Communism in Asia. In this context, opening up China seemed to be a good bet. In 1965, a Canadian businessman invited Nixon on a trade mission to China, but the State Department vetoed that opportunity.[44]

In 1972, following Mao's summit with Nixon, a joint statement promised the expansion of economic and cultural contacts between the two countries. A reform-minded Deng Xiaoping pitched for improved cooperation in agriculture, industry, technology, and defence—the pillars of China's 'Four Modernizations' in late 1970s. Shortly, Coca-Cola—which many on the Global Left saw as the ultimate symbol of US imperialism—would ink a deal to sell its beverages in the mainland.[45] The decision to start 'special economic zones' in Guangdong and Fujian drew foreign capital and managerial expertise, which then helped build China's industrial base.[46]

China's rise and the amplification of its comprehensive power is therefore a direct result of three factors: the US propagating its 'values' frontier, Kissinger's foreign policy principles that privileged ends over means, and the 'Nixon Doctrine' of outsourcing the fight against Communism to regional partners. These helped China hide its capacities and bide its time, till it was propitious to challenge its benefactor. This sentiment was not about a single individual, but an Establishment sensing that a geopolitical schism could be effected in the communist bloc.

Many view Kissinger's initiative to open up China as a fait accompli presented to successive US administrations. Each US president has believed in 'constructive engagement' with China, hoping that it would lead to a more democratic nation that will adhere to the principles of a free market.[47]

Kissinger's thesis—that a China which is more integrated in the world system will be a responsible stakeholder—became a bipartisan credo for the Republican and Democratic parties of the US. In the immediate aftermath of the Tiananmen incident of 1989, describing himself as an 'old friend', Republican President George H.W. Bush beseeched China to behave like a 'civilized' country.[48] Bush's successor, the Democrat Bill Clinton, glossed over human rights issues and renewed China's 'most favoured nation' status.[49] This sentiment would be taken to illogical extremes with the Obama administration informally exploring a duopoly to manage global affairs.

In 2018, when US President Donald Trump launched a pushback against China, it led former State Department official Susan Thornton to blame her own government for the rupture in bilateral ties. She argued that President Xi Jinping's 'China Dream' is rooted in the desire to be like the US, and that adept diplomacy would make China a responsible global player.[50] In November 2018, then White House adviser Peter Navarro alleged that Wall Street bankers were pitching in for China following reports of officials from financial services companies like Goldman Sachs and Morgan Stanley meeting the Chinese leadership.[51] The 'Kissinger realpolitik', replaced an old rival but helped to create a far more efficient adversary—one adept at using America's resources against it.

The central flaw was in Kissinger's construction of his power politics. While he heeded President de Gaulle's counsel of connecting with China, he perhaps disregarded Rockefeller's caveat that the US engaging in a triangular equation with Soviet Union and China would guarantee peace. This would have guaranteed that the US remained the most important international actor for both China and present-day Russia. Kissinger's narrow and obsessive focus on Moscow was a seminal error that has pushed the Eurasian power, Russia, which possesses the second-most powerful military force in the world, into China's corner.[52]

Since then, the expectations that China will cooperate with the West have been belied with China's nourishing of anti-US regimes like North Korea.[53] China is a master of deception in that it is able to make its contenders believe that their aims are being met.[54] Its economic planners have adapted the ideas of free trade to its brand of authoritarian capitalism, creating a dependency for US corporations on its market and then using it as a weapon.[55] There is a strong view emerging that China portrayed itself as a backward nation only to secure technological and economic assistance while working towards supplanting the US by 2049—the centenary of Mao's revolution.[56] In other words, America's underwriting of China's development in the last century has been an investment in creating its most potent threat in the next. Kissinger's China gambit continues to implicate the US's approach to the Asian giant to this day. Future students of international affairs may well view Kissinger as having laid the foundations in the twentieth century for America's decline in the twenty-first. Can Kissinger's realpolitik be now put to bed?

REGIONAL PERSPECTIVES

11

Kissinger in China, 1971–2021

IGOR YURGENS

I HAVE KNOWN HENRY KISSINGER since 2009 when I hosted him in Moscow during his visit to Russia. The think tank which I led at that time worked for the then president of the Russian Federation, Dmitry Medvedev, and Kissinger was interested in the new developments in the upper echelon of our power structure. I was lucky to have the opportunity to talk to him on a number of occasions in Russia and abroad, and the views he expressed were always both original and consequential.

Kissinger is an American patriot with deep European roots, and knowledge of history and traditions. For many years, as the national security advisor and secretary of state, he defined the notion of America's permanent national interests and defended them with great skill and brilliance. One of the undisputed triumphs of his diplomatic career was the opening of relations with the People's Republic of China (PRC) and the policy of détente with the Soviet Union. While both were important for the changing world order, synchronization of the two was the best way to serve US national interests.

The concept itself seems pretty linear: there was nothing new in pitting one enemy against another. The most eloquent definition of such continental alliances was offered by Winston Churchill in his famous book *The Gathering Storm*:[1]

> For four hundred years the foreign policy of England has been to oppose the strongest, most aggressive, most dominating Power on the continent … we always took the harder course, joined with the less strong Powers, made a combination among them, and defeated and frustrated the Continental military tyrant whoever he was … It is a law of public policy which we are following, and not a mere expedient dictated by the accidental circumstances, or likes and dislikes or any other sentiment.

This was the rationale for US diplomacy exploiting the Sino–Soviet rift, which reached its climax in the early 1970s. The period we are examining in this book was called 'a revolutionary moment in US history' by Kissinger himself in his book *On China*. It was the most acute stage of the confrontation of the two communist giants—the USSR and People's Republic of China, when the US decided it could not adopt a position of neutrality, but should use the conflict to its advantage.

Looking back at my personal experience at the time, I distinctly remember the atmosphere of fear and stupefaction. Fear, because the country was declared by its leaders to be on the threshold of the big war, probably a nuclear one, and stupefaction because the enemy was a neighbour that just ten years earlier had been perceived as the closest friend and ally.

I entered Moscow State University in September 1969. Just six months before that, the Soviet and Chinese militaries had confronted each other on the disputed island of Damansky on the Ussuri river—the border between the two countries. Our leaders from the regional young communist organization called upon us, Soviet students, to protest in front of the Chinese Embassy in Moscow. Some of us were given bottles of ink to throw at the windows of the embassy. I should confess that even the strongest among us could not hit the intended target because the fence was too high and the building was too far away. But we felt that truth and justice were on our side because since the mid-1960s, when the so-called Cultural Revolution began in China, Soviet television regularly showed massive anti-Soviet demonstrations in front of our embassy in Beijing.

The history of relations between the two countries had never been easy or comfortable. In 1860, Russia joined other European powers in securing territorial concessions and additional privileges from the weakened Qing dynasty after the Opium Wars. Russia acquired the territory of the Outer Manchuria, which represents a large part of its southern Far East. China never forgot the 'unequal treaties' of Aigun (1858), Peking (1860), and Tarbagatai (1864). Even today one can find in China's textbooks the results of those wars described as Russian seizure of 1.5 million square kilometres of Chinese territory.

After the October Revolution in Russia and the emergence of the Chinese Communist Party (CCP) led by Mao Zedong, the ideological togetherness went side by side with personal rivalries and tactical conflicts. The Soviet leader Joseph Stalin supported the CCP but for a long time favoured its enemy—the Chinese National Party (Kuomintang) under Chiang Kai-shek, whom he needed against Japan. Stalin always regarded the position of CCP in the international communist movement as junior, never missing a chance to cut Mao down to size.

After the allied victory over Nazism and the establishment of the People's Republic of China in 1949, a powerful Sino–Soviet block was created. Together with the East European countries that fell into the Soviet orbit, one could say that two-thirds of the world became communist and anti-Western.

After Stalin's death in 1953, Mao began to develop his theory of Soviet revisionism and claimed leadership of the international workers' movement while the new Soviet leader Nikita Khrushchev declared friendship with China to be the cornerstone of a common struggle against imperialism. Khrushchev wanted, on the one hand, to outshine Stalin, accusing him of all the evils of the totalitarian regime, and to use the alliance with China for his own international posture, on the other. Khrushchev launched a major development assistance programme for China, including the transfer of nuclear weapons technology. But things went sour pretty fast. Mao despised Khrushchev and wanted to be independent of the Soviets. By 1960, all Soviet advisers were withdrawn from China. The Soviets and the Chinese were accusing each other of deviating from the true Marxist–

Leninist line and ended up in a series of border clashes, the Damansky Island incident being the most dangerous one.

On the night of March 1969, Chinese army units with 300 soldiers crossed the Soviet border and tried to occupy the Soviet island of Damansky, which the Chinese called Zhenbao. Thirty-one Soviet servicemen were killed, while China lost seventeen men. The clashes continued for fourteen days. Finally, the Soviets used the Grad missile system, which was secret at the time, burning down several kilometres of Chinese territory and killing hundreds of Chinese military.

In China, a massive anti-Soviet campaign was launched in April 1969 at the IX National Congress of CPC. The delegates formally ratified the purge of Soviet sympathizer Liu Shaoqi and moderate Deng Xiaoping, and elevated Mao's radical allies to power. First Vice Chairman of CPC Marshal Lin Biao delivered a report praising the ideology of 'continuous revolution'. Chairman Mao in his speech at the Congress appealed to 1512 delegates to prepare for war.

That was the historical context in which Henry Kissinger proposed to use the Soviet threat as an additional reason to establish relations with China and to counterbalance the Soviet Union's growing military build-up and assertive international behaviour. After the Damansky episode, the USSR placed forty combat divisions with nearly a million soldiers and nuclear weapons along the Chinese border. One should keep in mind that the newly formulated Brezhnev Doctrine was used in Czechoslovakia in 1968, according to which the USSR, as the standard-bearer of the world communist movement, had a special right to use military power to enforce its unity—which was totally unacceptable to China and the US.

The other side of the coin of the geopolitical competition and confrontation was the US–USSR arms race. At the end of the 1960s, an unprecedented build-up of strategic armaments by the USSR and the US started, with the American concept of a 'disarming missile strike'[2] as its point of departure. Both countries were pursuing massive ballistic missile defence projects, which led to the unravelling of the whole idea of nuclear disarmament. Multiple attempts to negotiate at the United Nations ended nowhere.

In the early 1970s, the Soviet leadership announced that it had achieved nuclear parity. Even before that, the US Secretary of Defence Robert McNamara stated in his famous speech in San Francisco that both sides had the ability to destroy each other even after absorbing a first strike.[3] At the time, the USSR and the US had 2,350 and 1,750 ballistic nuclear missiles respectively.

Preparing for his first secret visit to China, Kissinger was convinced that using Chinese leverage, the Soviets could be induced to take a more moderate stance both in the geopolitical competition and in the Asian conflict. This was the time of the Vietnam War, and America's withdrawal from Indochina appeared as one of the obvious outcomes. Richard Nixon's promise of an honourable peace, on which he was elected President of the US two years earlier, was becoming an empty phrase. Isolating Hanoi and weakening the USSR in the region were among his objectives.

The USSR supported the Democratic Republic of Vietnam (North Vietnam) from the very beginning. Soviet Prime Minister Alexey Kosygin publicly said in 1965 that one day of Vietnamese military operations cost the Soviet Union 1.5 million dollars. The USSR delivered to North Vietnam 687 tanks, 317 airplanes and 7,500 anti-aircraft missiles. Russian military advisors accompanied Vietnamese troops in many combat operations. To weaken the Sino–Soviet front in Vietnam was one of the objectives of US diplomacy. Was this goal achieved? After the Nixon's visit, the Chinese aid to Vietnam was drastically reduced and reoriented to Khmer Rouge, who undermined North Vietnam's struggle. As we all remember, this confrontation led to Vietnam's military conflict first with Kampuchea and then, in 1979, with China. From the tactical point of view, the mission was accomplished, but the war was lost.

In 1990, the records of negotiations between Mao and Nixon were declassified. In the beginning of the discussion, Chairman Mao avoided the concrete issues of bilateral or multilateral relations with other countries. He jokingly suggested discussing 'philosophical issues' instead. Then, however, it became clear that the Americans wanted to give the impression that they were putting China on an equal footing with the US and emphasized the anti-Soviet vector of this effort. The price the US paid for tacit acceptance of this alliance by Mao was Taiwan, which the US previously recognized as the government of all China.

Mao's insistence on the recognition of the People's Republic and its One China policy was firm and irreversible. For the Chinese, unification of Taiwan with the mainland was a 'sacred national obligation'. During the discussion in 1972, Mao ironically said that reunification might happen in a hundred years; it could be suspended for tactical reasons, but never abandoned. Since 1972, all American presidents have reaffirmed America's commitment to the One China policy while emphasizing that the problem should be solved peacefully. The rejection of the use of force by either side was included in the Taiwan Relations Act of 1979, which makes it American law.

The final communiqué signed during the US president's visit specifically mentioned 'resistance to Soviet hegemony'. Dr Kissinger's book *Does the US Need a Foreign Policy?* described his ultimate objective thus: 'The challenge for the US was to make sure that it always had more options than either of the other two parties within the triangle. This obliged the US to stay closer to both Moscow and Beijing than they were to each other, with a tilt toward Beijing since it was the Soviet Union which represented the more immediate and by far the more powerful threat.'[4]

From the Soviet perspective, Richard Nixon's 1972 visit to China formalized Sino–American partnership against the Soviet Union with a view to keeping America's hands free to pursue its own geopolitical objectives. To ensure a proper balance, Kissinger, with Nixon's consent, began intense preparations for a US–Soviet summit meeting. A confidential channel of communication was established between Kissinger and the Soviet ambassador to Washington, Anatoly Dobrynin, with a secret telephone line between Kissinger's office and the embassy. As Dobrynin wrote in his memoirs *Strictly Confidential* (1997): 'Kissinger was always business-like, sharp … could give you a headache, but was never boring or bureaucratic.'[5] The Russians knew about the Chinese contacts and considered them as 'a dynamic game in the strategic triangle of China,

USSR and the US, with the Chinese card being a weighty argument on the American side.'[6]

The results of these 'parallel' activities were impressive: the Strategic Arms Limitation Treaty (SALT-1), signed in 1972, successful talks at the Biological Weapons Convention in the same year, the Anti-Ballistic Missile Treaty, and the beginning of the SALT-2 talks, culminating in the official visit to Washington of the General Secretary of the Soviet Communist Party Leonid Brezhnev in June 1973.

Can one say that Kissinger's endeavour was a success? Definitely, yes. In spite of the Watergate scandal, Nixon's impeachment process and Chinese doubts about the reliability of their American partners, the dialogue continued for twenty years during the mandate of five US presidents. It certainly rebalanced the equilibrium in Asia and affected the Soviet Union's international positioning. One can presume that this was one of the reasons why the policy of détente and its ultimate success—the Helsinki Final Act of 1975—came to fruition.

The American bipartisan consensus on China policy was altered by two events—Mikhail Gorbachev's arrival to power in the USSR and the brutal suppression of the student uprising in Tiananmen Square in China.

In March 1985, Gorbachev came to power in the Soviet Union with the concept of 'new thinking' in Soviet foreign policy. He decided that the USSR would be constructive in its dialogue with all countries and would not seek unilateral advantages or military superiority. The USSR unilaterally undertook important disarmament measures, intensified bilateral talks with the US, and approached Germany, Great Britain and France with far-reaching initiatives to improve relations. In Gorbachev's inner circle of advisors, this was called 'the tactics of stimulating the partners'. One of the members of this inner circle, Evgeny Primakov, was given the task of designing a new Soviet strategy in the Asia–Pacific region. Mr Primakov, the director of the Soviet Academy of Sciences' Institute of Oriental Studies, included me in his group of experts, and in 1986–90 we worked on the concept of a 'Soviet pivot to Asia', which was impossible without a reset with China.

As one of the best experts on China, Bobo Lo from Lowy Institute in Sydney, very eloquently put it: 'China, by virtue of its population, history, culture and geographical position, is an indispensable component of a constructive Asian policy, and this requires a settled policy, not a slogan. Confrontation should be the last resort, not a preferred option.'[7] That was exactly the bottom line of Primakov's recommendations to the Soviet leadership more than thirty years ago. Mr Primakov later became minister of foreign affairs and prime minister of the Russian Federation. Kissinger's articles on China were among Primakov's favourites.

At the same time, after the Tiananmen events, the US hardened its position on the issue of human rights in China. Many in the US, Republicans and Democrats alike, began to view China as an adversary. I would go so far as to say that Gorbachev's example of reforming communism peacefully played a role in the American perception of China. Deng Xiaoping embraced economic policies favourable to market forces and the West, but the internal struggle within the top echelon of the Chinese Communist Party did not allow for political democratization. Consequently, even President Bush, who was the head of the US Liaison Office in Beijing in mid-1970s and knew China well, could not save Kissinger's doctrine. With the arrival of Bill Clinton to the White House, the issue of human rights became predominant.

At the same time, on the Russian front, first Gorbachev and then Yeltsin as the president of Russia drew much closer to the US. From this point of view, the balance and equilibrium in the triangle remained intact. By contrast, in Russia–China relations we witnessed a reversal of traditional roles, as the Soviet Union and its successor Russia weakened considerably and China rose as a new global power.

The arrogance of the Soviet elite towards China was replaced by a mood of Russian insecurity. Chinese economic power creates in Russia a feeling of erosion of sovereignty in the Russian Far East, creeping further to the Urals. The demography is hard to deny: China's northern regions are populated by more than 140 million people, while the neighbouring Russian Far East has the population of 6 million at best, and this imbalance tends to deteriorate.[8]

Relations at government-to-government level are excellent on the surface. Both Presidents, Vladimir Putin and Xi Jinping, call them a 'strategic alliance' and rightly so. And yet, we have a dichotomy of perceptions. On the one hand, on paper, signed by the two leaders, we have the 'Sino–Russian comprehensive strategic partnership of cooperation'. On the other hand, the lack of trust and the heritage of many years of hostility make the relationship at lower levels of the two societies more complicated.

China does not view Russia as a real superpower that can compete with it and the US for global leadership. In private talks, Chinese pundits (rarely officials) describe Russia as a country in decline with big demographic problems, horrendous corruption and an unhealthy dependence on exports of raw materials. On the Russian side, Sinophobia is just below the surface. Among the most recent examples, Russia closed the 2600-miles-long border between the two countries because of the COVID-19 outbreak and ordered the deportation of Chinese students. Russians fully understand that China uses Russia's rift with the West to strengthen its geopolitical, military and technological influence. Russia's soft underbelly—the countries of Central Asia—are fully exploited through Chinese economic dominance and the Belt and Road megaproject. China welcomes Russia's oil and gas, but refuses to provide strategic assistance against EU and US sanctions.

Nevertheless, Russia has no other option but to be China's close partner. This partnership includes similar positions on international issues and common external threats, whether real or imaginary, but first and foremost it rests on the authoritarian tradition and practices of governance. With the arrival of Donald Trump in the White House, the US strategy of engaging China, designed by Henry Kissinger, was brutally destroyed. The Chinese Communist Party was declared to be the enemy of the free world, and rivalry with China became the priority of US foreign policy.

Henry Kissinger, the architect of triangular dynamic stability, has not remained indifferent to it. In October 2020, speaking at the Economic Club of New York, he stated: 'Our leaders and their leaders have to discuss the limits beyond which they will not push threats. And then they have to find a way of conducting such a policy over an extended period of time.'. Answering a question from the audience, he added: 'You can say that it is totally impossible. And if it is totally impossible, we will slide into the situation similar to World War I.'[9] He said he had grown increasingly alarmed over a New Cold War developing between China and the US, which he attributed to technological advances that drastically changed the geopolitical landscape. Kissinger once again stressed that the goal of US–China rapprochement in 1972 was to create a balance against the Soviet Union.

Today, Washington will not be able to turn the US–China–Russia triangle to its advantage, as it was able to do in the 1970s. We do not know whose advice Trump was listening to, but he tried hard to establish good relations with Vladimir Putin. This move could potentially serve the purpose, if not of turning Russia against China, at least of making it a valuable partner in the new rebalancing. But, as things stand now, Washington has nothing to offer Russia. Democrats who control the Congress handcuffed Trump by imposing the most severe sanctions on Russia, which the Trump administration could not override, and they may become even worse with Joe Biden in the White House.

It is now Russia's turn to try to use the US–China conflict, which is often called the New Cold War, to its advantage. Vladimir Putin played with the idea of a Yalta 2.0, using the analogy of the 1945 Yalta Conference at which Roosevelt, Stalin and Churchill divided the spheres of influence. From time to time, Russian pro-Kremlin experts assert that there are only three independent centres of global power—the US of America, the Russian Federation, and the Chinese People's Republic. A Yalta 2.0, with Xi substituting for Churchill, would put Putin at the high table of international politics and make Russia the balancing force between the two superpowers.

The all-time low in Russian–US relations will not allow this to happen, however much Putin and Trump may like each other. Russia has to reconcile itself to the position of China's junior partner, in substance if not in form. Another option for Russia to make itself useful and equal would be to reach out to other players like the European Union or Japan and maintain functioning relations with the US. That has become even less likely, however, after the annexation of the Crimea and serious worsening of tensions with the West on issues such as the Belarusian crisis, Russian Opposition leader Alexey Navalny's poisoning, interference in the US elections, and so on—the list is long.

The Soviet demise and China's rise could not be predicted in the 1970s when Kissinger tried to alter the course of the Cold War. He certainly helped to mitigate big tensions by exacerbating smaller ones. The Soviet Union's confrontation with China was a smaller evil than a nuclear conflict between the USSR and the US, no matter how hypothetical it seemed when Nixon came to power in Washington.

We are now going through a period of increasing escalation in the Sino–American Cold War. The two powers are now on a confrontation course in all dimensions, including technological, military, societal and geopolitical. Things will not become easier even with the more balanced Joe Biden as president. The risk of the Cold War escalating into a hot war is also growing, with China's aggressive behaviour in Hong Kong, its border clashes with India and sabre-rattling in the Taiwan Strait. Many in the West are now quite alarmed by China's growing ambitions and military capabilities. Taiwan has become a very contentious issue. On 1 January 2019, Chinese President Xi Jinping delivered a speech proclaiming that 'unification between the two sides of the Strait is the great trend of history' and that he would 'make no promise to forego the use of force and retain the option of taking all necessary measures'.

The administration of Donald Trump had also been provocative. It had announced that it was considering a US $7 billion package of arms sales to Taiwan, breaking the understanding with Beijing not to ship modern arms there. The US Secretary of State Mike Pompeo led the charge against Beijing, calling the Chinese Communist Party 'the central threat of our time'. He insisted that the US mission is 'securing our freedom from the Chinese Communist Party'. We all hope that the US, China and its partner Russia will somehow manage their rivalries. We hope that the European Union succeeds in consolidating its positions and becoming an even more important international actor. The irreversible course of history proves that freedom is better than unfreedom and democracy is more efficient than autocracy.

And yet, today one can say that it would be a serious mistake to underestimate the powerful impact of the dynamic mix of autocracy, technocracy and nationalism of the contemporary East, and the loss of common purpose of the West. We need people of Henry Kissinger's calibre now as much as we needed them fifty years ago, to make the world a safer place. At the very least, we should learn from their experience.

12

Nixon's Outreach

Coming to Terms with Reality

BILL EMMOTT

WHATEVER YOU MAY THINK OF Britain's wartime leader and keen imperialist, it is hard to deny that Sir Winston Churchill left behind a marvellous stock of quotations. A favourite Churchillism for any English person writing about the US is this: 'You can always count on Americans to do the right thing—after they've tried everything else.'[1] Given that as well as having a gift with words, Churchill was also a far-sighted strategic thinker, it feels likely that had he still been alive in 1971, Sir Winston would have applied his own maxim to President Richard Nixon's opening of relations with Mao Zedong's China, adding, perhaps, 'But what on earth took you so long?'

The United Kingdom, albeit under the Labour government that so brutally displaced Churchill's Conservatives in office in 1945, was among the first countries to recognize the new People's Republic of China (PRC, commonly known as 'China'), doing so on 6 January 1950, just behind India and Pakistan but ahead of all other Western nations. From Britain's point of view, then and with hindsight now, America's failure to do the same until more than two decades later represented a historic strategic mistake. Nixon's opening to China was not the act of courage or brilliance that it is often depicted as, but rather a belated acceptance of failure, a correction of a long-running error.

Recognition of a country's actual government, connecting legitimacy to the reality of holding power, is a basic tool of diplomacy and a simple fact of international relations. David Wolf, writing in the *Journal of Contemporary History* in 1983 about the decision to confer recognition to the Communist government,[2] opens with another Churchill quotation which feels just as apt: Churchill said in a speech in the House of Commons on 17 November 1949, 'The reason for having diplomatic relations is not to confer a compliment but to secure a convenience.' What is extraordinary and consequential is not that Britain secured this convenience in the case of the People's Republic (PRC), but rather that the US did not.

The then Foreign Secretary, Ernest Bevin, evidently agreed that to switch British recognition from the Nationalist regime of Chiang Kai-Shek to Mao's Communists following their victory in the Chinese civil war was just such a convenience. This was despite a strong antipathy in the Labour Party against the Chinese Communists, and despite the fact that the decision broke Britain away from the China policy of the US, a divergence that then lasted for a further twenty-one years.

The US refusal to accept reality in Asia's largest country proved a severe inconvenience during those decades for Britain, but also for other allies. To see how, it may be useful to compare the impact on Britain with the impact on another US ally, Japan, which has since defeat and occupation in 1945–52 been the US's closest ally in the Pacific. Both countries' experience leads one to see American policy and behaviour towards China as being inherently selfish, conducted in a way that disregarded the interests and sensitivities even of its closest allies. Britain's refusal to support the US militarily during the Vietnam War is surely not unrelated to a reaction during the 1950s and '60s against perceived American selfishness. Japan, in its turn, was shocked by Nixon's sudden overtures to China and shaken by America's decision not to consult or even inform its closest Asian ally about its change of mind and tack. Yet despite bearing such costs and such wounds, each has nevertheless stuck to their intransigent Yankee friends before and after the watershed of 1971, even during the past four years when the former President Donald Trump made doing so more embarrassing than at any stage since 1945. Neither, really, can afford to turn their backs on the US.

Nonetheless, looked at from the standpoint of those two island nations, on opposite sides of the world, US stubbornness over China can be taken to confirm that it is really the US that should be called insular, not either Britain or Japan. It is the great insular continental power protected, by two oceans and the world's most formidable economy, from the need to face up to reality or, many times, to make awkward choices.

This is not to argue that relations with Communist China would have been particularly straightforward for any of the three—Britain, Japan and the US—if the Americans had done the right and sensible thing by conferring recognition on Mao's government in 1950. American stubbornness nevertheless imposed a cost both on Britain, whose China policy did diverge from that of the US, and on Japan, which stuck loyally to the American line until 1971–72. Both countries were caught in a sort of limbo by American intransigence.

Britain's formal request in 1950 to open diplomatic relations with the PRC was refused, meaning that the countries did not exchange ambassadors but rather established semi-diplomatic relations by sending Chargés d'Affaires, deputy ambassadors, instead and Britain opened an embassy in Beijing that was officially known just as a 'legation'. This was because the UK was unwilling, or in truth thanks to US obstruction, unable, to fully denounce the Nationalist 'government-in-exile' in Taipei, Republic of China (ROC, now commonly called 'Taiwan'). Despite having their own permanent seat on the Security Council of the newly born United Nations, the British stood no chance of forcing the Republic of China to relinquish the Chinese seat it had occupied since 1945, given American objections. This inevitably tarred the British with the sins, in Communist China's eyes, of their US allies. Only in 1972, once the PRC took over the United Nations Security Council seat, was Britain granted full diplomatic relations and the exchange of ambassadors. The nastiest consequence came in 1967 during the Cultural Revolution when Red Guards laid siege to and then burned down the British legation.

In the case of Japan, recognition in 1949–50 would have been impossible given that the country was and then remained under US occupation for a further two years. Early diplomatic recognition could anyway hardly have salved the wounds of history, for Japan had been fighting the Chinese in varying degrees of intensity since 1931, and had left behind a legacy of atrocities such as the Nanjing massacre of 1937 where an alleged 300,000 Chinese were killed by Japanese soldiers. Those wounds continue to fester to this day.

Japan did engage with China's new rulers in the 1950s to negotiate the repatriation of Japanese residents of the former colony of Manchuria and to resume trading links, albeit at a modest level. However, under American pressure as well as tempted by the scent of commercial opportunity, the Japanese government and businesses then spent two decades establishing stronger trading links and closer ties with their other former colony, Taiwan, the economy of which was beginning to industrialize, especially during the 1960s. Any real restoration or renovation of Sino–Japanese relations following their decades of bitter conflict was thus both delayed and distorted by the effect of America's decision.

Why did Britain recognize the PRC?

It seems natural to ask why the UK chose to move so swiftly to 'secure a convenience' by recognizing the PRC. Yet, with hindsight, the question seems upside-down: What really requires explanation is the decision of other Western countries to follow the US by refusing to acknowledge what an Englishman might term 'the bleedin' obvious', namely that the People's Republic, and not the Republic of China on Taiwan, was the established, legitimate and for all intents and purposes permanent government of China. The natural thing for all Western powers to have done would have been to recognize the new government, as Churchill said, not as a compliment but as a convenience.

Few, if any, can have seriously believed that Chiang Kai-shek still stood a chance of fighting on and prevailing. Some might have believed that the Communist regime was weaker than it seemed, but that belief became untenable after Mao's successful intervention during the Korean War in October 1950, inflicting a major defeat and humiliation on the United Nations' forces led by the US. As the decade went on, it became even more untenable when the PRC successfully turned its 1950 intervention in Tibet into full annexation in 1959, and then in 1962 prevailed in its border war with India. Even so, among major Western powers, only France broke ranks and after a long delay opened diplomatic relations with the PRC in 1964.

Various hypotheses can be put forward as explanation for why Britain acted in the way that it did to try to open full diplomatic relations in 1950, against the US policy. One is that it represented a continued British imperialist pride, a desire to show it could still strut its own stuff on the world stage, regardless of its post-war dependence on the US. Another is that it may have been driven by a desire to protect British commercial interests in China, which were much larger than those of the US or other Western powers: from 'treaty ports' such as Shanghai, Tientsin, Tsingtao and Guangzhou, British traders had been active and prosperous for more than a century. British commercial property and investments in China in 1948 had an estimated value of £300 million,[3] which in 2020 pounds was equivalent to £11 billion. That is not a fortune, but is significant enough to give its owners some lobbying power with government.

A third, arguably more significant, explanation can be found in Hong Kong. That British Crown Colony, held since 1841 and with part of it held on a 99-year-long lease from the then Chinese imperial government in 1898, gave Britain what seemed at the time to be a continued opportunity to influence events in Asia and, in particular, to own a beacon of capitalism and trade. With the US promising to retain a dominant position from its base in Japan, the UK could hope to prove its importance as well as its influence from its possession of Hong Kong, as well, at that moment, as its hold on Malaya. The fall of both Singapore and Hong

Kong to Japanese forces in 1941 had been a humiliation. At least at that time, in 1950, even as imperial possessions such as India and Burma were gaining independence, there was no acceptance in London that the British Empire as a whole was at an end, either in Asia or elsewhere. There were, however, understandable fears that Communist Chinese forces might seek to emulate the Japanese and take control of Hong Kong. This provided a motive for securing the convenience of a negotiating channel to the new PRC government and for making the positive, peace-making gesture that the offer of recognition represented.

What all these hypotheses add up to, however, is a more general point: For more than a century, Britain had been the most influential foreign power in Asia and so had developed habits as well as interests that it was unlikely to shake off in a hurry. One of those habits was to think strategically and with a global perspective, even if with no longer the true power or reach to match thoughts with actions. David Wolf's paper in the *Journal of Contemporary History* in 1983, on which much of this chapter is based, benefited from the opening up of British government records from 1950 and surrounding years, under the thirty-year rule. What those records show is that as early as 24 October 1949, the Foreign Secretary, Ernest Bevin, presented a position paper to Cabinet in which he argued that although continued recognition of the Republic of China provided the Allies with a favourable vote in the United Nations Security Council, this was 'an advantage which cannot be maintained indefinitely'. He argued that the longer the UK delayed recognition of the PRC, the harder it would be to maintain British trade with China. Most tellingly, however, Bevin also argued that, in Wolf's words, 'A delay in recognition ... improved the chance that the Communist government would turn to the Soviet Union.'

That, of course, is exactly what did happen. Nevertheless, proven right though it was by history, British recognition failed to deliver many of the hoped-for benefits, even if it did symbolize the country's continued independence of mind and the perceived importance that an influential position in Asia played in Britain's foreign policy. British commercial assets in China were expropriated by the Communist government.

British trade with and from China dwindled, although perhaps thanks to recognition or to historical ties, British firms proved able to be among the first allowed to get involved again with the modest amount of trade that did resume, with what was then called the 48 Group of Companies being formed in 1954, alongside the British government's own Sino–British Trade Council, which many years later merged to become what is now the China–Britain Business Council.

Why the US didn't recognize the PRC?

While Britain, India, Burma, Pakistan and a handful of other Western or non-aligned countries did recognize the new People's Republic of China, the US considered doing so, according to British cabinet papers, but then chose not to. The decision not to do so became more understandable after the Korean War, yet less meaningful since by destroying General Douglas MacArthur's reputation the Red Army had surely proven the new regime's viability. In the light of that conflict, there was no prospect that US aid would or could have been offered to Communist China, making it arguably inevitable that Mao's government sought aid from the Soviet Union. The rush of events in that period of the late 1940s and early '50s, with the Cold War getting under way, the Berlin Blockade by the Soviet Union having just occurred in 1948–49, were hardly conducive to risk-taking or even, perhaps, to cool strategic thinking.

Nevertheless, George Kennan had already sent in 1946 his famous 'long telegram' to the State Department from the embassy in Moscow, laying out the case for what became the strategy of containment. The huge question this leaves hanging is: Why, in 1949, when the Communists prevailed in China's civil war, without yet having been truly intimately connected to the Soviets, the US did not opt to at least try to choose China as one component of that containment. If there was a strong case for doing so two decades later, wasn't there an even stronger case for doing so in 1949–50?

From a British standpoint, the failure to do so was and is a historic strategic mistake. More than even that, it is a mistake that took an enormously long time to be acknowledged and corrected. How to explain it? Three main hypotheses come to mind, although they inevitably overlap to some extent.

The first is ideological. The birth of the Cold War and the shock to both the US and Britain of the complete fracture of their wartime alliance with Stalin and the Soviet Union, turning allies into adversaries, generated a much more ideological reaction in Washington than it did in London. The British viewed it pragmatically, albeit with dismay. So did the US at first, but then the febrile world of US politics turned the Communist threat into an existential one. Under the Moscow Declaration of December 1945, Britain, the US and the Soviet Union had all pledged themselves to a policy of non-interference in China, and hence to recognition of the Nationalist government in Nanking as, at that time, the legitimate authority. Logically, such a pledge of non-interference should have led automatically to the recognition of the PRC, when it became plainly the new established authority. But while Britain and the Soviet Union followed that logic, fear of and hostility to communism had taken hold in the US.

The second hypothesis is about the power of vested interests in creating inertia in US policymaking. Some of that power and inertia was already there in Washington in the 1940s, following years of political and material support for Chiang Kai-shek and the Nationalist Kuomintang. While Chiang, his entourage, and above all his wife, Soong Mei-ling, were well-known in the US, Chairman Mao and his Long Marchers were far more remote figures, known through the writings of Edgar Snow and other journalists, but not directly. Madame Chiang even made an eight-month speaking tour of the US during 1943 to rally support. Then, once the Nationalists became a government-in-exile, really the de facto government of Taiwan, the cause of industrial development on that island and the support of its defence became strong vested interests of their own.

Once such interests take hold, especially if buttressed by ideology, a policy can become remarkably difficult to change in Washington. The nearest equivalent, albeit of far lesser strategic importance, is that of the US embargo on Cuba. It is many decades since that embargo made any political or security sense for the US. Yet it took until the administration of President Barack Obama in 2008–16 for the trade embargo and travel ban to be relaxed and for diplomatic relations to be established, and even then President Donald Trump was able to partially rescind in 2017 what he saw as US concessions.

This brings in the third hypothesis that in foreign affairs, such intransigent, self-harming, ideologically and vested-interest-driven policies can be maintained for decades simply because the US is powerful enough and secure enough to absorb such mistakes without undue pain or concern. The US could maintain what now looks like the absurd fiction that the Republic of China was the true government of China, that it would in due course return and deserved to hold China's permanent seat on the Security Council of the United Nations, simply because it could do so without apparent consequence. Post-1945 the US was not at all isolationist. But it could nevertheless be extraordinarily insular.

The consequences of this mistake

We cannot of course know how history might have evolved if the US had followed Britain's example by recognizing the PRC and had accepted the Communist Chinese as the legitimate wielders of a vote on the Security Council. It is reasonable, however, to speculate that by providing Mao and his government with another option, with more leverage over the Soviet Union and with some more incentives to play an official role in world affairs, the evolution both of China and of the Cold War could have been different. Perhaps not greatly different, but different nevertheless. More securely, we can speculate that some processes would have been accelerated, or at least brought forward.

This can be well seen from the British and Japanese points of view. Britain had a declining interest in Asia thanks to the dismantling of its empire and so perhaps endured the costs of American intransigence fairly easily. But still, earlier and less rancorous communication channels between London and Beijing could have allowed the two countries to achieve earlier understandings on the status of Hong Kong. Japan had a rising interest in Asia commensurate with its economic and political rehabilitation in the 1950s and 1960s. The chance to establish diplomatic channels with China at an earlier stage, when China too was weak economically and politically, could have enabled Japan to make early amends for its wartime conduct and to open up a more balanced commercial relationship. The fiction of Chiang Kai-shek as the once and future rightful leader of China did Japan no favours.

But then, the US didn't care about the consequences of its China policy for either Britain or Japan because it had no need to care. It retained Japan as home to its principal military bases in Asia–Pacific, and even retained its occupation of Okinawa until 1971. Britain was no longer a significant influence in Asia, and in any event British and US policies in Asia had clashed repeatedly, with the UK notably refusing to lend military support to US forces during the Vietnam War. At least in Asia, the US owed the British no favours.

It did, however, owe favours to itself. Few, if any, future historians will conclude that by maintaining the Kuomintang Nationalist fiction for twenty-one years the US did the right thing, or even helped its own interests. The counterfactual must always remain unknown. But what can be known is that this fiction served no useful purpose, made US policy look vindictive as well as unrealistic, and threw away all chance of using China as early leverage against the Soviet Union. When Henry Kissinger and then President Richard Nixon finally went to China, they were correcting a historic failure.

13

China's Rise and Japan's Awakening

TSUTOMU KIKUCHI

HOW TO DEAL WITH ITS giant neighbour, China, has been the most important issue in Japan's foreign relations for more than a millennium. After its defeat and occupation, Japan rejoined the international community as a member of the Western camp and, in accordance with the US policy of containing China, did not recognize the People's Republic of China. Relations with mainland China remained informal until normalization of diplomatic relations in 1972.

Japan suffered the humiliation of not being informed of Nixon's visit to China by the US government until shortly before the announcement. However, the moves by Nixon and Kissinger to improve relations with China provided an opportunity for Japan to once again tackle head-on the challenges posed by mainland China. Japan rushed to normalize diplomatic relations with China and expanded exchanges with it under the slogan of 'Japan–China friendship'. Reflecting a sense of guilt for its actions during the war, Japan responded with the utmost respect for China's wishes. Since China's adoption of the policy of reform and opening up in the end of the 1970s, Japan has helped China to participate smoothly in the international community.[1]

China's rise to great power poses a serious challenge for Japan. A particular problem for Japan is the sense of 'historical humiliation' that China has. China has now set as its goal the realization of the 'Chinese

Dream', or the great rejuvenation of the Chinese nation. Its dream will not be realized simply by having a national power that surpasses that of the US. Perhaps, for China, with its glorious history of civilization, redressing the 'humiliation of history' is an important component of the 'Chinese dream'. China has already begun this project in Hong Kong.

China is a country that has a vivid memory of the historical humiliation it suffered from Japan. What does the 'humiliation of history' mean to China? It is probably the fact that it was unable to stop Japan's military advance and overthrow Japan by its own hands. China has indeed become one of the victorious nations in their war against Japan. However, it was the massive military power of the US that made this possible, not China, which spent most of its time in civil war.

Japan, which once learned a lot—culture to governance systems—from China and was once a tributary state of that country, sent its military into China, overran the land and plunged it into chaos. Despite this past, Japan was not severely punished and quickly achieved economic recovery after its defeat, becoming one of the economic powers of the world. Moreover, after China's transition to the era of reform and opening up, China depended to a large extent on Japan for aid, investment, markets, and technology. It is not hard to imagine that this must have been a 'double humiliation' for proud China.

Shinzo Abe was the first Japanese prime minister to tackle this Chinese challenge head-on. Capitulation to China is not an option for Japan. Nor can Japan contain China. However, Japan may be able to impose some constraints on China's behaviour by working with such countries as the US and those in Southeast Asia, South Asia and Oceania that have concerns about China. It may be difficult to establish mutual trust with China, but it may be possible to manage mutual distrust.

The 'Nixon shock' and Japan

The news of President Nixon's visit to China came to the Japanese government just before his press conference, and has been long remembered in Japan as the 'Nixon shock'. The fact that Nixon and Kissinger did not consult with Japan beforehand indicated that they did not recognize Japan as a player in power politics, even though it had become a global economic power.

The shift in US policy toward China, however, provided new opportunities for Japanese diplomacy. First, it paved the way for the normalization of diplomatic relations with China. Japan, under intense US pressure, had signed a peace treaty with the Republic of China led by Chiang Kai-shek in 1952, keeping relations with the People's Republic of China (PRC) on the mainland informal. There was a growing consensus in Japan that normalization of diplomatic relations was urgently needed, in order to properly deal with the historical issues caused by Japan's military intrusion and to build stable relations with the big neighbour.

While the US government was cautious about normalizing diplomatic relations with China (PRC), Japan rushed to normalize diplomatic relations with it. Reflecting its guilt over its past history, Japan took a low-key stance toward China to avoid any dispute or conflict with it as much as possible, and worked to bring the relationship closer under the mantra of 'Japan–China friendship'. Sino–Japanese relations developed rapidly, and Japan became the biggest donor of official development assistance to China.

Second, China accepted the supremacy of the US in Asia. As the confrontation with the Soviet Union intensified, China, seeking to cooperate with Japan and the US, came to accept the supremacy of the US in Asia and to positively evaluate the Japan–U.S. alliance, which it had severely criticized until then, as a powerful means of checking the Soviet Union.

While struggling with the Vietnam War, the US was still overwhelmingly powerful and deeply involved in Asia. China's national power was small. It was easy for Japan to reconcile the strengthening of Japan–US relations with Japan–China friendship.

Third, the space for Japan's Asian diplomacy expanded. In the background of the shift in US policy toward China, there was a pressing need of getting out of the quagmire of the Vietnam War. The new US policy toward Asia, announced as the 'Nixon Doctrine', raised concerns in Japan about the US 'withdrawal' from Asia, but at the same time, it made Japan's diplomacy in Asia more active.

The Nixon Doctrine pointed out the importance of Japan's role for peace and development in Asia. Japan sought a new role, not only in the economic field but also in the political area, by normalizing diplomatic relations with North Vietnam and strengthening relations with ASEAN (Association of Southeast Asian Nations).

Bringing China into the international community

Japan has supported China's policy of 'reform and opening up', which was adopted at the end of the 1970s, shifting from a policy of nation-building that emphasized self-reliance to a policy of enhancing national strength through interdependence with the international community.

In the wake of the Tiananmen Square incident in 1989, Japan strongly expressed the risks in isolating China from the international society. Japan opposed proposals to impose severe sanctions on the country and urged a moderate response to it at the G7 summit. In addition, Japan responded to China's request and realized the Emperor's visit to China in 1992, when the aftermaths of the Tiananmen Square incident were still lingering.

After overcoming the temporary setback that followed the Tiananmen Square incident, China once again pursued its policy of opening up to the outside world, but during this period, the international political and economic landscape was undergoing major changes. China's participation in the international community proceeded in an environment where the Cold War was over and the unipolar structure dominated by the US was in place, and where the 'convergence of East and West'—democracy in politics and a market economy in economics—was seen to be the 'global standard'. China has sought to develop under the specific environment of a free, open and rules-based international order led by the US.

Under this order, on the one hand, China has made the most of and benefited the most from the free and open political and economic systems of other countries. This international order, however, was quite intrusive, containing elements directly touching on domestic rules and institutions of China. Principles and norms such as the rule of law, transparency and good governance are incompatible with China's governing regime. The great divergence between the basic principles and rules that make up the international order and those of China has caused deep concerns within the country and delayed its integration into the international community.

Japan has taken these Chinese concerns into consideration and has supported China's smooth adjustment to the international community. Japan has not always believed in China's slogans of 'peaceful development' and 'establishing a win-win relationship', but it has maintained its stance of support for China, believing that a prosperous China in the international community is preferable to an economically stagnant one.

China has been the largest recipient of Japan's official development assistance, and Japanese companies have entered the Chinese market in large numbers. Japan's economic interdependence with China has developed, and China has become Japan's largest trading partner. Japan's security environment has also improved. The Japan–US security arrangement, which was 'redefined' after the end of the Cold War, was further strengthened, and the US commitment to the security of Japan and Asia was solidified. China's actions to challenge the alliance system had not yet become apparent.

The awakening of Japanese diplomacy

Today, Japan has both concerns and expectations about the future of the Indo-Pacific. First, the future of the two major powers, the US and China, is causing concern. China, which once advocated 'peaceful development', is becoming more assertive and aggressive. As its power grew, China also sought to downplay and rewrite the rules of the international community that were undesirable to it. China has come to behave in a manner characteristic of a 'revisionist state'.

Moreover, there is a great sense of uncertainty about the future of the US. The domestic consensus that has underpinned US foreign policy is shifting due to a variety of factors, including a mountain of domestic issues, the reluctance of public opinion to engage in foreign affairs,

Washington's fiercely partisan politics, and the emergence of political leaders who prioritize domestic concerns.

Will the US continue to be a 'staying power in Asia'? Will the US continue to be as deeply involved in Japan's defence as it has been in the past? A sense of uneasiness about US policy is emerging in Japan. The Obama administration's half-hearted 'rebalancing policy' and the Trump administration's 'the US first' policy have intensified such concerns in Japan.

Second, Japan's anxiety about the future of US–China relations is on the rise. Japan cannot accept either the formation of Chinese regional hegemony or a Cold War between the US and China, or the creation of a US–China condominium (G2). In any case, the manoeuvrability of Japan's foreign policy must be limited.

How is Japan responding to this challenge? Japan's Indo-Pacific strategy is a response to this challenge. There are three pillars in Japan's strategy. The first is to strengthen the alliance with the US. Japan has become more proactive in the area of security in recent years, and its once restrained and passive stance is changing. In particular, under the second Abe cabinet inaugurated at the end of 2012, the constitutional interpretation of successive administrations was changed to allow Japan to exercise the right of collective self-defence. It also enacted security-related legislation to expand the role of the Self-Defense Forces, especially expanding defence cooperation between the US military and the Self-Defense Forces. Furthermore, the guidelines for Japan–US defence cooperation were revised to enable its smooth functioning in the contingency of Japan needing it.

In the past, measures to strengthen the Japan–US alliance were often taken at the initiative of the US side, but a notable feature in recent years is the increasing number of cases in which Japan is taking the initiative.

It is clear that Japan's concern about China is behind the series of measures it has taken. However, there seems to be a new element behind the recent activism by the Japanese government. There is a certain anxiety about the US commitment to defend Japan against China.

The most pressing issue for Japan is the dispute with China over the Senkaku Islands. For China, the Senkaku issue is deeply tied to the 'humiliation of history'. The US government has repeatedly stated that the

Senkaku Islands are under Japanese administrative authority, that they are subject to Article 5 of the Japan–US Security Treaty, and therefore the US obligation to defend Japan is applied to the Senkaku Islands.

The Japan–US relationship is close, and for the US, failure to fulfil its defence obligations would damage its global credibility. It is believed that the US would keep its promise.

However, for the US, it would mean going to war with China to protect Senkaku, 'a small island with no human inhabitants and only goats living'. This is a critical decision with the fate of the nation at stake. Bearing in mind the fragmented domestic politics of the US and the inward-looking orientation of its citizens, it is not surprising that Japan has some concern about the US fulfilling its defence obligations. The US possesses enormous power, but the political will to exercise that power seems to be unstable.

How should we respond to this situation? This is one of the key security policy issues that Japan is facing today. An important task for Japan is to convince the government and people of the US of the importance of supporting Japan. Today, for the first time since the end of World War II, Japan recognizes that it must seriously consider a strategy to 'entrap' the US into Japan's wars.

One of the hottest debates about Japan's post-war security has been how to keep Japan out of US wars. The various restrictions on defence policy (for example, constitutional interpretation of the right of collective self-defence) were also good excuses to stay out of it.

An alliance does not work on a piece of paper (a treaty). To ensure mutual defence cooperation in the event of an emergency, the alliance must be revitalized through constant efforts. What makes an alliance work is mutual trust and confidence in the other side.

There is criticism in Japan that the Abe cabinet's security policy was 'following the US'. In reality, however, the opposite is true. Japan has made the proactive moves to 'entrap' the US in a direction that is desirable for Japan's security. The revitalized Japan–US alliance is also useful in encouraging US involvement in Asia, given the alliance is the cornerstone of US engagement in the Indo-Pacific.

The second is the 'new South-bound policy', or the strengthening of ties with States and regional organizations in Southeast Asia, South Asia, and Oceania, as well as with Taiwan. Although these actors cannot be the main players in the formation of regional order on their own, they have a substantial national power and the potential to increase their national powers in the future, and they are located at important strategic junctures and are trying to proactively participate in the 'Great Game' over the future of the Indo-Pacific. They are not weak entities that sit as bystanders on the sidelines of great-power politics.

For Japan, these countries have a common interest in a desirable regional order and can be important partners in promoting the maintenance and strengthening of a rules-based regional order.

A feature of recent years has been the development of new bilateral, trilateral, and quadrilateral multilayered cooperative relationships in the political, economic, and security fields among these countries. Japan is also actively promoting these partnerships. The goal of these new networks, in addition to strengthening their own resilience (in terms of capabilities such as defence and maritime security, as well as economic development), is to keep the US in the region and at the same time mitigate its unilateral actions.

This, for example, can be said to be the aim of new state partnerships, such as the Japan–US–Australia–India (the Quad), Japan–US–Australia, Japan–US–India, and so on.

The third is to establish a constructive relationship with China, based upon the rules-based order. China now has as its goal the realization of the Chinese Dream, or the great rejuvenation of the Chinese nation. Perhaps, for China, with its proud history of civilization, redressing the 'humiliation of history' is an important component of the Chinese Dream.

There is a deep-seated conflict over history and sentiments between Japan and China, which cannot be easily reconciled. The 'humiliation of history' is deeply seared into the memory of China. It may be difficult for an empowered China to suppress its desire to redeem this past. In this regard, Japan is facing an enormous challenge to establish rules-based constructive relations with China.

Conclusion

China's role is important for regional and global peace and development. Although China has become more assertive and coercive, Japan has not slackened its efforts to encourage China to act in a way that respects the rules of the international community. The networks of alliances connected with the US will continue to be indispensable in maintaining and strengthening the rules-based order in the Indo-Pacific.

At the same time, however, these networks are inadequate to cope with the new situation in the region, which includes the rise of China, the increasing uncertainty of US involvement in the Indo-Pacific region, the strengthening of the resilience of South Asian, Southeast Asian and Oceania countries and their changing external orientation, and the constructive role of ASEAN as a regional organization.

Japan cannot 'contain' China, and any attempt to do so would seriously undermine Japan's peace and prosperity. However, Japan can contribute to shaping a regional environment that will influence China's choices, through partnerships with these countries and institutions.

The US-centred 'hub and spokes' type of arrangement will be transformed into a networked one, supported by new overlapping bilateral, trilateral, and quadrilateral relationships with other Indo-Pacific partners, while maintaining alliances.

The opening of China's doors by Nixon and Kissinger provided an opportunity for Japan to once again directly face the challenge posed by mainland China, a challenge that Japan had experienced for a long time. After fifty years of normalization with China, Japan is now awakening to meet this challenge. Japan is regaining the pride of behaving as a meaningful nation in the international community that it seemed to have lost with its defeat in the war

I hope that the 'sense of skin' and diplomatic wisdom that Japan has accumulated through more than a thousand years of interaction with China will empower Japan's constructive awakening.

14

Kissinger to Xi

Engage and Constrain

PETER VARGHESE

HENRY KISSINGER'S OPENING TO CHINA was arguably the most consequential event for Australian foreign policy in the last fifty years. Not that Australia knew anything about it. To the deep embarrassment of Australia's then prime minister, news of Kissinger's secret meetings came soon after our (Australia's) prime minister had launched a full-throated attack on the Australian leader of the Opposition for having the temerity to make a visit to China and promise diplomatic recognition if elected. Australia had flirted with diplomatic recognition of China in the 1950s but it was the Nixon–Kissinger opening to China which set in train China's re-entry into the global economy under Deng, its emergence as both a strategic and economic power and its rise to become Australia's largest export market by far.

It has become fashionable today to say that we made a terrible mistake in thinking that China's participation in the global economy would make it a more open political system. That may have been an expectation in Washington, but I do not think that Australian policymakers suffered any such delusions. Some of our political leaders may have been intellectually attracted to the proposition that China's opening to the world would ultimately lay bare the contradiction between an open economy and a closed polity. But for the most part Australia's China policy was framed around judgements about economic opportunities for Australia, together with a belief that a growing Chinese economy was good, not only for the hundreds of millions of Chinese living in poverty, but also for regional and global trade. The calculus was predominantly economic and it was largely accurate.

There were years when we imagined and hoped China might become a 'responsible stakeholder', but we certainly did not see this as inevitable. We observed that while political space was tightly controlled, China's economic opening meant personal space was expanding from the days of Mao suits and bicycles. China's leaders even went through a period when they thought that by bringing more democracy to the party, they could avoid bringing democracy to the people. But that did not last very long, and the one thing we knew for certain about China—then and now—was that the party was determined never to relinquish its monopoly on power, which is what defines a Leninist system such as China's.

Also, the middle class that China's growing economy created was not, unlike their European historical counterparts, in the vanguard of a push for more representative institutions. For the most part, they were the beneficiaries and defenders of the status quo shaped both by the rapid rise in their own standard of living and a deep historical fear of instability. Kissinger's opening to China was a strategic calculation made on the chessboard of the Cold War. But China's economic rise, which the opening enabled, has created its own post-Cold War strategic consequences. How to manage those consequences is the big geopolitical challenge of our times.

From hide and bide to coercion

To face this challenge, we need a new policy framework. Since Deng's opening of the Chinese economy in 1978 until recently, engaging China has been the primary axis of policy. Economic engagement was at its core.

In the 1950s and '60s, Australia saw China as a strategic threat. captured by the caricature of the 'yellow peril'. However, with the opening of the Chinese economy the focus shifted from strategic threat to economic opportunity. It is not that we were blind to the logic of economic power expanding strategic reach, but there was no sense of urgency in facing up to this reality. Also, China's international behaviour before Xi gave us no cause to do so.

In part, this was because China itself was content to abide by Deng's advice to 'hide and bide' and eager to convince us that its rise would be peaceful. To the extent that we were not convinced of this, we had reserve strategies of balancing and hedging. Bear in mind that the US–Japan–Australia trilateral grouping goes back to 2002 and the Quad as a China-balancing group was first proposed by Japanese Prime Minister Shinzo Abe in 2007. Even the reaching out to India by the US, Australia, and Japan, well before President Xi's ascension to power, was at least in part a recognition of India as a natural balancer of China. The same was true for the courting of Vietnam.

We knew that an economically powerful China would not be like Japan, content to be a large economy but a sublimated strategic power. But what type of strategic power China would become was less clear. Our judgement was that it was unlikely to be a classic revisionist power, not least because it had been a huge beneficiary of the international system. But we also knew that China would not forever live by rules which it had no part in framing and would also want to create new institutions with China at the centre.

All this began to change, first with the global financial crisis and then with the ascension of Xi. The former recalculated and accelerated China's view of the correlation of forces. Prior to the global financial crisis, China thought the shelf life of US strategic primacy was long and the power gap between the US and China would remain wide for a long time. After the crisis, China began to think that the US was on a steeper decline trajectory than previously thought and that the window of opportunity for China was therefore opening up sooner. Under Xi, this judgement has deepened.

China has abandoned 'hide and bide' because it believes its time has come and so it no longer needs to hide its ambitions or bide its time.

This may well prove to be a spectacularly flawed judgement but it is no less real for that. The rising tide of a Chinese nationalism determined to reverse a century of humiliation has reinforced this instinct for a more assertive posture. China, which well before Xi had made an art of convincing the world that it was more powerful than it was, now seemed to convince itself this was the case.

The point here is not that the Chinese system has fundamentally changed. It has since 1949 been an authoritarian one-party state with the Chinese Communist Party absolutely determined to keep a tight grip on its monopoly of power. What has changed is its behaviour, which shifted from trying to reassure us that its rise would be peaceful to demonstrating that there is a price to be paid for crossing China. And when China's behaviour changes so should our policy. It is clear that hope-for-the-best engagement is no longer a viable strategy for dealing with the situation we find ourselves in. The problem, however, is that while we have strayed from this framework, we have yet to settle on what should replace it.

Engage and constrain

The biggest risk is that we will over-correct and move from engagement to containment, wrapped in a hard decoupling. That would be both economic and geopolitical folly. Instead, we need to find a way forward which both engages China but also constrains it when necessary. This requires a new strategic equilibrium in the Indo-Pacific, which recognizes China's great power status but which also makes clear that coercive behaviour will be collectively opposed by a core group of states which, for differing reasons, do not wish to see China become the predominant power. It is that reach for predominance in the Indo-Pacific, and perhaps beyond, which drives the need to twin engaging China with constraining China.

For Australia, our concerns lie at the intersection of interests and values. China is not Australia's enemy in the sense that it directly threatens us or has designs on our territory. But predominance means an outsized capacity to set the rules and shape the strategic culture of the region. So long as China remains a one-party authoritarian state, the prospect of it dominating the Indo-Pacific region is not an attractive one. Put simply, we do not wish to see leadership in the region shift to an authoritarian state.

China would have us believe that history and time are on its side and that its predominance is inevitable. It seems to want to reach back to the Middle Kingdom where harmony was a hierarchy with China at its peak. Other states knew their place and they would quickly see the logic of not acting in ways which ran counter to China's interests. For China, the past is the future, broken only by a century of humiliation and four decades of economic catch-up.

A return to the Middle Kingdom is, however, neither feasible nor desirable and it is utterly incompatible with the multipolar world which is the more likely shape of the future. There is also nothing inevitable about China regaining predominance. It would be a mistake to assume that its economic trajectory will simply be a continuation of the last four decades of rapid growth. There is a brittleness at the heart of the Chinese system, which invites caution rather than certainty about its future trajectory. And even if China overtakes the US in economic size, its predominance will be largely devoid of allies and in a different world with many more major powers than the US ever had to contend with.

It is of course in China's interest to paint the US as in terminal decline—a narrative which the current political dysfunction in the US only reinforces. But the US has been written off before. And while its internal divisions are getting worse, the US is more than the dysfunction which Trump personified. It still retains enormous strengths, even if the margin of US power has peaked.

The US economy has great depth and flexibility, much more so than China's. It is a powerhouse of innovation and quality education. Its military firepower and global reach are unmatched and likely to remain so for decades, even if China is catching up in East Asia. And the US has a history of regeneration that should never be underestimated.

China, on the other hand, faces big challenges. Its leadership no longer talks of big economic reforms, even though without them the 'compact' at the centre of the Chinese system is at risk. It rested on the assumption that the people would accept the Party's monopoly of political power provided it continued to deliver rising living standards. But without market reforms, how is this to be delivered? Maybe a 'dual-circulation' economy driven by domestic consumption will fit the bill but that is far from certain.

Internal contradictions can have a long shelf life but they cannot survive forever. China's contradictions are less the tension between an open economy and a closed political system than between an economy that needs market reforms and a political system which seems to have concluded that market reforms would weaken the Party's position. This considerably narrows China's options. The risk here is that a slowing economy will erode the party's economic legitimacy, which leaves the party's role as the vanguard of nationalism as the only alternate source of legitimacy.

Nevertheless, let us assume that China's leadership is smart enough to keep the economic bicycle upright and China continues to shift relative strategic weights in its favour. Let us also assume that China's instinct to leverage economic power (real and imagined) for strategic gain continues to fuel a more assertive and coercive foreign policy.

Enter the Quad

To break through the dead-end debate on whether China will overtake the US, why not start from a different and far less contentious position? Namely, there is no way that China can be stronger than the aggregate weight of the US, Japan, India, Australia (the so-called 'Quad') plus any other country which judges that China's strategic predominance is not in their interests and are prepared to act accordingly.

This last requirement will probably exclude most but not necessarily all Southeast Asian countries, including Indonesia. As a grouping, ASEAN does not want to take sides. It wants to see a strategic balance between the

US and China. So, it is not uncomfortable with the emergence of various mechanism to balance China but it will not want to be an explicit member of any grouping seen by Beijing as aimed at constraining China. More likely, ASEAN will quietly cheer from the sidelines.

The Quad is not a grand anti-China military alliance in the making. It is not an Asian NATO, even if it is likely to see more military cooperation among the four countries. Indeed, one member, India, is allergic to the very idea of alliances. Rather, the Quad is a means of managing China's ambitions in a way which puts some constraints on how far it is prepared and allowed to go. It signals that leverage is a two-way street.

Of course, to exercise leverage, the Quad will have to do more than meet and issue communiqués in support of the peaceful resolution of disputes, the upholding of international law, and the eschewing of coercion. It will have to be prepared to make it clear that it is willing to impose costs on China for unacceptable behaviour. These costs might range from diplomatic through to economic all the way to collective measures to uphold principles such as freedom of navigation and the Law of the Sea.

Each member of the Quad brings a different perspective and motivation to its dealings with China. For the US, it is a means of helping blunt China's ambitions for predominance and reinforcing the absolute determination of the US to stay number one. For Japan and India, both of which carry historical baggage when it comes to China, it is a shared concern that a predominant China will narrow their strategic options and room for manoeuvre.

The one member of the Quad for whom the core issue is the character of the Chinese system is Australia. Indeed, Australia is perhaps the only member of the Quad whose anxieties about China would likely disappear if China were a liberal democracy. After all, what would be the basis of our concern in those circumstances? Australia does not have any objection in principle to the concept of a predominant power in our region. Quite the contrary. We have historically seen US strategic predominance as the bedrock of our security and also as the great enabler of economic growth in Asia.

The US may speak the language of a new ideological cold war but the reality is it is driven more by its determination to hold on to strategic primacy than a battle against an authoritarian system. The US would be just as determined to remain number one if China were a liberal democracy. Neither India nor Japan, for reasons of history and geography, would be at ease with a democratic China as the predominant power in the Indo-Pacific. We may be in the same Quad bed, but we each have very different dreams.

So, the Quad is one means of moving from 'hope for the best' engagement to 'engage and constrain'. It is saying to China that we want a relationship of mutual benefit, but we also want China to pursue its interests in a way which respects the sovereignty of others and avoids coercion. If China behaves otherwise, there will be collective pushback from countries which are capable of effectively doing so.

China portrays the Quad as containment by another name but we should not give China a veto over our strategic policy. Besides, constraining China differs from containment whose ultimate logic is a complete rejection of engagement. Containment seeks to thwart China. Constraining seeks to manage China.

Constraining China will take time to construct. It is unlikely the Quad will ever reach the NATO-like point where an attack on one is considered an attack on all. Indeed, the Quad currently has neither the unity of approach nor the will for serious collective action. But China's behaviour is shifting perceptions as more countries see with discomfort what an assertive China looks like. This has both hastened the urgency of pursuing arrangements such as the Quad and reduced the caution about offending China.

China currently seems determined to behave in ways which are quickly losing it friends and respect. Polling shows this is evident across the globe with negative sentiment about China rising substantially. Yet China seems not to care. This is either the arrogance of a nation which believes that its time has come and it can do as it pleases, or it is a judgement that the domestic benefit to the party in China being seen to call the shots exceeds any diplomatic costs. I suppose all of us who have worked as professional diplomats have learnt that domestic considerations beat foreign policy most of the time.

For all except the US, we are only too aware that unilaterally resisting Chinese pressure is hard and unilaterally constraining China impossible: better to do it collectively and certainly a better option than the unilateral US containment of China. I say unilateral because I cannot see Japan, India or any country in Southeast Asia supporting containment and I hope Australia will have more sense than to embrace it. Under a Biden administration containment is a less likely policy. But if China continues to favour coercion over persuasion, we should not underestimate the policy momentum that containment might develop in the US.

COVID-19 and deglobalization

It is not easy to contain a country as integrated into the global economy as China, unless of course your strategy is to dismantle that global system and the supply chains which support it, which is precisely what some advocate. For most countries the costs of decoupling would be obvious. Certainly, for Australia, decoupling our largest trading partner from the global economy would be sheer folly, irrespective of the legitimate complaints levelled at China's trade and economic behaviour.

Even before COVID-19 there were signs of deglobalization. Now that trend is accelerating. Some deglobalization makes sense, including diversifying supply lines for critical goods. Technology may also make it easier to onshore what has up to now been offshored. There will even be times when we choose to make things at home which may be made more cheaply abroad because we put social or political objectives ahead of efficiency.

But at the heart of globalization sits comparative advantage in trade and the efficient allocation of resources, and we abandon these concepts at our economic peril. Australia has been a beneficiary of globalization, and we have managed its politics and the equitable distribution of its benefits better than most. Mr Trump had become president largely because the US did not.

Our wealth as a nation and the living standards of our citizens are best served by an open economy, rising levels of productivity and a liberalizing trade system. COVID-19 does not change that and neither does China's strategic ambitions or economic behaviour.

But COVID-19 may have changed the politics of open economies. By reinforcing an instinct for self-sufficiency, by pointing to vulnerabilities in supply chains, by highlighting the drop in manufacturing and by sanctioning a vastly expanded role for government, COVID-19 has made it easier to push the politics of protectionism and to denigrate the economic logic of global supply chains. This will only exacerbate the already immense economic impact which COVID-19 lockdowns have had almost every way.

In this sense, COVID-19 will make it easier for populism to gain ground. One feature of populism is that it turns bad policy into good politics and we are likely to see a lot of debt-fuelled bad economic policy in the wake of COVID-19. We will have to reprosecute the case for an open economy because COVID-19 will have strengthened its opponents.

For Australia, we are now also facing up to the consequences of our considerable trade dependence on China. That trade was one factor in Australia enjoying an unprecedented thirty-year stretch of economic growth, broken only by the COVID-19 recession. Australia did well out of globalization in large part because we did well out of trade with China.

Are we too dependent on China? The answer will not be found only in percentages. China takes well over a third of Australia's exports, more than the next five export destinations combined. In an earlier age, before it joined the then EEC, the UK took an even larger share of our exports but the difference is the political character of China. It is an authoritarian system prone to threatening trade consequences if we do or say something China does not like. Usually this is bluster designed to make enough nervous business leaders go running to the government to warn that we need to be nicer to China.

But China's most recent moves against Australian exports of barley, wine, beef and coal signal that this is now more than bluster. And the longer-term effect of a dual-circulation economy in China may also have significant consequences for Australia's exports to China. So, it makes sense for Australia to diversify its trade connections: not by deliberately slowing trade with China, which would not be in our interest, but by growing trade with other countries, such as the US, Japan, Korea, India, Indonesia, Vietnam, and a post-Brexit UK.

Trade diversification is a worthy national objective but it is markets, not governments, that drive trade. Some products would struggle to find alternative markets, including iron ore, which is by far Australia's largest export to China. It is also unrealistic to expect individual Australian businesses to turn their backs on trade opportunities with China, but the government can help business pursue other markets through pushing for trade liberalization, negotiating Free Trade Agreements and, most importantly, putting in place domestic economic settings which make Australian firms more internationally competitive.

Conclusion

Nixon and Kissinger's opening to China was a bold strategy anchored in the logic of the Cold War. Together with Deng's subsequent opening of the Chinese economy, it transformed our economic and geopolitical world. The salad days of the China growth story, when we could reap the economic rewards without confronting the strategic costs, are now behind us. The strategic consequences lie ahead.

Australia cannot unilaterally reset the terms of engagement with China. But we can frame the relationship around an 'engage and constrain' strategy with domestic, bilateral and geopolitical components anchored in the following principles and realities:

1. China will likely remain either the largest or second-largest economy for decades ahead.

2. Its leadership is determined to retain the political monopoly of the Chinese Communist Party and the authoritarian structures that sustain that monopoly.
3. We cannot change China's system from the outside, so we must engage with China where our mutual interests are served and, over time, look to expand areas of engagement and cooperation including in regional and global organizations.
4. China will not simply embrace a system based on global rules. It will be selective in how it engages in regional and global institutions, but the United Nations system, G20, East Asia Summit and APEC provide ready platforms to build on multilateral engagement with China.
5. We must hold firm to our values and strengthen our national capacity to resist coercion, whatever the source. This should include an increased investment in defence and diplomacy. Both are vital to our future, but in Australia only one is being resourced adequately.
6. We should not treat China as an enemy or a threat, but quietly abandon the notion that we can have a comprehensive strategic partnership with China as long as it remains an authoritarian state seeking regional predominance. Such a partnership assumes an alignment of strategic interests which simply does not currently exist.
7. We must work with the US, Japan, India and others, especially in Southeast Asia, to construct a new strategic equilibrium in the Indo-Pacific with the capacity and commitment to collectively constrain coercive behaviour by China and to impose costs for such behaviour.
8. We should make it clear in Washington and elsewhere that Australia will not support a policy of containing China or decoupling China from global supply chains, but we will support greater diversification of those supply chains.

9. We need to lower Australia's trade dependence on China by expanding access to other markets. Our objective should be diversification not diversion, achieved through trade promotion and liberalization in other markets and through domestic economic reforms that raise productivity, builds national resilience and lifts our international competitiveness.

15

The Strategic Legacy in Southeast Asia

HOO TIANG BOON AND QUAH SAY JYE

IN 1971, US NATIONAL SECURITY Advisor Henry Kissinger landed in China for secret talks with Chinese Premier Zhou Enlai, laying the basis for President Nixon's historic meeting with Mao the following year. The rapprochement between the US and China astounded the world. But more that that, the Nixon–Mao summit paved the way for the normalization of relations between two adversaries that had fought during the Korean war, a monumental story that upended the global order and resulted in the entry of the People's Republic of China into the United Nations at Taiwan's expense, with the former becoming a 'tacit ally' of the US in Asia.[1] It was the 'week that changed the world', Nixon famously declared.

Fifty years on, those changes are viewed with much more scepticism in the US. A bipartisan consensus has emerged that casts the PRC as America's primary strategic competitor, with Americans questioning the wisdom of integrating a communist-party-led China into international society. The Sino–American rapprochement, sparked by Kissinger's 1971 visit, is seen by many Americans as emblematic of a policy approach and strategic error that culminated in the rise of a China that remains autocratic and is a direct challenge to US global primacy and democracies around the world.[2] Such perceptions are backed by American public sentiments, with polls indicating that negative attitudes toward China are among the highest in the US in recent times.[3]

Given this contemporary relevance, it seems apt for us to revisit the subject of the geopolitical legacy of Kissinger's historic visit. In doing so, however, this essay will not approach the discussion from an American angle, a conversation that may well have more twists and turns as the US grapples with China's global ascendancy. Instead, it will unpack Kissinger's visit and the subsequent rapprochement through the relatively-ignored window of Southeast Asia, focusing on the impact and implications of these epochal developments on the region. We proceed by first contextualizing our discussion with an account of the perceptions and fears that many Southeast Asian nations had of China in the 1950s and '60s. This is followed by analysis of the repercussions that the Sino–American rapprochement wrought on Southeast Asia. The essay concludes with thoughts on how the rapprochement should be evaluated amidst the backdrop of rising US–China rivalry in Southeast Asia in the contemporary period.

The early fears

The Cold War is generally seen as a global ideological clash between capitalism, embodied by the US and its allies, and communism, as represented by the Soviet Union and its allies. This bipolar order structured competition between the two blocs for influence around the world, including in Southeast Asia. In Southeast Asia, however, it was the PRC and not the Soviet Union that was the principal communist protagonist during the Cold War,[4] though this is not to say that the Soviets had no role to play. The Chinese role in the region was shaped by a complex web of factors, including geography, nationalism, local politics, and ethnic ties. While contact and engagement between leaders during the 1955 Bandung Conference managed to soften perceptions and create a modicum of trust in Beijing amongst some Southeast Asian countries,[5] this dynamic was short-lived. This was not surprising. Since the establishment of the PRC under communist leadership in 1949, non-communist governments in Southeast Asia had long been wary of communist China. Mao's foreign policy was based on a desire for China to be the base or 'headquarters' of communist revolution in Asia, establishing contacts and support for communist parties or revolutionaries in the region.[6] Chinese Communist Party (CCP) leaders believed that China's revolutionary experience was of international significance, serving as a model for other foreign revolutionaries at a time of rapid decolonization around the world, including in Southeast Asia.[7] The success of these revolutionaries would further establish China's ideological credentials and leadership in the socialist bloc, along with boosting the international prospects of the communist cause.[8]

Thus, throughout the 1950s and '60s, the CCP supported and funded communist parties in Southeast Asia, including the Malayan and Burmese communist parties.[9] Many of these parties were at the forefront of nationalist struggles in the region. Chinese support of these parties, including armed elements, created problems of national security for many Southeast Asian states as these local insurgencies could both topple existing governments as well as spill over and foment a wider regional communist threat. Several Southeast Asian leaders subscribed to US President Eisenhower's domino theory: the idea that if one country succumbed to communism, it could easily lead to other regional states falling under the spell of communist ideology.[10] They, therefore, keenly watched political developments in neighbouring Southeast Asian countries, and worked not only to combat internal communist threats, but also considered the issue through a regional lens. This translated to poor relations between non-communist Southeast Asian states and China.

The Philippines, the country most closely allied with the US, was perhaps the clearest example of this. Relations between China and the Philippines were mostly suspended in 1949, the year the PRC was founded. Commercial ties were cut, and travel and immigration were banned.[11] The Filipino government went on to fend off domestic communist guerrilla forces throughout the 1950s and '60s. Thailand, another beneficiary of US military and economic support, also had a very poor relationship with China in the 1950s and '60s. Less than 100 kilometres from China, Thailand had always harboured traditional concerns of potential Chinese aggression.[12] Conversely, Beijing developed stronger ties with the communist Hanoi, and provided considerable military and propaganda support throughout the 1960s.[13] During that period, Beijing also supported Cambodia under King Sihanouk, providing military aid as Cambodia facilitated the transfer of arms to Hanoi.[14] Cambodia was thought to be dependent on China for most of the 1960s until, inter alia, Beijing's refusal to stop disseminating communist propaganda within Cambodia, which led Sihanouk to pursue formal relations with the US.[15] Sino–Cambodia relations became increasingly complicated as a result.

Ethnic factors also came into play during this period and coloured the relationship between a number of Southeast Asian nations and China. Singapore was the only ethnic Chinese-majority nation outside of China (and Taiwan), while Southeast Asian countries such as Indonesia, Thailand, and Malaysia had sizeable ethnic Chinese minorities. Significant numbers of these Southeast Asian Chinese populations, typically Chinese migrants and their descendants, were still attuned to developments within China. Mao's famous statement that the 'Chinese people had stood up', for example, had brought about a surge of ethnic pride among this group, causing the kind of emotional pulls that complicated the nation-building efforts of Southeast Asian governments.[16] Furthermore, Beijing pursued a policy of 'jus sanguinis' (law relating to blood) citizenship in 1955, which declared that all ethnic Chinese around the world could choose to be citizens of China. This blurred the line between 'overseas Chinese' and ethnic Chinese living outside of communist China, arousing suspicions of the political loyalties of the latter groups within their resident states in Southeast Asia.[17]

Ethnic issues were perhaps most acute in Indonesia during the tail end of President Sukarno's reign. Disputes and controversy over citizenship, where Chinese Indonesians had to choose between Chinese and Indonesian citizenship, led to distrust and suppression of ethnic Chinese within Indonesia, including large-scale violence.[18] The distrust amongst the 'pribumi', or indigenous peoples, towards the ethnic Chinese, remains deep-seated till this day.[19] Such ethnic tensions coloured relations between

China and Indonesia, and made Beijing an easy scapegoat for Jakarta's domestic troubles. This was notably seen during the transition from the Sukarno to the Suharto regime in 1965, when CCP influence was blamed for the failed coup which led to a major anti-communist purge. Under Sukarno, despite tensions over ethnic matters, relations with the PRC were still relatively stable, as both countries took on a strong anti-imperialist line as part of the 'Jakarta-Phnom Penh-Hanoi-Pyongyang-Peking axis'.[20] Relations with Suharto's Indonesia were the opposite, as the domestic and foreign policies of Jakarta turned deeply anti-communist.

On a regional scale, concerns over the Chinese communist threat led several Southeast Asian states, openly or otherwise, to ally themselves with the US, forming a so-called 'arc of containment' around China.[21] The fear of the Chinese threat was also a key reason behind the formation of the Association of Southeast Asian Nations (ASEAN), the primary regional organization.[22] A number of Southeast Asian states, including Singapore and Malaysia, wooed the US as a security guarantor, who in turn also cultivated strong ties with the leaders of these non-communist governments. Under Suharto, Indonesia adopted a strong anti-China and pro-Western stance and was a regionally influential supporter of the 'arc'. Such ties helped boost the legitimacy of US intervention in Southeast Asia, particularly its role in the Second Indochina War, through the expression of public support and political arguments in favour of a sustained US presence in the region.[23]

Meanwhile, brewing beneath the surface was a growing antagonism between the Chinese and the Soviets, culminating eventually in an open Sino–Soviet split by the 1960s. While full details of this fracture will not be discussed here, tensions between China and the USSR had become most clearly evident in 1969 when border disputes resulted in military clashes that left an acute sense of insecurity between both.[24] This led the Soviets, who took the border clashes as evidence that the Chinese planned to eventually annex Soviet territory,[25] to contemplate a nuclear strike on China.[26] On the flip side, the PRC was compelled to see the Soviet Union, with whom it shared long borders, as its principal security threat instead of the US. Combined with the domestic chaos that came during the Cultural Revolution, this geopolitical insecurity prompted Mao to consider rapprochement with the US, which will be elaborated next.

After the rapprochement: A new calculus in Southeast Asia

In the late 1960s, CCP leaders attempted to hint to American officials that Beijing was open to dialogue and a shift in the bilateral relationship.[27] At the same time, sensing an opportunity to exploit the Soviet–Sino split, as well as undercut Chinese support for Hanoi with a view towards enabling the US to pull out of the region, some Americans began questioning Washington's diplomatic isolation of China. One of those voices was Nixon, who hinted at considerations over a new modus vivendi with China as early as in 1967 (before becoming president) in a *Foreign Affairs* article. Those sentiments were concretized in the form of the Nixon Doctrine in July 1969, which alarmed US allies in Southeast Asia, who saw the doctrine as a major policy turn that signalled Washington would be less willing to provide regional security or abide by previous commitments and treaties. During his visits to Indonesia, the Philippines and Thailand, Nixon was bombarded with questions about the content and implications of the Nixon Doctrine, and had to constantly reassure these allies that they would not be abandoned.[28]

With the assistance of Pakistani intermediaries and some 'ping-pong diplomacy'[29] the rapprochement was set in motion when US National Security Advisor Henry Kissinger and Chinese Premier Zhou Enlai held secret talks in Beijing in July 1971.[30] While full diplomatic relations between China and the US were achieved only in 1979, Kissinger's visit broke decades of frozen relations between the two countries and set up Nixon's monumental meeting with Mao in 1972, which established concrete steps to develop formal ties, including economic relations, between the two former adversaries. Alongside the benefits that came with gaining recognition from the international community as a permanent member of the United Nations Security Council, the rapprochement, crucially, opened doors for China to gain access to vast amounts of global capital and technology that were important for its economic modernization.[31] In the US, the Kissinger–Nixon move was noted from changing the complexion of the Cold War, from one guided by ideological conflict to one guided by realpolitik considerations.[32]

For Southeast Asia, the significance of the rapprochement in fundamentally altering the strategic context of the region in the 1970s was noted by several scholars.[33] Even before the rapprochement fully unfolded, Southeast Asian governments reacted to the news of Kissinger's visit and the prospect of a subsequent Nixon visit with a regional dialogue to address the developing situation. To that end, a special meeting was convened by the foreign ministers of the ASEAN countries (the five founding members) in October 1971.[34] Participants at the meeting agreed there was a need to reevaluate their countries' respective outlooks towards the two great powers, but no immediate consensus on the appropriate way to respond emerged. Eventually, building on Malaysia's push for the region's 'neutralization' with regard to extra-regional powers, negotiations led to the declaration of Southeast Asia as the Zone of Peace, Freedom and Neutrality (ZOPFAN), which affirmed ASEAN's objective to be 'free from any form or manner of interference by outside powers'. The US and China both accepted the ZOPFAN proposal, with Washington confident that the US-allied 'arc of containment' would still ensure Western primacy in the region.[35]

In effect, Nixon's impending visit and the prospect of a US–China rapprochement had confirmed to ASEAN leaders that American involvement in Indochina was about to wind down as the Nixon Doctrine had suggested. This mandated a re-evaluation of the strategic trajectory of Southeast Asia,[36] especially consideration of the prospect of multipolar competition—as opposed to a bipolar one—within the region as American withdrawal implied a bigger Chinese, Soviet, and possibly Japanese regional influence.[37] Believing that a balance of power was the most desirable situation in these circumstances, Southeast Asian leaders sought a relationship equidistant between the great powers. For many Southeast Asian states, this meant rethinking their frosty dynamics with China. To that extent, the rapprochement paved the way for these states to pursue relations with China as it implied that the US had tacitly given the green light to do so. SarDesai cites the Nixon–Mao meeting and the subsequent withdrawal of US troops from the region, as 'crucial events' that 'radically influenced the international relations of Southeast Asian states'.[38] Before the rapprochement, Southeast Asian states fretted that developing relations with China could risk alienating the US.[39] This could have entailed costs for these nations, as not only were they dependent on the US for arms and trade, vitally, the US was their principal security guarantor. With Washington establishing relations with Beijing (and the latter even becoming a 'tacit ally'),[40] Southeast Asian governments were free to pursue their own ties with China, without any fear of compromising their own relationship with the US.

The Sino–US rapprochement, therefore, made conditions ripe for the establishment of formal diplomatic ties between China and Malaysia (1974), Thailand (1975), and the Philippines (1975).[41] The official documents underpinning these new relations, notably, included an 'anti-hegemony' clause that was also a feature of the Shanghai Communiqué signed between China and the US in 1972.[42] The clause stated that the signatories were 'opposed to any attempt by any country or group of countries to establish hegemony or create spheres of influence in any part of the world',[43] alluding to a commitment towards a stable balance of power in the region. Importantly for ASEAN states, the rapprochement diminished perceptions of the communist threat in the region. While it took time for China to fully wind down its support for regional communist movements, the normalization of relations between China and ASEAN states essentially relieved the latter governments of a major internal security threat.[44]

In Singapore's case, while the island state did not establish official ties with Beijing until October 1990, it took the rapprochement as the cue to establish better relations with China right from the start. Hence, both countries engaged in their own version of 'ping-pong' diplomacy in 1972, with Singapore's Minister of Foreign Affairs S. Rajaratnam visiting Beijing in 1975.[45] Addressing the motivations of that visit later, Rajaratnam pointed out that Nixon's meeting with the Chinese leadership had set a precedent while the ensuing rapprochement transformed the strategic landscape for Southeast Asia.[46] Acutely aware of its vulnerabilities as a small nation, Singapore sought for a manageable balance of power in the region. With the withdrawal of the US, cultivating stronger relations with China become paramount for ASEAN nations, which saw Beijing as acting as a counterweight to looming Soviet involvement (via its proxy Vietnam). Those new ties would also be helpful for Southeast Asia to be involved in the anticipated rise of the PRC once the latter had come aboard international society.[47] Singapore was, nevertheless, cautious about establishing formal relations with China out of a sensitivity for the perceptions that this might generate among its neighbours as the only ethnic Chinese-majority nation in Southeast Asia, and took care to wait until Indonesia had first established diplomatic ties with China in August 1990 before doing so itself.

Not every Southeast Asian country welcomed news of the Sino–American rapprochement. Notably, Vietnam reacted negatively to news of Kissinger's visit and the impending Mao–Nixon summit; for them, this was akin to a betrayal and almost a repeat of Chinese actions in 1954. Hanoi requested that the Chinese government call off the summit, which Beijing refused.[48] Subsequently, the rapprochement led to a downward spiralling of relations between Beijing and Hanoi, and was a factor in compelling the Vietnamese to accept a settlement with the US in 1972.[49] But this increased Vietnamese insecurities in the process, and was a consideration for Hanoi to fully throw its geopolitical lot with the Soviet Union by 1978 when it signed a treaty of friendship and cooperation with the latter.

It should be qualified that while the rapprochement, sparked by Kissinger's initial visit to China, was significant in influencing the calculus of Southeast Asian states vis-à-vis Beijing, its impact should not be overstated as some of these considerations predated Kissinger's and Nixon's visits and were already being deliberated in regional capitals. As a case in point: in the 1960s, Thai leaders felt that the US's military presence in Indochina prohibited them from establishing relations with both Beijing and Hanoi.[50] Hence, following the events in 1968, which included the Tet Offensive and Lyndon Johnson's decision to not run for another term as president, Foreign Minister Thanat Khoman publicly raised the prospect that Thailand was considering of exploring relations with Beijing and should not be blamed for doing so.[51]

Fifty years on: So, what for Southeast Asia?

Might today's Southeast Asian leaders 'regret' the Kissinger–Nixon decision to pursue rapprochement with communist China, as some in the US evidently do? This may seem like a moot point; after all, Southeast Asia's then leaders were reacting to great-power machinations that were largely outside of their control during the Cold War. Yet, put differently, it is fundamentally a question about whether Southeast Asia today would perceive the consequences of the rapprochement as beneficial for the region.

We suspect the answer is less than straightforward. It is true that the rapprochement effectively meant that communist China had become less of a political or security threat to Southeast Asian states (with the exception of Vietnam). And although China and Vietnam fought a short border war in 1979, for most Southeast Asian states, the rapprochement ushered in a period of relative stability in the region, particularly from the 1980s. A prime reason for that is the subsequent economic rise of China, a story not unconnected to the consequences of the rapprochement. Of course, the sources of this ascendancy are multifaceted,[52] and a key part relates to Deng Xiaoping's domestic reforms and opening-up programme, which released the shackles of the Chinese economic race horse. But an important part of the story is also about the more favorable external environment which the rapprochement engendered for China, allowing the country to integrate into the international community and benefit from access to global capital, technology, education, and other resources that had not been available when it was isolated.

Fifty years on, politically, China remains communist but it is no longer keen to export its ideology to Southeast Asia. Economically, however, China has been open for business and that is what principally matters for Southeast Asian governments (many of whom, while not communist, veer towards varying degrees of autocratic governance). ASEAN states have been keen to profit from Chinese economic opportunities, and trade between China and the region has flourished over the years. Today China is the largest trading partner for most ASEAN states, and 'plays the most important role for ASEAN in terms of investments, trade flows and economic relationships'.[53] In 2019, the ASEAN–China Free Trade Agreement (FTA) was upgraded, an agreement that first became operational in 2010 and established the world's third-largest free-trade area based on trading volume. Such transnational economic linkages are expected to burgeon even further after the signing of the Regional Comprehensive Economic Partnership (RECP) in November 2020, an omnidirectional economic pact that builds upon the ASEAN-plus-one framework to also connect China to other FTA partners of ASEAN.

Yet, economics only tells one aspect of the story. Arguably, no ASEAN country is putting all their eggs in the Chinese basket (even if states such as Cambodia and Laos are strategically closer to Beijing than others). All Southeast Asian states want to ride the Chinese growth train. However, they also worry about whether the now economically (and militarily) more successful China will flex its muscles to impose its will on them when it deems fit, a concern borne out of periodic frictions relating to overlapping territorial or maritime claims between China and a number of ASEAN states in the South China Sea.[54] To that extent, every ASEAN state is 'hedging' against negative China scenarios in one form or another, the only difference being the degree of hedging.[55] This apprehension, among others, explains why ASEAN leaders see the US as a critical offshore balancer and indispensable factor for stability in the region, with ASEAN support for continuing US presence in Southeast Asia remaining strong.

Herein lies another dilemma for ASEAN leaders: Amidst growing Sino–US competition for influence in Southeast Asia, they worry about a time when they are compelled to choose between the two.[56] Because of the extent to which the region shares deep linkages with both powers, ASEAN can ill afford to take sides between the US and China. ASEAN leaders recognize that if Southeast Asia is turned into a proxy battleground of the great powers, the bloc will bear the most collateral damage, including the fracturing of its unity. What is worse, an outright US–China conflict, particularly a military one, will destabilize the wider regional environment, leading to conditions that could imperil ASEAN's growth. A twenty-first century 'Kissinger' and a new US–China rapprochement may well be high on the wish list of ASEAN leaders if these scenarios come to pass.

16

Triangulation and the Tilts

Nixon's China Rapprochement and the 1971 India–Pakistan Crisis

TANVI MADAN

ON THE MORNING OF 12 December 1971, President Richard Nixon met with National Security Advisor Henry Kissinger and Deputy National Security Advisor Alexander Haig to discuss the ongoing India–Pakistan War. Kissinger proposed a public statement labelling India the aggressor 'to impress the Russians, to scare the Indians, to take a position with the Chinese'. Nixon was very clear about his priority, saying, 'Chinese. That's the main thing.'

This China factor on Nixon's mind—and Kissinger's—led to an extraordinary conversation between them. They discussed whether or not Beijing would and should move militarily against India on behalf of Pakistan, and what the US should do to deter the Soviet Union from acting against China if Beijing took that step. Nixon asked Kissinger whether it would require the US to '[s]tart lobbing nuclear weapons in'. The National Security Advisor clarified that was not what he meant, but asserted that the US could not let 'the Soviets move against [China] … and succeed' because if they did, 'we'll be finished'.[1]

This conversation reflected the prism through which, since spring 1971, Nixon and Kissinger had seen the developing crisis over East Pakistan (later Bangladesh). Their particular concern was the crisis's potential to scuttle their China rapprochement. That, in turn, they believed would harm their triangular diplomacy, which was designed to change the balance of power in the US–Soviet–China triangle, giving Washington leverage with Moscow that could help bring the Vietnam war—or at least America's involvement in it—to an end. Nixon and Kissinger saw this triangulation and the required rapprochement with China as crucial, not just for strategic reasons but for Nixon's 1972 re-election prospects as well.

In a background briefing to the US Congress after the onset of the India–Pakistan war in December 1971, Kissinger refuted the notion that 'US policy is motivated primarily by (a) considerations of China policy or (b) a gut-loathing for the Indians'.[2] The latter has often been pointed to as the reason for Nixon and Kissinger's attitude towards the 1971 crisis. However, it was indeed the first factor, that is, their desire to engage Beijing in order to create space with Moscow, that was the crucial determinant of the American approach. More facetiously, the political counsellor in the US embassy in Pakistan in 1971 lamented years later that the US policy towards that crisis got 'hung up' in Nixon and Kissinger's 'globaloney'.[3]

Counterfactuals are hard to prove. However, knowing what we now know, it is a good bet that the US approach to and involvement in the India–Pakistan crisis would not have been the same had the 1971 Bangladesh crisis not coincided with Nixon and Kissinger's quest for a China rapprochement. Their 'triangulation' priority led to the US 'tilt' to Pakistan, and contributed to the Indian 'tilt' to the Soviet Union. And these tilts cast a long shadow, with effects that have lasted to this day.[4]

Washington's tilt

When Nixon was Dwight Eisenhower's vice president, he was known as a 'Cold Warrior', committed to countering the Sino–Soviet communist bloc. In this guise, he had criticized India's engagement with the Soviet

Union and China in the 1950s. But subsequently, this vantage point had also led to Nixon's desire to ensure that democratic India won the 'fateful race' with communist China. In May 1959, he had joined then Senator John F. Kennedy to support aid for India. Nixon had asserted, 'What happens in India ... could be as important or could be even more important in the long run, than what happens in the negotiations with regard to Berlin.' The result of the competition between 'two great peoples in Asia' would have a global impact.[5]

However, Nixon's view of what it would take to win the Cold War would change. And this in part drove his desire for a China reset. As a presidential candidate, in a 1967 *Foreign Affairs* article, he had mentioned his interest in exploring engagement with China. Asia, to him, was 'where the action is'. And '[a]ny discussion of Asia's future must ultimately focus on the respective roles of four giants': China, India, Japan, and the US.[6]

Subsequently, as president, Nixon saw China as important not just for its own sake, but also because of his administration's other two priorities: Dealing with the Soviet Union; and the Vietnam War. At a time when US dominance, and its strategic and economic superiority were under threat, Nixon and Kissinger directed their foreign policy efforts towards maintaining America's global standing. Based on Vietnam-era geopolitical and domestic realities, and the belief that a balance of power would produce global stability, Nixon's foreign policy came to revolve around what was called triangular diplomacy—the 'calculated management of policy on mutual relations between and among the US, the Soviet Union, and China', as Raymond Garthoff put it.[7]

Neither Chinese hostility nor the threat had disappeared, including in Vietnam. But Nixon and Kissinger saw Beijing as potentially helping solve their Southeast Asia problem. Furthermore, they believed that bringing China in from the cold made a potential China threat 'more manageable and predictable'.[8] Finally, given Sino–Soviet friction, they could use Beijing to out-manoeuvre Moscow.

So, early in his administration, Nixon sought to re-evaluate US policy towards China. There were sceptics, including Kissinger initially, but the President persisted. His approach involved two elements: (a) preparing the ground at home for a reset; and (b) signalling China. The strategy to make Beijing aware that Washington was interested in improving relations also involved a two-pronged effort on the part of Nixon, Kissinger, and a close circle of advisors: (a) sending a message through public proclamations; and (b) secret diplomacy.

This secret diplomacy is what linked Nixon's China rapprochement effort with South Asia. Two decades before, India had been a US channel to China; now Nixon and Kissinger saw Pakistan as that channel. What had earlier been Pakistan's greatest liability in US eyes—its close partnership with China—had become its greatest asset. And from late 1969 through summer 1971, Islamabad passed Washington's messages to Beijing.

Thus, in March 1971, when the Pakistani military in Bengali-majority East Pakistan launched a crackdown on the Awami League and demonstrators, who were demanding implementation of national election results and greater autonomy, the White House's major objective was to 'maintain Pakistan's goodwill' in order 'to preserve the channel to Peking', as Kissinger later put it.[9] In early April, Beijing's invitation to an American ping-pong team to visit China pleasantly surprised Nixon and Kissinger. They were even more delighted when, at the end of month, Pakistani officials conveyed Chinese premier Zhou Enlai's invitation for Nixon or an emissary to visit China.[10]

Subsequently, unbeknownst to the State Department, planning got underway for Kissinger to travel through Pakistan to China in July. Thus, even as the situation in South Asia deteriorated, Nixon instructed that nothing be done to 'squeeze' West Pakistan.[11] He wanted to maintain the Pakistan channel to China, and also believed he needed to demonstrate to Beijing that Washington could be a reliable friend. Nixon told US ambassador to India, Kenneth Keating, in June 'for reasons we can't go into … we've got to take up here—for reasons that go far beyond India–Pakistan relations—another position'.[12]

Then in July, while Kissinger was in the midst of the trip that would take him to Delhi, Islamabad and (secretly) Beijing, the President resisted congressional calls for pressure on Pakistani leader Yahya Khan to moderate his approach towards the Awami League and find a compromise. The White House also found workarounds to a congressional embargo on economic aid to Pakistan, took a liberal attitude towards Pakistani debt rescheduling and stated that Pakistan would get military equipment that the US had earlier sanctioned.[13]

This reluctance to push Yahya towards compromise continued after the White House had established direct channels to China. Nixon and Kissinger were grateful for his role in establishing the channel. They were also concerned that US pressure on Pakistan 'might be misunderstood in Peking' and seen as a joint US action with the Soviet Union, which was backing India. Thus, in subsequent meetings with the Chinese leadership, Kissinger repeatedly emphasized that the US was supporting Pakistan.[14]

Could Sino–US rapprochement have survived increased US pressure on Pakistan? China had its own motivations for the rapprochement. Furthermore, Beijing's own support to Islamabad had not gone beyond some military supplies, and rhetorical and political backing.[15] As early as March, a US interagency group had assessed that Chinese military intervention to help Pakistan was highly unlikely since Beijing would consider it 'high risk, low benefit'.[16] At a meeting in July, Zhou had told Kissinger that 'if India commits aggression, we will support Pakistan' but left the nature of that assistance ambiguous.[17] Defending his perspective, Kissinger later noted that he believed that China was more seriously committed to Pakistan because of his interpretation of a statement that Zhou made to the effect that 'China would not be indifferent if India attacked Pakistan'.[18] With this assumption, Nixon and he believed that China would see a 'victory of India over Pakistan' as 'the same as a victory of the Soviet Union over China'.[19]

As September and October unfolded, opportunities for a peaceful resolution of the crisis dissipated as the stakeholders became increasingly inflexible. Nixon and Kissinger continued to view the crisis through global glasses, worrying about China's reaction to their stance. Kissinger insisted in November, 'We are willing to do anything if the Indians will give us six months to turn around in.'[20] That period was crucial because of the President's upcoming trips to Beijing and Moscow ahead of the

1972 elections. Thus, Kissinger rejected suggestions by National Security Council staff and State Department contingency planners that the US warn Beijing that provocative Chinese border incidents in the event of India–Pakistan hostilities would adversely affect Sino–US relations.[21]

But, given the August 1971 India–Soviet treaty of friendship and cooperation, any Chinese desire to intervene militarily in such a way now had to take into account Moscow's reaction. Thus, while Beijing publicly pledged support for Pakistan, its actions were relatively restrained. In October, a surprised Kissinger noticed 'less passion and more caution' from Zhou on Pakistan. In November, he tried unsuccessfully to draw out Huang Hua, the Chinese permanent representative at the United Nations, further on the subject.[22]

As the prospects of an India–Pakistan war grew, Kissinger told Secretary of State William Rogers that the President 'would like to tilt towards Pakistan'.[23] When war broke out in early December, the administration announced it would remain neutral, but Nixon privately asserted to Kissinger, 'Of course, we're not neutral.'[24] The US held India responsible, cancelling loans and sales of military spares, and delaying approving food aid to India. Simultaneously, the White House suggested to America's Middle Eastern allies that, while Washington could not sell or permit them to sell US equipment to Pakistan, it would be 'obliged to protest, but … will understand' if they supplied Pakistan with American arms.[25]

With the Pakistan army's defeat in the east imminent, Nixon and Kissinger became convinced that India would try to destroy West Pakistan next, despite substantial contrary analysis within the US government.[26] The White House thought China was watching the US response closely. Kissinger told Nixon that if Pakistan broke up, Beijing would conclude that the US is 'just too weak' and it might 'drop the whole idea' of engaging with Washington.[27]

With China on their mind, on 9 December, Nixon and Kissinger discussed sending an aircraft carrier to the Bay of Bengal.[28] The administration subsequently deployed a naval task force led by USS *Enterprise*, ostensibly to deter New Delhi and to demonstrate to Beijing that it was willing to oppose India and step up for its friends. This was a far cry from 1962, when the US had contemplated deploying an aircraft carrier to the Bay of Bengal to deter China and show support for India. It was also a far cry from the 1965 war, when the US had warned China against attacking India and had dusted off its contingency plans to support India in case Beijing did so.

Indeed, this time, the US tried to urge Beijing to move against India, despite the State Department and allies' expectation that Chinese reticence would persist.[29] When the Pakistani army was on the verge of surrendering in the east, Kissinger suggested to Huang Hua that India needed to be 'intimidated' to prevent it attacking West Pakistan. He urged a coordinated China–Pakistan–US effort to confront the India–Soviet action. Encouraging China to increase its military commitment, Kissinger passed along Nixon's message that if China 'were to consider the situation on the Indian subcontinent a threat to its security, and if it took measures to protect its security, the US would oppose efforts of others to interfere with the People's Republic'. Beijing's permanent representative reiterated that China was prepared to defend itself if attacked. But, given the concern that taking any action against India would give the Soviet Union an excuse to attack China, he repeatedly emphasized that Beijing wanted to persist with efforts underway at the United Nations—where China and the US had been coordinating—to resolve the situation.[30]

Chinese military intervention did not materialize, but the war did have other outcomes. For one, the creation of Bangladesh. Significantly, it also resulted in US–India relations arguably reaching their lowest point. Indian Prime Minister Indira Gandhi, at least, had little doubt about the cause: She told *The New York Times* that America's approach towards India changed 'when your policy towards China changed'.[31]

New Delhi's tilt

It is unlikely Nixon and Kissinger's China rapprochement would have had such a negative impact on US–India relations had it not unfolded almost simultaneously with the 1971 crisis. The fact is it also resulted in India's tilt towards the Soviet Union, with the signing of the India–Soviet treaty.

Dealing with deteriorating Sino–Soviet relations, Moscow had proposed such a treaty to India in early 1969 as 'very good insurance against any possible aggression by China or Pakistan.'[32] However, Indira Gandhi had been reluctant because of the potential US, Chinese, and domestic reactions. She had worried that the treaty would be seen as a move away from non-alignment or 'directed against a third party'. So, while Gandhi had agreed to 'exploratory talks', the idea had subsequently been shelved.[33]

When tensions rose between India and Pakistan in the summer 1971, one of New Delhi's key concerns involved the possibility of Chinese intervention if war broke out. India sought assurances from the superpowers to deter Beijing or to ensure that it would be prepared if China went beyond supporting Pakistan diplomatically. In early June, Indian Foreign Minister Swaran Singh raised the issue on a trip to Moscow, but his Soviet counterpart Andrei Gromyko was not willing to give something in return for nothing, and revived the idea of a treaty.[34]

Given the US–India Air Defense Agreement (ADA) of 1963, which included a provision for mutual consultations in the event of a Chinese attack on India, New Delhi also reached out to the US. In July, Defence Minister Jagjivan Ram asked Kissinger about what the US would do if China intervened against India.[35] His question reflected Indian awareness of the changing US assessment of China. The Soviet chief of mission in London had told his Indian counterpart in March that the US was seeking an agreement with China.[36] When Kissinger met with Indira Gandhi in New Delhi in July (just before he secretly travelled to China), he also indicated that it was Nixon's policy to 'gradually … establish a relationship with Communist China'. He added that there 'could be significant developments in the months ahead'. They 'were not directed at India', but due to the need to bring China into the international community.[37]

The prospect of rapprochement alone did not bother Indian officials, but doubts arose about its potential impact on US support for India. Indira Gandhi's Principal Secretary P.N. Haksar was 'puzzled' by Kissinger's implication that if China intervened in an India–Pakistan conflict, New Delhi would 'have to rely on' Moscow.[38]

The Sino–US rapprochement, made public on 15 July, in and of itself did not make an India–Soviet treaty inevitable. Indira Gandhi indeed 'welcomed' the beginning of Sino–US normalization.[39] Rather, the treaty was the result of a confluence of conditions: The Bangladesh crisis with a real chance of an India–Pakistan war and the possibility of Chinese intervention, the Indian need for deterrence and the Soviet desire for a treaty in return for providing that deterrence, the lack of availability of the US as an option as a result of the Sino–US rapprochement, and Indira Gandhi's expanded domestic political capacity.

The impact of the China rapprochement on the attitude of the US towards the Bangladesh crisis was of particular concern. A few months earlier, influential defence expert K. Subrahmanyam had assessed the 'probability of Chinese intervention' as 'low'. Even if Beijing intervened, he argued, 'the chances of Super Power support to India appear to be fairly high in the current circumstances'.[40] But the altered Sino–US dynamic suggested American support against China might not be forthcoming. And this concern was only fuelled by Kissinger's indication to Indian ambassador to the US, L.K. Jha, at a meeting on 17 July that India would be on its own if it took action in East Pakistan and China intervened.[41]

For New Delhi, the India–Soviet treaty now became more desirable—as morale booster, deterrent to China, source of fuel and military supply, and support at the United Nations. The treaty had also become more feasible. The American stance had strengthened the hands of treaty advocates in the Indian government, who stressed that the Sino–American détente increased the urgency for an agreement with Moscow. Foreign Secretary T.N. Kaul noted that India had 'no alternative left' and it needed the Soviet treaty to have a 'reliable friend'. Hoping to seal the deal, Soviet officials, on their part, fuelled Indian concerns about the US and the possibility of Chinese intervention.[42]

The crisis, as well as Indira Gandhi's major electoral victory in 1971, also made the domestic political conditions more favorable for the treaty.[43] Furthermore, by August, the Indian public attitude towards the US had deteriorated. In a survey, only 40 per cent identified the US as friendly towards India, while the Soviet Union scored much higher at 60 per cent.[44]

And when the treaty was announced on 9 August, even Jan Sangh leader Atal Bihari Vajpayee—usually a critic of Indira Gandhi's government—acknowledged that India now had a much-needed 'friend at a critical juncture'.[45] That treaty and that critical moment cemented India's tilt.

The long shadow

The confluence of the 1971 crisis and Nixinger's China rapprochement cast a long shadow on India's view of and relationship with the major powers.

Views of the US: Perhaps the most significant impact was on India's perceptions of and ties with the US. For many Indians, the USS *Enterprise* sailing into the Bay of Bengal represented a stark demonstration that Washington had ranged itself against New Delhi on the side of both of India's adversaries, China and Pakistan. That alone contributed to the view that persisted for decades—one that Moscow exploited—that the US was determined to block or hinder India's interests and its rise.

This Indian view was only reinforced by America's cooperation with Pakistan and China after the Soviet invasion of Afghanistan in 1979. This resulted in, at best, the Reagan administration looking the other way as Beijing assisted the development of the Pakistani nuclear programme. At worst, President Reagan's Cold War priorities provided cover for that proliferation. Simultaneously, American economic and military cooperation with China was strengthening India's other rival.

The Nixon administration's approach to the 1971 crisis also helped erase the memory of US assistance to India during the 1962 War with China. Even less remembered were the billions of dollars of economic assistance Washington provided in the 1950s and '60s to ensure that democratic India succeeded.

Views of the Soviet Union/Russia: Soviet military supply to—and utility for—India preceded the 1971 war. But it was that crisis and the treaty that cemented the India–Soviet relationship. The Indian public and elite came to view Moscow as a reliable friend, erasing memories of the lack of

Soviet reliability during the 1962 War, and of its flirtation with Pakistan in the mid-to-late 1960s.

In the US, meanwhile, the treaty cemented the view that Indira Gandhi was pro-Moscow and that India was on the Soviet side. The agreement was far more visible and required more obligations from India than the 1963 ADA with the US. And New Delhi's assertions that it remained non-aligned had few takers.

Diversification: Nixon's China rapprochement, the 1971 crisis and its consequences reminded Indian policymakers of the importance of the strategy underpinning non-alignment, that is, diversification. The idea behind maintaining a diversified portfolio of partners had been the hope that it (a) would allow India to benefit from various partners; (b) would minimize too much dependence on any one partner; (c) would reduce the demands of dependence in terms of the strings attached to external assistance—or the necessity to go along with a particular partner's interests and actions because India had no choice; and (d) would protect against the questionable reliability of any one partner.

To Indian policymakers, the 1971 crisis both highlighted the unreliability of one partner (the US) and the wisdom of not having given up the other (Soviet) partner. Those lessons, however, also made India wary of subsequent overdependence on the Soviet Union. That concern fuelled India's desire to develop its own capabilities, including an independent nuclear deterrent, and ease its China threat by re-engaging Beijing. New Delhi also tried to revive its US option—but it found that its earlier utility for the US as a geopolitical counterbalance and democratic contrast to China had diminished considerably because of Nixon's China rapprochement.

Concern about a G-2: Indian concern about US unreliability vis-à-vis China—and particularly the concept of a G-2—can be traced initially to Nixon and Kissinger's China rapprochement. From partnering with the US to balance China in the late 1950s and '60s, New Delhi suddenly found itself dealing with a US–China partnership that was backing Pakistan against India in a crisis. More broadly, the US reset with China required a major reassessment of India's balancing strategy vis-à-vis China.

This need to reevaluate was only fuelled by the Shanghai Communiqué that emerged from Nixon's visit to Beijing in February 1972. At best, Indian officials saw it as Washington endorsing a Chinese role in South Asia. At worst, India's ambassador to the US told Kissinger, the communiqué left the door open for US acceptance of Chinese hegemony in South Asia.[46] Privately, he expressed his larger concern to the Indian foreign secretary—the possibility that Nixon and Mao had reached a secret understanding about 'sphere[s] of influence'.[47] This concern—of a G-2 or a US–China condominium—lurks to this day in India. And fifty years after Kissinger first went to Beijing, it means that New Delhi continues to closely watch and analyse every step in US–China relations.

17

Kissinger and India's Geopolitics

C. RAJA MOHAN

GEOPOLITICS HAS NOT BEEN AT the centre of thinking on international relations in Independent India. Free India did inherit a strong tradition of geopolitics from the ancient tract of *Arthashastra* and a more immediate legacy of realpolitik from the British Raj. But the dominant influence of liberal internationalist thought on the Indian national movement, especially the first prime minister Jawaharlal Nehru, saw New Delhi struggling to reconcile the ideals of internationalism and the challenges of conducting foreign policy in a nasty and brutish world.

This essay explores the challenges presented by Kissinger's visit to China in 1971, the nature of India's adaptation to it and the ideological resistance to seizing opportunities for dealing with the US on a more practical basis in the 1970s and since. Kissinger's geopolitics would again figure prominently in the rearrangement of the bilateral relations in the twenty-first century as New Delhi and Washington concluded a historic civil nuclear initiative in 2005. President George W. Bush's willingness to break much political and bureaucratic resistance in Washington to ending the nuclear dispute with New Delhi was widely seen as similar to the Nixon–Kissinger outreach to Mao Zedong's Beijing. But New Delhi had trouble acting decisively on the possibilities. By the time India had acquired the will to discard the 'hesitations of history', the wheel of great power relations was turning again. In the last few years, the idea of balance of power and geopolitical equilibrium so central to Kissinger's worldview has begun to seep into India's own strategic calculus. But the task of managing great power politics and inserting itself confidently into them has just about begun.

Geopolitical discomfort

Although Jawaharlal Nehru's foreign policy articulation was essentially in terms of liberal internationalism, pacifism, and the ideal of a One World, his diplomacy could not totally disown the legacy of geopolitics of inherited from the Raj. While Kautilya's *Arthashastra* was not on its mind, the new elite that took charge of New Delhi could not transcend the geopolitical DNA shaping the mental make-up of India's security establishment, including the colonial-era Political Department (the predecessor of the Ministry of External Affairs). After all, Independent India simply absorbed the old bureaucratic structures into the new framework of governance. But the tension between Nehru's 'Asianism' and the Raj geopolitics persisted through the last century. It expressed itself most vigorously in India's China policy. The flip side of this tension was the approach to the West in general, and the Britain and the US in particular. That itself was rooted in the presumption that India is obliged to support China in the name of Asian solidarity and find ways to jointly stand up against the West.

The first among the multiple instances that presented themselves was in how to deal with the continuous turmoil in great power relations in the 1930 and '40s. In the late 1920s, the anti-colonial solidarity brought the Indian and Chinese nationalists in the international forums against imperialism. Yet, when the Second World War came, the two could not cooperate. Gandhi refused to accept the personal appeal from the China's Jiang Jieshi (Chiang Kaishek) to join forces with Chinese nationalists in fighting the Japanese imperialists. Jiang offered to support the Indian nationalists against the British after the defeat of Japanese occupation. For Gandhi, however, the priority was to defeat British imperialism.

As Mao's communists took charge of China, there were deep differences in New Delhi between Nehru and Patel on assessing the character of the People's Republic of China's and its implications for the Northern frontier. Nehru's reluctance to confront Chinese power became very much part of the Indian elite's thinking. Reflecting this difficulty were a number of policy issues that New Delhi confronted—India's role in the Korean War, securing the Himalayan kingdoms (Nepal, Sikkim, and Bhutan) against Chinese expansionism, vacillations on Tibet, and unilateral assumptions about China accepting India's border claims. Nehru's insistence on wooing Chinese premier Zhou Enlai at Bandung and ending Beijing's regional and international isolation, reluctance to accept the US proposal on taking China's place in the UNSC, the reported rejection of Kennedy's offer to assist with a nuclear weapon programme, signing of the partial test ban treaty in 1963 amidst signs of China's nuclear weapons intent, all underlined Nehru's profound misreading of China's nationalism and its strategic ambitions. If Nehru underestimated the threat from China, he overestimated the threat from the US Cold War alliances in Asia and was reluctant to pursue strategic cooperation with Washington. This paradigm would endure in India's international relations, well into the early decades of the twenty-first century.

Much in the manner that India struggled to deal with great-power politics in the 1930s, it was unprepared for the Sino–American rapprochement. Nehru is often given credit for seeing through Chinese communist ideology to recognize its nationalism and his prescience in seeing the Sino–Soviet split. But his successors did not extend that logic to see that a China threatened by the Soviet Union would have no problem turning to the US. New Delhi also underestimated the importance of America's realpolitik.

India's ideological framing of the international situation as an irreconcilable Cold War between the East and the West, and an enduring conflict between North and South, meant there was little attempt within the policy establishment or the academic community to think of the world in terms of power and assessing its dynamics in terms of shifting great-power coalitions. While India was compelled to turn to the US and later

Soviet Russia to cope with the Chinese challenge after 1962, it seemed unprepared to recognize the possibilities for Sino–US normalization amidst the deepening Sino–Soviet split in the late 1960s, and America's difficulties in Vietnam and Southeast Asia.

After 1971: The marginalization

India signed a peace and friendship treaty with the Soviet Union on 9 August 1971, barely three weeks after President Nixon announced in July 1971 that his National Security Advisor Henry Kissinger had made a secret visit to China. On the face of it, the move seemed a decisive geopolitical response to the shifting great-power landscape. But a more compelling factor was India's immediate need for support from the Soviet Union in preventing the United Nations Security Council from intervening in India's planned liberation of East Bengal from Pakistan. The Soviet Union gave just enough support in the December 1971 by delaying the UNSC call for a ceasefire and Nixon ordered the USS *Enterprise* to sail into the Indian Ocean, to save Pakistan. India's success in liberating Bangladesh solidified two geopolitical narratives in New Delhi—the reliability of the Soviet Union and the hostility of the US. India's decision to conduct a nuclear test in May 1974, so soon after the liberation of the Bangladesh, and the treaty with the Soviet Union, seemed to reinforce the image of a new India that had shed its Nehruvian idealism and was ready for a confident and pragmatic realpolitik on the world stage.

The reality, of course, was far more complicated. Three factors shaped the reduction of India's geopolitical room for manoeuvre in the 1970s. First was India's marginalization in the great-power dynamics. Having opened up to China, the US enhanced its leverage with both Beijing and Moscow. In countering the Soviet threat, Mao sought to weaken the Soviet influence in Asia and divided Left movements around the world. While fending off the Chinese challenge, the Communist Party of the Soviet Union was more than eager to consolidate the new détente with the US. For Moscow the symbols of parity with Washington—strategic nuclear arms control, the Nuclear Non-Proliferation Treaty and, more broadly, the sense of joint management of the world order—became ever more important. By convincing itself that the Soviet Union was the most important external partner, New Delhi neglected the importance of finding sufficient common ground with the US and the West. As the distance between New Delhi and the West increased, and the relations with China remained frozen, India's marginalization in the major power constellation began to grow.

Kissinger's visit to India in 1974 offered the means to reconstruct the relationship with the US after the bitter legacies of 1971 and the harsh US response to India's nuclear test. But India's ability to do so was undermined by the deepening suspicion of the US and an inability to understand Kissinger's realpolitik premised on power. For India, new wariness of the US had become so intense as to prevent taking a more differentiated view of realists like Kissinger and the ideologues of liberal internationalism in the Democratic Party. Nor was it willing to see the new constraints operating on Nixon and Kissinger—the strains on the Bretton Woods system, domestic political turmoil triggered by an increasingly unpopular and costly intervention in Vietnam and the weakening US alliance system. India was overly obsessed with the fear of the US or the United Nations somehow separating Kashmir from India. While the story of the Cold War was mostly about the United Nations being largely powerless, New Delhi could not shed the fear of 'internationalization'. As New Delhi prepared to host Kissinger, Indira Gandhi ostentatiously flew to Kashmir to signal Indian resolve. Kashmir was probably the last thing on Kissinger's mind. He was trying to reposition the US amidst the quagmire in Vietnam. New Delhi's lack of realism was also evident in calling its first atomic test a 'peaceful nuclear explosion' and believing that the rest of the world would believe this deception. To make matters worse, New Delhi was engaged in self-deception. It did not follow through with additional tests or call itself a nuclear weapon power. India provoked the world into reacting—for example, China's atomic assistance to Pakistan—and invited sanctions without actually exercising the nuclear option. If there was a chance of using Kissinger's realism to close the nuclear dispute with the US and reframe the relationship, New Delhi seemed utterly unwilling to explore such a possibility. When New Delhi tested nuclear weapons again a quarter century later in 1998, Kissinger would be the first to call for an atomic accommodation between Washington and New Delhi.

Second, India's changing ideological orientation in the 1970s made its geopolitical position even worse. At home, India's economic turn to the Left steadily eliminated the possibility that commercial cooperation could compensate for political differences with the US and the West. India's turning to 'socialism' and greater state control of the economy steadily limited the possibilities for engaging the Western capital. India threw out IBM and Coca-Cola from the country and rejected the offer of Siemens to transform India's power plant production capacity. As China was preparing to open its economy by the end of the 1970s, India moved purposefully towards closing it. India's relative economic decline now seemed irreversible and reinforced India's geopolitical marginalization. As anti-Americanism became politically correct, reversing productive academic and scientific collaboration with the US, which flowered in the 1950s and '60s, became politically correct. Anyone who talked of engaging the US was automatically dubbed a 'CIA agent'. Visas for US academics became ever more difficult to obtain. Just as China was warming up to the US and Chinese studies were beginning to take off in the US, New Delhi did all it could do make the pursuit of Indian studies in the US rather hard. Indira Gandhi's declaration of Emergency in 1975 snapped the Western empathy for India as a struggling democracy. The radicalization of India's foreign policy led to an intense diplomatic focus on opposing the US and the West in the name of championing the Third World (now called the 'Global South'), represented by a more radical Non-Aligned Movement. At the United Nations, India was voting more often against the US than even the Soviet Union. At the global level, India demanded for a change in the global rules (the New International Economic Order) while shunning all possibilities for taking commercial advantage of the existing order.

Third, any power political analysis would have shown there was no way the Soviet Union could compensate for the declining cooperation with the West. But the imagery of symmetry between the East and West and a sense of self-righteousness in denouncing the US at every opportunity left no room for self-doubt or credible internal criticism of the policies adopted by New Delhi. The liberal opposition was too weak to challenge New Delhi's new orientation. The Jan Sangh, which seemed to offer a conservative criticism of India's Left turn at home and abroad under Indira Gandhi, made peace with that drift. At home it moved towards adopting 'Gandhian socialism' and discovered the virtues of economic populism. The Jan Sangh and the parties that came together to form the Janata Party that captured power in the 1977 elections, criticized Indira's tilt towards the Soviet Union, denounced the friendship treaty and called for genuine non-alignment. While the Jan Sangh's Atal Bihari Vajpayee got charge of foreign ministry in the first non-Congress government in New Delhi, he did not really challenge India's Soviet drift. The attempted correction eventually came from Indira and Rajiv Gandhi in the 1980s, but it was not decisive enough to construct a more realistic geopolitical framework for India.

India's strategic inertia

Angry with the Soviet Union for supporting the Janata Party during 1977–79 and recognizing that India had moved too close to Moscow in the previous decade, Indira Gandhi, who returned to power in 1980, sought a diversification of India's foreign and security policies by reaching out to the US, Europe, and China. At home, she sought to tone down the radical economic policies and initiated the early debates on reforming the Indian economy. Rajiv Gandhi, who succeeded her in 1984, pursued that path with greater vigour. Yet, the engagement with the West remained hesitant and tentative, while New Delhi did not move quickly enough to explore the possibilities for a boundary settlement with Deng Xiaoping, who was bringing China out of a prolonged and debilitating Cultural Revolution. And as the US began to rearm Pakistan in the 1980s, India's dependence on Soviet weapon supplies steadily increased. Moscow, which opposed New Delhi's rapprochement with Beijing in the late 1970s, began to make peace with China amidst the backlash against its geopolitical overextension and mounting pressure from Washington. India was surprised again by the turn in great-power relations and found itself on the margins once more. Meanwhile, the costs of the alliance with the Soviet Union were increasingly visible after it intervened in Afghanistan. Although New Delhi did not endorse the Soviet intervention, its silence sent negative signals in India's extended neighbourhood—especially in the Muslim world.

It was only with the collapse of the Indian economy along with the Soviet Union that New Delhi could find a way to break out of its marginalization. India's rapid economic growth and the end of the Cold War allowed India to restructure its geopolitics. Successive prime ministers in the reform era—P.V. Narasimha Rao, Atal Bihari Vajpayee, Manmohan Singh, and Narendra Modi have invested much political capital and diplomatic energy in strengthening the strategic partnership with the US. Growing commercial cooperation and the influence of the Indian diaspora create positive conditions for advancing the relationship. If the Kashmir question and the nuclear dispute continued to trouble bilateral ties in 1990s, President George W. Bush found a way to resolve these tensions in the early years of the twenty-first century. But the historic civil nuclear initiative he signed with Manmohan Singh was not just about ending India's atomic isolation after the 1974 test. It was premised on the assumption that it was in US interest to assist India's rise to great power status. Instead of seeing this opportunity to strengthen itself, New Delhi was paralyzed by the fear of violating the presumed canon of Indian foreign policy—non-alignment and strategic autonomy. Notwithstanding Manmohan Singh's eagerness to transform the relationship with the US, the Congress Party seemed utterly reluctant. While Indira and Rajiv began the search for a productive engagement with the US in the final decade of the Cold War, Sonia Gandhi and Rahul seemed determined to avoid it. The decade-long rule of UPA (2004–14) that had begun with great promise saw New Delhi consciously limit strategic cooperation with the US.

Modi, in contrast, was ready to move the relationship forward since he became prime minister in 2014. But the institutional inertia in the security establishment tended to slow the pace of progress. India's inability to take full advantage of the US partnership in the twenty-first century was reinforced by New Delhi's misreading of great-power relations. India's decision to join the Russia and China in pursuit of a 'multipolar world' might have been justified in the 1990s, when the US policies on Kashmir and nuclear proliferation directly threatened India's security. But the steady improvement in India–US ties in the early years of the twenty-first century and the US willingness to set aside activism on Kashmir and resolve the nuclear dispute did not seem to make a difference to India's pursuit of multipolarity (the code word for constraining US power). While the Russian and Chinese interest in multipolarity was quite evident, it has not been clear why India should persist with a forum that is by design targeting the US, which was rapidly emerging as a valuable external partner in the twenty-first century. Sheer strategic inertia arising out of the choices made in the 1990s, seemed to nudge India in the 2000s towards supporting and expanding the ambit of the RIC (the Russia, India, China Forum) and the BRICS (Brazil, Russia, India, China, South Africa Forum).

Beyond the path dependence, New Delhi was unwilling to question the assumptions about the US being the principal external challenge for India, the reliability of Russia, and the benign nature of Chinese power. It was only after China blocked India's entry in the Nuclear Suppliers Group in 2016 and the confrontation with China at the Doklam plateau in the summer of 2017 that there was a rethinking on the nature of Chinese power, the consequences of Beijing's expanding economic and political influence in the subcontinent as well the Indian Ocean, and the threats from China's growing weight in the international institutions. After China responded to the Indian move of changing the constitutional status of Jammu and Kashmir in August 2019 by raising the question in the United Nations Security Council and its aggression in the Ladakh sector in the summer of 2020, there was little room left for ambivalence about Chinese power and the unprecedented problems it poses for India. But having woken up late, New Delhi finds the China challenge daunting. Thanks to the underestimation of China's power and the rapidity of its rise in the twenty-first century, New Delhi's power differential with Beijing has become massive. (China's GDP in 2020 is more than five times larger than that of India. Beijing spends four times more than New Delhi on its armed forces.) Although Washington has extended much support for India in coping with the Chinese aggression and Russia continues to sell arms to India, New Delhi once again finds itself in tricky place among the great powers. Given the deepening tensions between Russia and the US, New Delhi's traditional ties with Moscow are beginning to cause concern in Washington. Russia's own room for manoeuvre between China and the US is shrinking and it is difficult to see how Moscow can escape the trap of becoming a junior partner to Beijing. While there is little appetite in the US to find a new modus vivendi with Russia, there are influential sections in the US that want to explore geopolitical accommodation with China in order to deal with economic challenges facing Washington, as well as climate change and other global issues. It is not clear if President Joe Biden's confrontation with China in early 2021 can be sustained. Put simply, China's leverages in relation to other major powers are indeed impressive, thanks to its economic strength and growing military power.

Between ideology and realpolitik

Henry Kissinger's 1971 trip to Beijing sent shock waves across the world because he and President Richard Nixon were replacing the ideological framework that animated the US during the early decades of the Cold War with a power-based political approach. It was not easy to sell the proposition in Washington that the US must align with one communist power to defeat another; after all the Cold War was supposed to be about the contest between the 'free world' and 'communism'. Kissinger's realpolitik was seizing on the opportunities opened up by the Sino–Soviet split in the 1960s. Together, the two developments that came in the wake of the border war between India and China in 1962 should have inoculated India against the dangers of an ideological approach to international affairs. Thanks to the radicalization of New Delhi's domestic and international politics in the 1970s, India became even more ideological. Although there were brief moves that reflected geopolitical thinking in the five decades since 1971, New Delhi remained reluctant to see the changes in great-power relations through the prism of power politics and remained too slow in adapting to the continuous shifts in great-power relations.

The Soviet Union joined Nazi Germany to fend off potential threats from Japan in 1939. Then it aligned with the West to fight Germany when the latter attacked Russia in 1941; but that coalition broke apart immediately after Hitler's defeat in the summer of 1945. Moscow and Washington found ways to cooperate at the peak of the Cold War and experimented with joint efforts to manage some challenges to the international system. Yeltsin's Russia tilted to the West after the fall of the USSR in 1990. Putin reversed that policy and Russia is now locked in an intractable conflict with the US and the West. China took Western support to fight Japanese imperialism. Mao's China aligned with the USSR in 1950 and fought a war with the US in Korea (1950–53). By the 1960s he was fighting the USSR, and by the end of the decade was seeking a rapprochement with Washington. Deng opened the door for economic engagement with the West, enriched China and facilitated its dramatic rise. Xi Jinping is now trying to nudge the US out of Asia and is seeking a new compact with the West that recognizes China's new weight in the international system.

Through all these extraordinary shifts in great-power politics, the Indian elite has pretended that non-alignment had all the answers to India's international problems. In defining 'strategic autonomy' as keeping distance from the West, New Delhi now finds Beijing is squeezing India's natural playing room in South Asia and the Indian Ocean. In emphasizing the pursuit of a multipolar world that would limit American power, India was blind to the prospects of unipolar Asia. Instead of balancing the near against the far, New Delhi revelled in countering the far in coalition with the near. But as the costs of this tradition mount, India's recent turn to realism has its task cut out. Understanding Kissinger's geopolitical legacy would certainly help.

18

Kissinger and the Rise of China

A South Asian Perspective

SUHASINI HAIDAR

THINGS WOULD HAVE TURNED OUT very differently for South Asia if Richard Nixon and Henry Kissinger had chosen Poland or France or Romania over Pakistan as a conduit for their plans to engage China. In the early months of his presidency, the Nixon administration made it clear to anyone it thought had a good line to Beijing, that the US was ready to engage. China was cold to the idea of using France, and after two meetings of US and Chinese diplomats in Warsaw, Mao Zedong shut down the Poland track as well, ostensibly over the US action in Cambodia.[1] Next, recounted Henry Kissinger, Nixon's National Security Advisor, they tried Romania, working through President Nicolai Ceausescu to reach out to the Chinese government, but hit an unexpected block.

'We went to the Romanians, thinking they were most independent of the East Europeans and they were communists and therefore the Chinese would like that. Turns out the one group the Chinese didn't trust were Communists,' said Kissinger, explaining that Beijing feared Romanian officials would divulge details to the Kremlin, who would attempt to sabotage the process.[2]

Eventually, it was Pakistani President Yahya Khan who delivered the Chinese to the Americans for talks, an event that left a lasting impact on not just the futures of the US and China, but changed the course of South Asian history. On 8 December 1970, the Pakistani ambassador to Washington brought a handwritten note from Premier Zhou Enlai, who referred to Nixon's assurance to Yahya a few weeks earlier that the US would not enter into a 'condominium against China' in its talks with the Soviet Union, and offering to send an emissary to a 'mutually convenient place' to arrange high-level contacts with China. Planning for Nixon's visit to China in February 1972, what he referred to as the 'week that changed the world', had begun. It later emerged that Zhou had also sent a copy of the same letter through Romanian channels, but it didn't reach the White House until a month later, and that ended that.

Events changing South Asia's landscape had begun as well. In November 1970, a powerful cyclone ripped through East Pakistan, submerging many parts of the state and killing more than 500,000 people. The cyclone didn't just expose the entire region to utter devastation, it exposed Pakistan leadership's inability and apathy in dealing with this much neglected part of its country that was granted to it in Partition by the British, but separated from it by the vast breadth of India. On 7 December, just a day before the letter from Zhou was delivered to the White House, Pakistan held general elections, in which Bengalis of East Pakistan, angered over the West Pakistani handling of the disaster voted 72 per cent in favour of Sheikh Mujibur Rahman's Awami League, which ensured it won a majority, 160 of the overall 300 seats. The result was a massive setback to Yahya Khan and to Zulfikar Ali Bhutto's PPP that won West Pakistan, and they stalled the process of swearing in the constitutionally elected new PM. Meanwhile, in India, Indira Gandhi's Congress Party faction won a landslide victory in February 1971 (the results were later questioned, which led to the Emergency), and she was consolidating her power both as a popular leader and as an international figure.

The battle drums were growing louder in South Asia, but Washington had its eye on the peace pipe with Peking (now Beijing). In March and

April 1971, the Pakistani military unleashed a massive pogrom, called 'Operation Searchlight' on East Pakistan, but the Nixon administration was more preoccupied by the Chinese invitation to the US ping-pong team to visit Beijing, along with US journalists, and what that signalled for their talks. Nixon's response to Kissinger's memo in April 1971 on options before the US—(a) support Pakistan; (b) maintain neutrality; (c) help Pakistan end the conflict—was unequivocal. 'To all hands, don't squeeze Yahya at this time,' he said, checking option (c).[3] On each occasion that the US consulate in Dhaka proposed the US intervene to stop the Pakistani government, the White House sought instead to firm up its Chinese opening, for which it needed the Pakistani government.

Events in the rest of South Asia in 1971 were no less tumultuous, some of which intersected with the India–Pakistan crisis, and others that added to the drama of the times for the Indira Gandhi government. Sri Lanka (Ceylon at the time), for example, witnessed an insurrection by the ultra-communist JVP that lasted several months in 1971, and saw Prime Minister Sirimavo Bandaranaike's government lose control of a number of cities and areas before Sri Lankan forces prevailed. Both Pakistan and, subsequently, India rushed troops, air support, and supplies to assist. In return for Pakistan's support, and possibly even in an attempt to play mediator, Bandaranaike allowed Pakistani planes to transit and refuel in Colombo on their way to East Pakistan. After a stiff warning to Colombo from New Delhi, they stopped the facility in August 1971.[4]

India's steadfast friendship with Bhutan was tested in other ways around the same time. In December 1970, Bhutan had applied for membership of the United Nations, the first such independent foray for the Himalayan kingdom that was still bound by (the now revised) 1949 agreement to be 'guided by the advice of the Government of India in regard to its external relations'.[5] To be sure, India sponsored Bhutan's application, but not after many years of misgivings in Bhutan about India's intentions. In 1964, Bhutan's queen, a powerful figure, had hinted as much in a conversation with Foreign Secretary T.N. Kaul.[6] 'We believe India is the only country that can help us to achieve our natural aspirations. But, any hesitation on India's part to get us into the United

Nations Organization naturally raises suspicions amongst our people. I can assure you that once India gets us into the UNO there will be no suspicions but complete trust between us,' Kaul quoted her as saying during his conversation with the queen when he wrote his memoirs.

Nepal had tensions with India on a different score, over the delayed renewal of the 1960 Treaty of Trade and Transit, which had led to an economic crisis and anti-India protests in Kathmandu. Nepal's King Mahendra watched the Bangladesh crisis clearly, with an eye on whether China would intervene in Pakistan's favour. 'China's inability to assist Kathmandu in any way in Nepal's trade treaty negotiations with India and even more, Peking's failure to come to the rescue of its West Pakistan ally exposed the limited economic, diplomatic and military capability of China South of the Himalayas. The emergence of Bangladesh in the face of Peking's determined—if only vocal—opposition is indicative of China's inability to directly challenge India's status as the hegemonic power in South Asia,' concluded noted Nepali diplomat Rishikesh Shaha in an article in February 1972.[7]

The idea that India was now unassailable in South Asia became the most important takeaway of the Bangladesh crisis. For decades, Indians had not even wished to use the term South Asia, as they felt the 'Indian subcontinent' gave India its 'rightful' place in the region's hierarchy. (This is also one of the reasons that New Delhi was suspicious about the creation of the South Asian Association for Regional Cooperation (SAARC), spearheaded by Bangladesh's Zia-ur Rahman, which it saw as a platform for the smaller South Asian countries to 'gang up' against it.)

Many officials believed that the South Asian construct was a US ploy to reduce India's influence in the region. This belief was fuelled by the fact that the first official reference to South Asia was at the US State Department, which published a report titled 'The Subcontinent of South Asia: Afghanistan, Ceylon, India, Nepal and Pakistan' in 1959.[8] This also fed into the many 'balance of power'[9] theories that meant that both the US and China's courtship of Pakistan in the decades after independence were driven less by bilateral concerns and more by a desire to restrain India from acquiring the ability to dominate the rest of the region.

Post-1971, India was able to send out the message loud and clear of its pre-eminent hold over the region. A few weeks after India's win against Pakistan in Bangladesh, the US embassy reported on an interview that Indira Gandhi gave to a journalist in which she said the US–Indian relations could return to normal 'if the US was prepared to recognize India's predominant position on the subcontinent.'[10]

'It's not just a question of India's case insofar as Bangladesh is concerned,' she is quoted by the US embassy as having said.[11] 'It's a question of recognizing what India is, what India stands for and what India wants to do. We have never accepted the theory of balance of power, and we have no intention [of] doing it now.'

Fifty years later

There are several factors that today stand in stark contrast from that period five decades ago, beginning with the US–India relationship. In December 1971, the US was willing to send its Seventh Fleet to the Bay of Bengal in a last-ditch attempt to save the situation for Pakistan, and so that its own dialogue with China not be harmed. In 1971, the US wanted the Chinese to move PLA divisions towards the boundary with India to threaten the Indian Army against trying to aggress on West Pakistan.[12] In 2020, when the Chinese PLA aggressed the boundary with India and occupied territory, the US government and military publicly spoke of supporting India with intelligence, surveillance technology, and supplies, something that would have seemed impossible all those years ago.[13] Fifty years later, little rancour remains, and trust, after the US declared India a major defence partner and India signed three foundational agreements for military coordination, has grown year on year.

The US–Pakistan alliance, which allowed the Nixon administration to turn a blind eye to the worst genocide the subcontinent had seen, is now a shadow of itself, and Washington's main objective with Islamabad now appears to be the facilitation of talks between the Taliban and Afghan leadership, and a smooth exit for US troops from Afghanistan.

The US–China relationship has retained its strategic tensions, but the US–China Shanghai Communiqué in February 1972, which recognized a

'One China policy' virtually giving up Taiwan's claims, set the course for China's arrival on the global economic stage. The transformation wrought by Kissinger's trips led not only to the rise of China in incalculable ways, it also saw US–China bilateral trade grow from about US $2 billion in 1979 (when the trade treaty was signed[14]) to US $635 billion in 2019.[15]

Meanwhile, the India–Pakistan relationship has reached its lowest point in the past fifty years, where despite there being no open conflict as in 1971, or the Kargil war in 1999, there are no talks, no public channels of communication, no exchanges amongst civil society, and no cultural, sporting or trade ties. It would not be an understatement to suggest that India–Pakistan ties today resemble US–China relations prior to Nixon's China visit, where even an invitation to a ping-pong team[16] or an interview to a journalist[17] from the other side seems difficult. The tenets of the Bhutto–Gandhi Simla Agreement of 1972, which sought to put the Bangladesh war behind them after India's release of 93,000 Pakistani prisoners of war (PoWs), which committed to a bilateral resolution of outstanding issues, are all but forgotten.[18]

One could go further afield, with some very imaginative license. If it is accepted that India's Soviet friendship treaty and testing a nuclear device in 1974 were precipitated by the insecurity Indira Gandhi felt over the linking up of US–Pakistan–China, then it may also be possible to argue that the Soviet invasion of Afghanistan, and subsequently, the joint US–Pakistan efforts to build a religious 'jihadi' counter to communism in the region were all part of the geopolitical jostling derived in some way from the events of 1971 and the choices that Nixon–Kissinger made in their pursuit of ties with China. It may be possible to even link India and Pakistan's nuclear tests of 1998, events that dramatically shifted strategic dynamics in the subcontinent, to those events in 1971. While any alternative to history is purely hypothetical, it would be hard to argue that the use of the Romanian channel instead of the Pakistani one by Nixon–Kissinger in engaging China in 1970–71 could have had such far-reaching consequences for the Indian subcontinent.

In his book *The India Way*, External Affairs Minister Subrahmanyam Jaishankar made a similar point, attributing India's successes to its ability to reading the 'geopolitical tea leaves' correctly after 1971.

'Indo–Soviet and later Indo–Russian relations are a direct product of our global strategizing. After 1991, so too has been the adjustment in our policy towards the US. Both the Indo–Soviet Treaty and the India–US Nuclear Deal were outcomes of a larger reading of world affairs. That is the case with correctives introduced in respect of the US in 1973 and China in 1976 to overcome the 1971 polarization with both,' he wrote.[19]

These shifts have been well-documented and commented upon, but what has perhaps not found as much scholarly attention is the complete change in the perception that Nepali diplomat Shaha referred to (earlier in this chapter)—that of India as the pre-eminent South Asian power in a region where China had no toe-hold—to one where China is in pole position.

India and China have three fronts or fault lines between them. The first is the historic and bilateral one, of the Line of Actual Control and the unresolved boundary of 3,500 kilometres they share. The second is the oceanic one, in the Indo-Pacific, which includes China's forays in the Indian Ocean region and India's quadrilateral alliance (the Quad) with the US, Australia, and Japan, as well as maritime partnerships with ASEAN countries like Singapore and Indonesia. The third, which has the potential to encircle India, is in the South Asian neighbourhood, one that was seen as India's sphere of influence, but one that China has assiduously courted in the last few decades.

If in 1971 China had little interest, investment stake, and political leverage in the entire South Asian region (except Pakistan), by 2021 it has all three in each of India's neighbours (with the exception of Bhutan). Beijing's strides in the region did not happen overnight, but at various points in the past half-century, the shift has become perceptible. For example, when Nepal's King Birendra sent a delegation to Beijing in 1990, to seek support against the economic blockade placed by the Rajiv Gandhi government as a protest against the Nepali king's decision to import weapons from China, the Chinese demurred. 'The Chinese felt sad over the situation in Nepal, supplied 10,000 litres of low-octane fuel as a token of respect to the king, but advised us to keep India in good humour,' recalled one of the delegates of that mission, according to one account.[20] He also added that the 'Chinese said they are not in a position to substitute India at least for the next thirty years'. King Birendra was left with little choice other than to repair ties with New Delhi. Twenty-five years later, when Nepal Prime Minister K.P. Sharma Oli made a similar request for support during India's economic blockade in 2015, however, Beijing no longer had any compunctions in helping. In a transit and trade treaty inked in March 2016 during a visit by Oli to China, which was later ratified with a protocol in 2019, Beijing made seven sea and land ports available to Nepal for third-country imports, and allowed exports through six dedicated transit points between Nepal and China, thus ending Nepal's complete dependence on India as a land route for bilateral and third-country trade. [21]

China's earlier policy of not showing its hand in the politics of other countries has also given way to overt confidence in dealing with the political structure of countries in India's neighbourhood. In 2005, despite a close relationship with Nepali King Gyanendra, who even pushed for China's membership of the South Asian Association for Regional Cooperation (SAARC), China did not come out openly to save the monarchy. In contrast, after Oli's decision to dissolve the parliament and the resultant split in the Communist Party of Nepal in December 2020, the Chinese Communist Party sent its own team to try and negotiate a truce. The effort was unsuccessful, but it underlined just how deep Beijing's stakes in Kathmandu are. Not just in Nepal, China's economic, military and political stakes in each of India's neighbouring capitals (with the exception of Thimphu), whether it is Islamabad, Kabul, Male, Colombo or Dhaka, have grown stronger. These were spurred by the development of its 'blue water navy', and the wide range of projects it is involved in through the Belt and Road Initiative (BRI), which includes the China–Pakistan Economic Corridor (CPEC) and China–Myanmar Economic Corridor (CMEC). China has entrenched itself.

The results can be judged from a number of parameters. Until 2014, India outflanked China on investment (FDI) with the three biggest South Asian economies other than Pakistan, but by 2018 China had outshot India on this count. If trade with all SAARC countries is taken into account, India now lags behind China by at least $20 billion (2018 figures).[22] The number of Chinese tourists, which grew 8.5 times in the past decade, caught up with numbers of Indian tourists in Bangladesh, Maldives, Nepal, and Sri Lanka by 2019.[23] The number of students from South Asian countries (Afghanistan, Myanmar, Maldives, Bangladesh, Nepal, Pakistan, and Sri Lanka) studying in China is nearly double the numbers in India.[24] Even if you don't count the students from Pakistan in China, who number about 19,000, from the comparison, India and China are even in terms of students from the other South Asian countries. This is possibly the most telling of all statistics, given that more South Asians share a common language with India than with China, and should feel more welcome in an open democracy than in a closely surveilled state.

In the past year, the Chinese government and its CPC party arms like the United Front Works Department (UFWD) have used the opportunities presented by the pandemic to push ahead with this quest. Apart from sending medicines and PPE kits, and promising vaccines to most SAARC countries as part of its 'Health Silk Road' initiative, China's vice minister has held three separate meeting with combinations of Afghanistan, Bangladesh, Nepal, Pakistan, and Sri Lanka, and discussed debt waivers with them. Chinese experts suggest that it is only a matter of time before Beijing holds a meeting of all SAARC countries (minus India and Bhutan), for they are all part of the Belt and Road Initiative (BRI), and even that they will be invited to join the fifteen-member ASEAN-led Regional Comprehensive Economic Partnership, which India declined to be a part of.[25]

None of this is to say that India is not matching China measure for measure. During the pandemic, in fact, the perception is that India has outdone China with its generosity in sending aid, supplies, and vaccines to countries in the neighbourhood. The point is that the power dynamics of South Asia have changed dramatically from the times of America's China opening. India's challenges are cut out, as S. Jaishankar acknowledged in a recent interview to *The Hindu*, and the success of its pushback will determine the future course of South Asia.[26]

'China today is, you know, in nominal terms, the second-largest economy in the world. It is impacting every region of the world in trade in connectivity and so, the South Asian region cannot be impervious, cannot be insulated from the rest of the world. When I see global changes, I can't say I don't like these global changes. I must gear up and be competitive myself. I should obviously improve my connectivity, my trade, my education, my medical travel, my institutional linkages. And that is precisely what I am doing. Look at our LOCs (lines of credit), our grants, our connectivity projects, the travel to India. So pretty much [if you] use any parameter, and you will see India–South Asia also going up,' the External Affairs Minister said.

Neither has the US sat idle in the face of the growing challenge in the region. US President Barack Obama's 'pivot to Asia', President Donald Trump's development of the idea of the Indo-Pacific and the Quad, the renaming of the US PACOM military command to the INDOPACOM, a new push to infrastructure and development assistance and its Millennium Challenge Corporation (MCC) foreign aid agency in Nepal and Sri Lanka are all measures towards reversing some of the power balance in the region, including in South Asia.

The changes for the region in this half-century are perhaps best summed up by comparing the words of the Shanghai Communiqué after Nixon's meeting with Mao Zedong in February 1972, with the present reality. The four-point agreement stated that:

1. Progress toward the normalization of relations between China and the US is in the interests of all countries;
2. Both wish to reduce the danger of international military conflict;
3. Neither should seek hegemony in the Asia–Pacific region and each is opposed to efforts by any other country or group of countries to establish such hegemony;
4. Neither is prepared to negotiate on behalf of any third party or to enter into agreements or understandings with the other directed at other states.[27]

It is plain to see that the communiqué, especially the last two points, no longer reflect the ground position in the region, nor the commentary in Washington and Beijing, which is increasingly confrontational.

No less interesting is the change in Henry Kissinger's own views towards India's role in the region, from when he once referred to Indians as 'the most aggressive goddamn people around [South Asia]'.[28]

Much more recently, in his last published book in 2014, *World Order*, Kissinger described India as 'a fulcrum of twenty-first century order: an indispensable element, based on its geography, resources and tradition of sophisticated leadership, in the strategic and ideological evolution of the regions and the concepts of order at whose intersection it stands.'[29]

19

Balancing Powers

AYESHA SIDDIQA

IN MARCH 2021, PAKISTAN ARMY Chief Qamar Javed Bajwa spoke about the need for the US to have a better understanding of the China–Pakistan Economic Corridor (CPEC) and view Islamabad as an essential connector between East and West Asia. By making those remarks he tried to restore Pakistan's ability to retain and balance its relations both with the US and China, two states it has always viewed as critical for its security and geopolitical balance in South Asia. In both instances, the linkage is driven by Pakistan's primary concern with India and desire to use the relationships to build the country's economic, geopolitical, and military prowess.

Though Islamabad always, and only, refers to its relationship with Beijing as strategic, its linkage with Washington is equally critical despite being more visibly unstable. This dichotomy also tends to make China appear to Pakistan as an essential balancer of power in South Asia and fill the gap created occasionally due to strategic divergence with the US. The Sino–Pak relations have been comparatively less boisterous and shrouded in a long-term cycle that demands greater patience. Indeed, Pakistan has watched and contributed to building China's military capacity and influence, and guarded a positive narrative regarding China.

From bridging the gap between Washington and Beijing in the early 1970s to sharing Western technology with China during the 1980s and developing a defence industrial partnership, Pakistan has added to its Asian partner's strategic advantage. Notwithstanding China's domestic sociopolitical and socio-economic changes that had an impact on how it dealt with its South Asian ally, Beijing also considers it strategically important as a source for reaching out to the world. This connection makes Pakistan's relationship fundamentally different from its links with the US. Nonetheless, Pakistan's key interest remains in maintaining ties with both powers and avoiding any collision between the two that would make those ties costly for it.

This essay will examine the evolution of Pakistan's ties with both China and the US since the 1970s.

The Cold War years, 1972–90

A glance at the archival material on Richard Nixon's 1972 visit to China shows that policymakers in both countries were anxious about Pakistan's security as being threatened by the Soviet Union. The India–Pakistan conflict and the role of the Soviet Union in support of the latter was viewed as Moscow challenging not just US, but also Chinese interests.[1] Washington looked adversely at the India–Pakistan war of December 1971. This war and the fall of Dhaka were presented as a conspiracy against China by the American deputy secretary to President Nixon on national security, Alexander Haig, to his Chinese hosts: 'They want to surround the People's Republic of China by bolstering some of your enemies and the enemies' proxies.'[2]

Haig's conversation during his visit in January 1972 to formalize agenda for the Nixon visit later that year was to assure China of US commitment to its security against any threat from Moscow and to present Washington as a reliable partner that would help against any Soviet adventurism. The pitch was to convince Beijing of Washington's reliability that felt obligated in case of its South Asian ally and not '... allow the Soviet Union to separate Pakistan'.[3] Though the US commitment could not stop the separation of then East Pakistan from the western wing and becoming Bangladesh, the Cold War was an essential frame to which Pakistan's leadership remained committed and found it beneficial to engage with both Beijing and Washington.

Pakistan's role as a frontline state against the Soviet Union not only provided it with economic and military assistance, but also the opportunity to play a significant role in the region. The ability to manage a dual partnership with two ideologically diverse but significant geopolitical players enhanced Pakistan's possibilities. The Kissinger–Nixon visits, during a period in which Pakistan was substantially weakened militarily due to the loss of its eastern wing, established the country's role not only as an interlocutor for Washington but also as a window for China to the West.

The Cold War was the primary plinth on which the US–Pakistan relations were constructed with the expectation that the relationship could not only become more solid but build Pakistan as worth representing US interests in the region. The US aid to India during the 1962 Sino–Indian war, however, demonstrated the shortcomings of this expectation: Pakistan was one of the significant partners but the relationship would not outweigh broader US interests such as its concern about communism. All the same, helping bridge some of the ideological divide between its two partners consolidated Pakistan's geopolitical value for both and it also secured Islamabad's own position, which helped it make gains without getting distracted by the ideological baggage of one partner versus the other.

The desire to maintain status quo regarding bilateral relations continued during the democratically elected government of Zulfiqar Ali Bhutto, who was reputed for the ideological Left leanings of his Pakistan People's Party (PPP), creating an impression that relations with China deepened during his tenure. However, many of the critical projects such as setting up of the Heavy Mechanical Complex (HMC) or the interest-free loan of US $217.4 million were given by China to the military government of General Yahya Khan. The funds were used to recover from the crisis of depletion of resources due to the 1971 war.[4] Pakistan remained the only non-communist country to receive assistance from China, which included free weapons.

This support was critical at a time when Bhutto struggled to improve relations with the US. Despite the Pakistani leader's two visits to Washington and assurance of commitment to bilateral relations, Nixon remained suspicious of Bhutto, whose removal from the Ayub Khan cabinet was linked to US pressure. This naturally made China important for Pakistan in filling the strategic gap vis-à-vis India. New Delhi's first atomic test at Pokhran in 1974 increased the technological gap between the two South Asian neighbours, which Bhutto earnestly wanted to fill—and Beijing was important for that.

The defence–technological angle became increasingly important as the Kashmir issue went on the back-burner in the Sino–Pakistan bilateral conversation. The procurement of arms from China during the 1960s and '70s allowed Pakistan to increase its quantitative capacity while it waited for an opportunity to acquire high-tech weapons from Western sources. Defence technological acquisitions from Europe were less affordable as compared to the US for which a convergence of strategic objectives was almost a precondition. The opportunity came after the Soviet invasion of Afghanistan, which led to the signing of two aid packages worth approximately US $6.6 billion.

Much more came into the country during the 1980s. According to senior Pakistani journalist Muhammad Zia-ud-Din, more than US $50 billion entered Pakistan's economy during this period.[5] There were five broad reasons for the geopolitical development in Afghanistan being important for Pakistan.

First, it reset the relations with the US and restored Pakistan's position as a frontline state and a critical US ally in South Asia.

Second, the war against the Soviet Union in partnership with the US and its allies created political space for Pakistan in Afghanistan. It established Pakistan as a significant player with interest in resetting Afghanistan's future and expanding its outreach to Central Asia. It gave

Islamabad the opportunity to deal with the problem of its historic fear of Afghanistan posing as a facet of a two-front challenge in a possible war with India.

Third, the American aid which poured in helped with an additional burden on Pakistan created due to a change in Chinese policy, which stopped interest-free loans and credit to its South Asian ally. Driven by domestic compulsions and the decision by Deng Xiaoping after Mao Zedong's departure to emphasize on building the Chinese economy, China put a stop to all free lunches. After 1979, Pakistan had to pay for Chinese weapons. Incidentally, this coincided with China improving ties with India, which resulted in disengagement of troops from the Sino–Indian borders. Though looked at cautiously by Pakistan, the easing of Sino–Indian tensions did not necessarily bring a strategic divergence in the Sino–Pak relations. Besides visits to Pakistan by Chinese dignitaries, there was cooperation between the two allies in the war in Afghanistan. Beijing had remained suspicious of Soviet ambitions during the 1970s, especially after Moscow's troops deployment in Afghanistan. China's leaders continued to blame Moscow for the 1971 break-up of Pakistan.[6]

Fourth, the war in Afghanistan of the 1980s brought the much-needed major military modernization to Pakistan. Unlike the 1960s, weapons given by the US were of better quality and state-of-the-art, which provided Pakistan with a technological push. The problem of the quality–quantity gap in defence technology that Pakistan had struggled with during the 1970s was resolved.

Finally, fifth, the technology injection bolstered Sino–Pakistan ties and added a new dimension—building up of a two-way defence–industrial cooperation that contributed to improving Beijing's overall defense-industrial capacity. For instance, the Pakistan Air Force (PAF) helped refine design perimeters of the JF-17 Thunder aircraft based on its experience of using both Chinese equipment and better quality western aircraft. While Pakistan's foreign secretary, Shahryar Khan, looked at the easing of Sino–Indian tension during the 1980s as 'romance going out of the relationship' between Pakistan and China, with a similar view expressed by author Ahmed Faruqi regarding the 1990s, the fundamental basis of the bilateral ties was adjusted but not changed. Beijing's abandonment of a zero-sum game approach in South Asia allowed not only for improving ties with New Delhi, but also cooperation with Pakistan.

Islamabad, on the other hand, continued to value its relations with Beijing and being mindful of its policies. For instance, in 1980, Pakistan closed its embassy in Vietnam in view of China's considerations.[7] Beijing's relations with Hanoi had deteriorated after war between the two in 1979. More importantly, Pakistan played a critical role in opening up the doors of Western technology to Beijing. Valuable material, ranging from US shoulder-fired Stinger missiles to the remains of the Tomahawk fired by the US in 1998 targeting Osama bin Laden, was shared with the Chinese.[8] The technological cooperation was both vertical and horizontal—from developing conventional weapons, an element which will be discussed in greater detail in the following subsection, to nuclear weapons.

Nuclear-weapon proliferation was a major contention between Pakistan and the US. Despite the fact that Washington was aware of Islamabad's activities in this regard and of the Sino–Pak cooperation, it was willing to overlook these developments, especially at the peak of Pak–US convergence on Afghanistan. For Islamabad, hence, the objective was to prolong the period of cooperation and use it to its benefit. Pakistan's military dictator General Zia-ul-Haq had told the editor of the *Far Eastern Economic Review* that the Afghanistan war, being between two superpowers, would never end, hence indicating his expectation of a long-term relationship.[9] The situation, however, changed dramatically after the signing of the Geneva Accords in April 1988. This was resisted not just because of uncertainty in Afghanistan, but lack of a framework which would allow for stable Pak–US relations. The withdrawal of Soviet troops from Afghanistan brought the US non-proliferation agenda to the fore, culminating in the arms embargo of October 1990.

After the Pressler Amendment, 1990–2001

Despite the popular narrative that decried yet another 'let-down' by the US, Islamabad seemed better poised for the much-feared shift in its relations with Washington that not only cut arms supply but also military training. Pakistan military's strategy during this phase was two-pronged. On the one hand, it tried to rekindle relations, especially resumption of arms sales. Efforts finally resulted in the passing of the Brown Amendment to the US Foreign Assistance Act, which allowed a one-time waiver to the Pressler Amendment.

The change would permit the US president to certify that Pakistan did not engage in further nuclear enrichment and so could be transferred weapons such as the F-16s and the P-3C Orion reconnaissance aircraft that Islamabad had paid for but which were stuck in the US. During the early 1990s there was discomfort in the armed forces, especially the Pakistan Air Force (PAF), on not getting the aircraft.

On the other hand, Pakistan got into a strategic snuggle with Beijing to develop its conventional and non-conventional defence capabilities. A number of co-development, co-production projects were launched with China, including developing a main battle tank and a fighter aircraft. Pakistan's links with the US were important as it sought help from US manufacturers for upgrade of Chinese fighter aircraft designs.

The defence industrial partnership was mutually beneficial as Pakistan contributed to improving Chinese designs. The cooperation also aimed to help China gain access to the Middle East with Pakistan's assistance. The more significant dimension of the cooperation pertained to nuclear technology that Islamabad was eager to develop. As the US tried to cap Islamabad's nuclear activities, the latter sought Beijing's help to fill its technology gaps that included obtaining medium-range ballistic missile technology from North Korea. The Ghauri-I was acquired in exchange for enriched uranium that North Korea needed. The Sino–Pak cooperation aimed at escaping nuclear blackmail in more than one way. It was not just competing with India but also ensuring that Pakistan became greatly self-reliant in delivery platforms and acquired sufficient enriched uranium if it faced greater US sanctions.

New war, new consequences, 2001–2015

India and Pakistan conducting nuclear tests in 1998 changed the strategic dynamics of South Asia. It also indicated America's inability to influence Pakistan, which was more affected by sanctions than India was. Not that Washington could dissuade Islamabad at that time; it didn't have the capacity to weigh in on the conversation and benefit from the difference of opinion inside the military on whether to test or avoid international sanctions. The then naval chief, Admiral Fasih Bokhari, for instance, argued against testing. Ultimately, the decision was to test because of the strategic symbolism. Not testing would have allowed India to walk alone from South Asia into the elite club of nuclear nations, where, as it was perceived, it would have been readily accepted.

The sanctions against India did not appear to Pakistan as critical as the ones against it. In fact, Chinese President Zhao Ziyang complained to President George Bush during his 1989 visit to China about the West's bias towards India versus Pakistan in the matter of nuclear proliferation.[10] Furthermore, Pakistan wanted to set the tone of its relations with the US emphasizing its significance as a US partner in the region.

With regard to the limited engagement between US and Pakistan, Washington was made aware of its limitation, caused by the disruption of the International Military Education and Training (IMET) programme, even more after the 9/11 terror attack in New York. Pakistan proved initially uncooperative, and had to be threatened with the message of 'Either you are with us, or you are with the terrorists' to force a quick response to cooperate. General Pervez Musharraf, the army chief and president then, realized his lack of options. Pakistan was conscious of its limited manoeuvrability at that time, since the strategic community in Washington viewed its South Asian ally with a lot of suspicion due to its engagement with global jihad, the Al-Qaeda, and the Afghan Taliban. Eager to reset relations with the US, Pakistan was aware this had to be done in a totally different scenario as compared to the past. It could not be accused of aiding and abetting communism or communist elements, which was the reason for the earlier engagement with the US. Now, post-9/11 was a different situation. After 2001, it was expected to fight the religious-right extremist forces that were cultivated to fight the earlier US wars.

Rebuilding ties also meant restrategizing to turn the weakness of its situation into strength. Islamabad intended to get into a strategic relationship with the US and try to hold it as long as possible, mainly because of Washington's power status but also with an eye on an injection of quality defence technology that it could not get from China. This meant recreating Pakistan's image as a willing partner but with the capacity which the US required for its war in Afghanistan. Even before 9/11, Pakistan had begun to use its knowledge of violent extremism compounded with the older formula of presenting itself as being susceptible to threat from religious extremism to find common cause with Washington.

A Rand Corporation team visiting Pakistan in February 2000 was informed about '16–17 per cent senior army officers having religious extremist tendencies'.[11] Musharraf's immediate willingness to cooperate was necessary to create room for Pakistan in US strategic plans, but then also use the opportunity to negotiate a greater space in carving Afghanistan's future. This required safeguarding Taliban interests and protecting them from being treated in the same way as Washington dealt with Al-Qaeda. In an interview with me in 2002, the director-general of Inter-Services Public Relations, Major General (retd) Rashid Qureshi said that Pakistan would cooperate with the US on Al-Qaeda but would like to retain the power to deal with the Taliban without any foreign intervention.[12] Pakistan was relatively successful in the earlier years of WoT as the US focused on the Arab terrorists and allowed Pakistan to deal with the Talibaan.

Pakistan's continued linkage with the Taliban was partly based on its understanding that the Americans would not stay in Afghanistan permanently. Their exit would make it imperative for Pakistan to look for reliable partners through whom it could re-operationalize the strategy to remain an influential player in Afghanistan and, through it, in Central Asia. The biggest concern was about the US giving a role to India in Afghanistan, thus rolling back Pakistan's military-strategic gains. There was much talk of accessing Central Asia, for which political control of Afghanistan was essential.

Pakistan depended upon silence from China in not publicly objecting to a strategy that also affected Chinese security interests. The congregation of militants from different parts of Central Asia in Afghanistan and Pakistan's northern areas were a direct threat to both China and Russia, which was dealt with through private diplomacy. It was only at times that the bilateral tension would become visible when China would close borders with Pakistan. This happened on a few occasions in the decade of the 2010s, especially as the Taliban operated close to the Sino–Pak border.[13] Unlike the US that gets attacked by Islamic jihad for deep ideological bias, China managed to secure a better relationship with the jihadis which can be attributed to its engagement with the various extremist and religious groups, but also allowing Pakistan to play the role of an interlocutor.

The US may not have got a better treatment or received some sympathy like the Chinese even if its behaviour was less pushy because of other issues such as an ideological bias of the Islamists and Pakistan military's decision-makers in general. Clearly, Pakistan dealt with both the powers that it was dependent upon in different ways. There was a tedious negotiation with Washington regarding different militant groups. This conversation also drove the Pak–US transactional relationship. The mutual suspicion intensified, particularly after the US military operation to capture and kill Osama bin Laden in Abbotabad in 2011, followed by a skirmish between US/Afghan and Pakistani forces in which twenty-eight Pakistani soldiers were killed at a check post in Salala. Pakistan shut down the NATO supply line for almost six months until the US Secretary of State Hillary Clinton apologized. There was so much suspicion that crept into the relationship that Pakistan did not take the bait of America's Asia pivot.[14] Washington's expansion of its mission in Islamabad as an expression of its long-term commitment towards Pakistan was viewed with suspicion and termed as part of some bigger India–US conspiracy.

With China, there was strengthening of a linkage that gave Pakistan the sense of 'letting its hair down' in a military-strategic sense. Notwithstanding Beijing's reservations about Islamic militancy, it continued to protect Pakistan's position regarding the militant leader Masood Azhar. China has continued to block any effort by India for the United Nations to declare Azhar as a terrorist.[15] Pakistan's military-strategic and defence-industrial dependency on Beijing also multiplied, which gave a new direction to the country's defence industry. Besides jointly improving its technological capabilities vis-à-vis India, Islamabad used the partnership to find export markets for collaborative defence production. The new market opportunities in Africa and Southeast Asia, though limited, were meant to establish new linkages and influence. For Pakistan's own security, it drew Beijing into developing the deep fishing port at Gwadar. It was initially offered for development in 2006. It is noteworthy that Zulfiqar Ali Bhutto had offered a similar opportunity to the US during the 1970s but had received no positive response.[16]

A new partnership, 2015–2021

Pakistan's increased dependence on China was also based on a realization of a deepening India–US relationship. I remember sitting through several conversations in Islamabad where the presence of Americans of Indian origin in US think tanks was talked about as New Delhi's grand plan to influence US thinking. Partly driven by its concern regarding the aforementioned development but mainly driven by its economic compulsions, Pakistan also signed the China–Pakistan Economic Corridor (CPEC) in 2016, which promised to bring an investment of approximately US $50 billion into Pakistan. This was a new set of politico-economic ties, the planning for which was dominated in the first couple of years by the political government rather than the military. The friction over control of the project coincided with the military changing the government in Islamabad and supporting a hybrid civil-military rule.

The inept handling of CPEC by the new government of Prime Minister Imran Khan resulted in a noticeable slowing down of the project, which did not achieve the aforementioned investment figures. This led to the bilateral relationship being split into two—more stable military-strategic link and a weak politico-economic relationship that by 2020 seemed to have been put on the back-burner. However, contrary to US political scientist Andrew Small's assertion that CPEC has lost steam,[17] the relationship remains a strategic milestone. For Pakistan, CPEC is a future investment, especially when Beijing's geo-political and geo-strategic power gains steam and overtakes the US, as it is expected amongst Islamabad's strategic community.

The slowing down of CPEC coincided with the US announcing its Indo-Pacific strategy that completely bypassed Pakistan and gave India the role of the new 'frontline' state in South Asia. India's role as part of the four-member Quad was aimed at countering China's growing power. However, it also indicated a US expression of mistrust of Pakistan as a strategic partner. It is not clear if the Pakistan army realized the extent of unhappiness in the Pentagon regarding Pakistan's role in Afghanistan. Pakistan's army chief, Qamar Javed Bajwa, expressed his resentment as he responded to announcement of the Indo-Pacific strategy: 'Pakistan does not need material or financial assistance from the US, but needs to be trusted and treated with respect.'[18] Such views denote discomfort over the US not recognizing Pakistan's sacrifices in the WoT, which has been Islamabad's core argument since the beginning of US operations in Afghanistan.

Since 2018, Bajwa has engaged in hectic efforts to improve ties with the US and convince it of the viability of CPEC. But Washington remains aprehensive of Pakistan walking into a debt trap and being forced to surrender to Chinese power.[19] Islamabad's position, on the other hand, is to argue that it needs the project to build its depleting economy that is affected by Financial Action Task Force (FATF) regulations and lack of much-needed investment. Since the US and the West at large will not invest, it cannot miss the Chinese opportunity that it is eager to legitimize geopolitically.

Conclusion

Though the Indo-Pacific strategy was noticed by the army chief, it has taken a long time to be comprehended in Pakistan. Islamabad certainly does not want to be caught in the crossfire of Sino–US rivalry as both relations are critical for it. Given that Pakistan remains part of the Western/US geostrategic constellation, it wants to benefit from Chinese investment without putting all its eggs in one basket. General Bajwa has been making efforts to mend fences with the US and start a dialogue that it could capitalize on, especially in case the Indo–US linkage does not take off. Its eyes are not on US resources but on Chinese, which it would like to capitalize on by reducing the controversy around it.

Acknowledgements

THIS BOOK IS A RESULT of a Zoom call last year with several diplomats on how a once-in-a-century pandemic would shape the world. One of the examples of events that reshaped our world that came up in the call was Henry Kissinger's secret visit to China, which triggered the idea of putting this volume together to mark fifty years of that event.

We would like to thank our contributors, all accomplished individuals, who took time out to put together the essays for this volume. Each of them brings a very different perspective on the subject at a time when China is seeking global supremacy.

The pandemic impacted both of us. One of us had to spend two weeks in hospital to recover from the virus; the other battled the virus at home and recovered. Our thanks to our families who helped us in this journey.

Our thanks to executive editor, Swati Chopra, and the team at HarperCollins India that helped us publish this book in time despite all the constraints imposed by the pandemic and the lockdown.

Thanks are also due to Vedika Gupta, our research assistant, who helped us coordinate with our contributors and added several nuggets of information where needed. She is soon set to join the Indian Air Force to follow her passion for flying, and has promised to keep a copy of the book in the cockpit with her.

Notes

Introduction to the Paperback Edition

1. The first edition was published in August 2021.
2. Bonnie Girard, 'From the Deal to Decoupling: Trump's Evolution on China', *The Diplomat,* 17 September 2020. https://thediplomat.com/2020/09/from-the-deal-to-decoupling-trumps-evolution-on-china/.
3. Edward Luttwak, *The Rise of China vs the Logic of Strategy* (Cambridge: Belknap Press of Harvard University Press, 2012), p. 47.
4. Ibid., p. 266
5. Robert Blackwill and Jennifer Harris, *War by Other Means: Geo-economics and Statecraft* (Cambridge: Belknap Press of Harvard University Press, 2016), p. 225
6. Ibid.
7. Ibid., p. 226.
8. *China Briefing*, 'U.S.-China Trade in Goods Hits a New Record in 2022 – What Does it Mean for Bilateral Ties', 15 February 2023. https://www.china-briefing.com/news/us-china-trade-in-goods-hits-new-record-in-2022-what-does-it-mean-for-bilateral-ties/.
9. Eric Martin, 'U.S. Wants to De-risk, Not Decouple From China, Biden Aide Says', 28 April 2023. https://www.bloomberg.com/news/articles/2023-04-27/us-wants-to-de-risk-not-decouple-from-china-biden-aide-says.

10. Janet Yellen, 'US decoupling from China would be disastrous', *Financial Times*, 20 April 2023. Accessed at: https://www.ft.com/content/b38478a6-7a30-47f0-a8f7-6c89dd77d324
11. Russel Flannery, 'U.S. Businesses Look To De-Risk, Not Decouple, Their China Ties', *Forbes*, 12 March 2023. Accessed at: https://www.forbes.com/sites/russellflannery/2023/03/12/us-businesses-look-to-de-risk-not-decouple-their-china-ties/?sh=599a7ca92294.
12. *AmCham White Paper on American Business in China, 2023*. Accessed at: https://www.amchamchina.org/white_paper/american-business-in-china-white-paper/. Quoted in *China Briefing, US-China Relations in the Biden Era*. Accessed at: https://www.china-briefing.com/news/us-china-relations-in-the-biden-era-a-timeline/.
13. *Economic Times*, 'India-China Trade Climbs To USD 135.98 Billion in 2022, Trade Deficit Crosses USD 100 Billion For The First Time', 13 January 2023. https://economictimes.indiatimes.com/news/economy/foreign-trade/india-china-trade-climbs-to-usd-135-98-billion-in-2022-trade-deficit-crosses-usd-100-billion-for-the-first-time/articleshow/96969775.cms.
14. Dong Yue, 'On China, Washington "can't have it both ways"', Xinhua, 26 April 2023. http://en.people.cn/n3/2023/0426/c90000-20011742.html.
15. Ibid.

1: Kissinger and China

1. Henry Kissinger, *Diplomacy* (New York: Simon & Schuster, 1994), pp. 702–735.
2. Kissinger, *Diplomacy,* pp. 17–29 and 703–733.
3. Walter Isaacson, *Kissinger: A Biography* (New York: Simon & Schuster, 1992), p. 334.
4. Kissinger, *Diplomacy,* p. 722; Henry Kissinger, *White House Years* (Boston: Little, Brown & Company, 1979). pp. 171–173.
5. Kissinger, *Diplomacy,* p. 19.
6. Kissinger, *White House Years,* pp. 684–693; Isaacson, *Kissinger,* 336–343.
7. Isaacson, *Kissinger,* p. 333.

8. Kissinger, *White House Years,* pp. 704–706.
9. Gary J. Bass, *The Blood Telegram: Nixon, Kissinger, and a Forgotten Genocide* (New York: Alfred A. Knopf, 2013), 302–303; Srinath Raghavan, *1971: A Global History of the Creation of Bangladesh* (Cambridge, MA: Harvard University Press, 2013), 205, 240–256.
10. Joint Statement Following Discussions with Leaders of the People's Republic of China, Foreign Relations of the United States, 1969–1976, vol. XVII, China, 1969–1972; website of the State Department Historian: https://history.state.gov/historicaldocuments/frus1969-76v17/d203
11. Kissinger, *On China* (New York: Penguin, 2011).
12. Kissinger knew this. I attended a function in Kissinger's honour about fifteen years ago, and went to say hello to him on the way to lunch, adding that I had worked for him in the State Department. Kissinger looked behind me and said, 'Funny, I don't see any scars on your back!'
13. World Bank website: https://data.worldbank.org/indicator/NY.GDP.MKTP.CD?locations=CN-US-IN-RU

2: Evil Liberalism versus Moral Pragmatism

1. Kishore Mahbubani, *Can Asians Think?* (Singapore: Times Books International, 1998), p. 148.
2. US Air Forces Central Command, *Airpower Summaries*; https://www.afcent.af.mil/About/Airpower-Summaries/
3. Watson Institute, 'Human Cost of Post-9/11 Wars: Direct War Deaths in Major War Zones', (13 November 2019); https://watson.brown.edu/costsofwar/figures/2019/direct-war-death-toll-2001-801000
4. George F. Kennan, *American Diplomacy: Sixtieth-anniversary expanded edition* (Chicago: University of Chicago Press, 2012).
5. John J. Mearsheimer, Introduction in *American Diplomacy: Sixtieth-Anniversary Expanded Edition*, George F. Kennan (Chicago: University of Chicago Press, 2012), p. xxiv.
6. Ibid.
7. Kishore Mahbubani, *Has China Won?* (Public Affairs, 2020), pp. 183–210.
8. Ibid., p. 186.

9. Andrew Ross Sorkin, 'Paul Volcker, at 91, Sees "a Hell of a Mess in Every Direction"', (23 October 2018); https://www.nytimes.com/2018/10/23/business/dealbook/paul-volcker-federal-reserve.html
10. Joseph E. Stiglitz, 'The American Economy is Rigged', (1 November 2018); https://www.scientificamerican.com/article/the-american-economy-is-rigged/
11. Martin Wolf, 'Democracy will fail if we don't think as citizens', *Financial Times* (6 July 2020); https://www.ft.com/content/36abf9a6-b838-4ca2-ba35-2836bd0b62e2
12. Stephen M. Walt, *The Hell of Good Intentions: America's Foreign Policy Elite and the Decline of US Primacy* (New York: Farrer, Straus and Giroux, 2018), p. 14.
13. John J. Mearsheimer, *The Great Delusion: Liberal Dreams and International Relations* (New Haven: Yale University Press, 2018), p. 168.
14. 'US Air Strike Wiped Out Afghan Wedding Party, Inquiry Finds', *The Guardian* (11 July 2008); https://www.theguardian.com/world/2008/jul/11/afghanistan.usa
15. Kishore Mahbubani, *Has China Won?: The Chinese Challenge to American Primacy* (New York: Public Affairs, 2020), pp. 2–3.

3: Kissinger's Secret Trip, China's Rise, and a New Bipolarity

1. This chapter draws on my recently published book, *India Versus China: Why They are Not Friends* (New Delhi: Juggernaut, 2021).
2. Jaw-ling Joanne Chang, 'United States–China Normalization: An Evaluation of Foreign Policy Decision Making', Occasional Papers/Reprints Series in Contemporary Asian Studies, Number 4-1986 (75), School of Law, University of Maryland, p. 26; https://digitalcommons.law.umaryland.edu/cgi/viewcontent.cgi?article=1074&context=mscas
3. Richard M. Nixon, 'Asia After Viet Nam', *Foreign Affairs*, vol. 46, no. 1 (September/October 1967), p. 121.
4. Yafeng Xia, 'China's Elite Politics and Sino–American Rapprochement, January 1969–February 1972', *Journal of Cold War Studies*, vol. 8, no. 4 (Fall 2006), pp. 3-8.
5. Ma Ke and Yang Xiao, 'China–U.S. 40 Years On: Kissinger's Secret Trip to China', *CGTN* (26 September 2019); https://news.cgtn.com/

news/2019-09-26/China-U-S-40-years-on-Kissinger-s-secret-trip-to-China-KihqiF2UVi/index.html

6. John Pomfret, *The Beautiful Country and the Middle Kingdom: America and China, 1776 to the Present* (New York: Henry Holt, 2016), pp. 447–449 (Kindle).
7. Ma Ke and Yang Xiao, 'China–U.S. 40 Years On: Kissinger's Secret Trip to China'.
8. Pomfret, *The Beautiful Country and the Middle Kingdom*, p. 458 (Kindle).
9. X (George Kennan), 'The Sources of Soviet Conduct', *Foreign Affairs*, vol. 25, no. 4, July 1947, pp. 566–582; Andre Amalrik, *Will the Soviet Union Survive Until 1984?* (New York: Harper Row, 1970).
10. Pomfret, *The Beautiful Country and the Middle Kingdom*, p. 482 (Kindle).
11. Ibid., p. 538 (Kindle).
12. See the writings of Michael Beckley: 'Rogue Superpower: Why This Could be an Illiberal American Century', *Foreign Affairs*, November/December 2020; 'Stop Obsessing About China: Why Beijing Will Not Imperil U.S. Hegemony', *Foreign Affairs*, September 21, 2018; and 'The United States Should Fear a Faltering China: Beijing's Assertiveness Betrays Its Desperation', *Foreign Affairs*, 28 October 2019.
13. Henry A. Kissinger, *World Order: Reflections on the Character of Nations and the Course of History* (London: Allen Lane, 2014), p. 367.
14. Pomfret, *The Beautiful Country and the Middle Kingdom*, pp. 453–455 (Kindle).
15. Harold Isaacs, *Scratches on Our Mind: American Views of China and India* (Abingdon: Routledge, 2015), p. 121 (Kindle). It was originally published by John Day in 1958.
16. Isaacs, *Scratches on Our Mind*, p. 353 (Kindle).

5: China's Rise and Asia's New Security Dilemma

1. Susan B. Glasser, 'Mike Pompeo, the Secretary of Trump,' *The New Yorker* (19 August 2019); https://www.newyorker.com/magazine/2019/08/26/mike-pompeo-the-secretary-of-trump
2. Henry Kissinger, *On China* (New York: The Penguin Press, 2011), (Kindle, location 8049).
3. Ibid., location 8071.

4. Ibid., location 8055.
5. Ibid.
6. Jeffrey M. Smith, 'Democracy's Squad: India's Change of Heart and the Future of the Quad', *War on the Rocks* (13 August 2020); https://warontherocks.com/2020/08/democracys-squad-indias-change-of-heart-and-the-future-of-the-quad/
7. Ibid.
8. Margaret MacMillan, *Nixon and Mao: The Week that Changed the World* (New York: Random House, 2007), p. 120.
9. Ibid., p. 122.
10. Ibid., p. 123.
11. Richard M. Nixon, 'Informal Remarks in Guam with Newsman' (The American Presidency Project, 25 July 1969); https://www.presidency.ucsb.edu/documents/informal-remarks-guam-with-newsmen
12. Ibid.
13. Ibid.
14. Ibid.
15. Nixon, 'Asia After Vietnam', *Foreign Affairs*, vol. 46, no. 1 (October 1967), p. 121.
16. Ibid., p. 123.
17. Winston Lord, 'Memorandum for Henry A. Kissinger, MemCons of the Final Sessions With the Chinese', the White House (National Security Archives, George Washington University, 12 August 1971), p. 2; https://nsarchive.gwu.edu/
18. 'Memorandum of Conversation', The White House (National Security Archives, George Washington University, 11 July 1971), p. 14; https://nsarchive.gwu.edu/
19. Ibid.
20. Ibid.
21. Javier C. Hernandez, 'Harsh Penalties, Vaguely Defined Crimes: Hong Kong's National Security Law Explained', *The New York Times* (30 June 2020); https://www.nytimes.com/2020/06/30/world/asia/hong-kong-security-law-explain.html.
22. Donald Clarke, 'Hong Kong's National Security Law: An Assessment', *China Leadership Monitor*, issue 66 (Winter 2020, 1

December 2020); https://www.prcleader.org/current-issues?utm_source=so&cid=9e51de47-103e-4eca-97c9-a87fccde0086

23. William Zheng, 'The Time for China's Rise Has Come, Security Chief Tells Law Enforcers', *South China Morning Post* (15 January 2021); https://www.scmp.com/news/china/politics/article/3117973/time-chinas-rise-has-come-security-chief-tells-law-enforcers
24. Ibid.
25. Shi Jiangtao, 'Congress Concludes with President Xi Jinping as Undisputed "Core Leader"', *South China Morning Post* (24 October 2017); https://www.scmp.com/news/china/policies-politics/article/2116830/congress-concludes-xi-undisputed-core-leader
26. Timothy R. Heath, 'The Consolidation of Political Power in China Under Xi Jinping: Implications for the PLA and Domestic Security Forces', Ct-503, Testimony presented before the U.S.-China Economic and Security Review Commission on 7 February 2019, p. 10.
27. Ibid., p. 3.
28. Shin Nakayama and Ken Moriyasu, '"Indo-Pacific Czar" Kurt Campbell Calls for Spreading Out US Forces', *Nikkei Asia* (15 January 2021); https://asia.nikkei.com/Politics/International-relations/Biden-s-Asia-policy/Indo-Pacific-czar-Kurt-Campbell-calls-for-spreading-out-US-forces

6: Kissinger and the Selling of America

1. Henry Kissinger, *World Order: Reflections on the Character of Nations and the Course of History* (London: Penguin Allen Lane, 2014), p. 9.
2. Kissinger (2014), p. 367.
3. Edward N. Luttwak, *The Rise of China vs the Logic of Strategy* (The Belknap Press, Harvard University Press, 2012), p. 285, footnote 1.
4. Henry Kissinger, *On China* (Penguin Allen Lane, 2011).
5. Ibid., p. 407.
6. Ibid., pp. 408–409.
7. Ibid., p. 480.
8. Ibid., p. 495.
9. Ibid., p. 495.

10. George Archibald, 'Old Hands Hold Hands with Beijing in Trade Policy', *Washington Times*, 3 March 1997; https://corpwatch.org/article/us-old-hands-hold-hands-beijing-trade-policy.
11. Members of Kissinger Associates Inc who served various US administrations include Bent Scowcroft, J. Stapleton Roy, Lawrence Eagleburger, Timothy Geither, Bill Richardson, John Brennan, William Sion and Willim Rogers, among others. Kissinger Associates Inc, Centre for Media and Democracy; www.sourcewatch.org/index.php/Kissinger_Associates,_Inc.#Kissinger_Associates.27_Associates. Heather Timmons & Ilaria Maria Sala, 'At 93 Henry Kissinger is still doing deals and courting controversy in China', *Quartz* (5 April 2017); https://qz.com/950103/at-age-93-henry-kissinger-appears-to-have-played-a-cruical-role-in-the-xi-jinping-donald-trump-summit/ George Archibald, 'US: Old hands hold hands with Beijing on trade policy', *The Washington Times* (3 March 1997); https://corpwatch.org/article/us-old-hands-hold-hands-beijing-trade-policy. Niall Ferguson, 'The Secret of Henry Kissinger's Success', *Politico* (20 January 2018); www.politico.eu/article/the-secret-to-henry-kissingers-success/ Leslie H. Geib, 'Kissinger Means Business', *The New York Times* (20 April 1986); www.nytimes.com/1986/04/20/magazine/kissinger-means-business.html
12. For a discussion of the role of US business in lobbying support for China's membership of WTO see Bob Davis and Lingling Wei, *Superpower Showdown: How the Battle Between Trump and Xi Threatens a New Cold War* (New York: HarperCollins, 2020).
13. Xinhua, 'Kissinger Says China's Accession to WTO Achievable in 1999'. http://en.people.cn/english/fortune99/speeches/speech.html.
14. Robert Lighthizer, 'What Did Asian Donors Want?', *The New York Times* (27 February 1997). https://www.nytimes.com/1997/02/25/opinion/what-did-asian-donors-want.html.
15. Lighthizer (1997).
16. Davis and Wei (2020), chap. 4 and 7.
17. Surjit Bhalla, Chinese Mercantilism: Currency Wars and How the East Was Lost, ICRIER Working Paper No. 45 (July 1998); https://icrier.org/pdf/Surjit%20S.%20Bhalla.PDF.
18. The original US support in 1945 for China's UN status as well as its shareholding in the Bretton Woods institutions, IMF and IBRD, predated the communist takeover of China. The US has had a long

history of relations with pre-communist China, and the two were allies during the Second World War. It was the overthrow of the Nationalist government and its flight to Taiwan that forced the US to break diplomatic relations with the People's Republic.

19. Dong Wang, 'China's Trade Relations with the US in Perspective', *Journal of Current Chinese Affairs*, vol. 39, no. 3: pp. 165–210; https://journals.sagepub.com/doi/pdf/10.1177/186810261003900307
20. Bohdan O. Szuprowicz, 'China Fever: Scrambling for Shares in a $600 Million Buying Spree', *Management Review* (8–16 May 1979), p. 9.
21. Reihan Salam, 'Normalizing Trade Relations with China Was a Mistake', *The Atlantic* (8 June 2018); https://www.theatlantic.com/ideas/archive/2018/06/normalizing-trade-relations-with-china-was-a-mistake/562403/
22. Robert Lighthizer, 'A Deal We'd Likely Regret', *The New York Times* (18 April 1999); https://www.nytimes.com/1999/04/18/opinion/a-deal-wed-be-likely-to-regret.html
23. Edward Luttwak, *Rise of China vs. the Logic of Strategy* (Harvard University Press, 2012); Robert Blackwill and Jennifer Harris, *War by Other Means: Geo-economics and Statecraft* (Harvard University Press, 2016).
24. Robert Kagan, 'Why the Rush to Favor China?' *The Weekly Standard* (20 March 2000); https://carnegieendowment.org/2000/03/20/why-rush-to-favor-china-pub-236
25. Robert Cassidy, 'The Failed Expectations of US Trade Policy', *Foreign Policy* (4 June 2008); https://www.bilaterals.org/?the-failed-expectations-of-us
26. Robert Blackwill and Jennifer Harris, *War by Other Means; Economics and Statecraft* (Belknap Press, Harvard University Press, 2016), p. 189.
27. Lighthizer (2010), p. 3.
28. Lighthizer (2010), p. 7.
29. Lighthizer (2010), p. 15.
30. Robert Lighthizer, *Testimony Before the U.S.–China Economic and Security Review Commission: Evaluating China's Role in the World Trade Organization Over the Past Decade* (9 June 2010); https://uschinatradewar.com/files/2017/01/LIGHTHIZER-2010-STATEMENT-US-CHINA-ECONOMIC-SECURITY-COMMISSION.pdf

31. 'Made by America in China', *Forbes* (25 June 2007); www.forbes.com/2007/07/20/elephant-dragon-meredith-oped cz_rm_0725dragonsix.html?sh=60988a341e9f
32. Davis and Wei (2020), p. 70.

7: Secrets, Subterfuge, Subordination

1. National Archives – Minutes of 19 July 1971 White House meeting.
2. Lucien Pye, 'About Face: A History of America's Curious Relationship With China, From Nixon to Clinton', *Foreign Affairs* (May/June 1999); https://www.foreignaffairs.com/reviews/capsule-review/1999-05- 01/about-face-history-americas-curious-relationship-china-nixon
3. Robert Blackwill, 'Trump's Foreign Policies Are Better Than They Seem', Council on Foreign Relations, Council Special Report No. 84 (April, 2019).
4. Ibid.
5. The China Deep Dive, Report on the US Intelligence Community's Capabilities and Competencies with Respect to the People's Republic of China to The House Permanent Select Committee on Intelligence, October 2020; https://intelligence.house.gov/uploadedfiles/hpsci_china_deep_dive_redacted_summary_9.29.20.pdf
6. Ibid.
7. Anonymous, 'The Longer Telegram: Toward a New American China Strategy', Atlantic Council; https://www.atlanticcouncil.org/content-series/atlantic-council-strategy-paper-series/the-longer-telegram/
8. 'Cold War, Warm Hearth', 'Postwar Politics and Cold War', 'Henry Kissinger and American Foreign Policy', The Gilder Lehman Insititure of American History; https://ap.gilderlehrman.org/history-by-era/seventies/essays/henry-kissinger-and-american-foreign-policy
9. Message from Nixon to Zhou, via Hillaly (10 May 1971), The National Security Archives; https://nsarchive2.gwu.edu/NSAEBB/NSAEBB66/ch-23.pdf
10. Yoav J. Tennebaum, 'China Power: Kissinger's Visit, 40 Years On', *The Diplomat* (8 July 2011); https://thediplomat.com/2011/07/kissingers-visit-40-years-on/

11. James Mann, *About Face: A History of America's Curious Relationship with China, From Nixon to Clinton* (Alfred Knoff, 1998), p.15.
12. Ibid.
13. Mann, *About Face*, p. 11,
14. Bradley A. Thayer and Lianchao Han, 'Kissinger's Folly: The Threat to World Order is China', The Hill (19 April 2020); https://thehill.com/opinion/international/491507-kissingers-folly-the-threat-to-world-order-is-china
15. Ibid.
16. Jeremy Page, 'How the U.S. Misread China's Xi: Hoping for a Globalist, It Got an Autocrat', *The Wall Street Journal* (23 December 2020); https://www.wsj.com/articles/xi-jinping-globalist-autocrat-misread-11608735769
17. Bradley A. Thayer and Lianchao Han, 'Kissinger's Folly: The Threat to World Order is China'.
18. Ibid.
19. Henry Kissinger, 'The Future of U.S.–Chinese Relations Conflict Is a Choice, Not a Necessity', *Foreign Affairs* (March/April 2012), vol.91, no. 2, p. 52.
20. Jeremy Page, 'How the U.S. Misread China's Xi: Hoping for a Globalist, It Got an Autocrat'.
21. Ibid.
22. Ibid.
23. The China Deep Dive, Report on the US Intelligence Community's Capabilities and Competencies with Respect to the People's Republic of China to The House Permanent Select Committee on Intelligence, October 2020.
24. Denny Roy, 'How China Squandered Its Chance for A Peaceful Rise', *The National Interest* (13 February 2021); https://nationalinterest.org/feature/how-china-squandered-its-chance-peaceful-rise-178116
25. Ibid.
26. The Longer Telegram.
27. Nicholas D. Kristof, 'The Rise of China', *Foreign Affairs* (November/December 1993); http://foreignaffairs.com/articles/asia/1993-12-01/rise-china

8: A Future beyond the Past

1. 'The Opening to China Part I: The First Opium War, the United States, and the Treaty of Wangxia, 1839–1844', Office of the Historian, Department of State, United States of America; https://history.state.gov/milestones/1830-1860/china-1
2. 'Chinese Immigration and the Chinese Exclusion Acts', Office of the Historian, Department of State, United States of America; https://history.state.gov/milestones/1866-1898/chinese-immigration
3. Pearl S. Buck, *The Good Earth* (New York: Open Road Integrated Media, first published 1931).
4. R.R. Leonhard, *The China Relief Expedition Joint Coalition Warfare in China, Summer 1900* (John Hopkins University, 1990); https://www.jhuapl.edu/Content/documents/China%20ReliefSm.pdf
5. Ibid.
6. Pearl S. Buck, *The Good Earth.*
7. E. Snow, *Red Star Over China* (New York: Grove Press, 1968).
8. Ibid.
9. 'McCarthyism and the Red Scare' (University of Virginia); https://millercenter.org/the-presidency/educational-resources/age-of-eisenhower/mcarthyism-red-scare
10. Henry Kissinger, *Peace, Legitimacy, and the Equilibrium: (A Study of the Statesmanship of Castlereagh and Metternich)* (Cambridge: Harvard University Press, 1954).
11. R.J.W. Evans and H.P.V. Strandmann, *The Coming of the First World War* (Oxford: Clarendon, 1990).
12. Henry Kissinger, *On China* (London: Penguin, 2011).
13. Ibid.
14. Ibid.
15. Ibid.
16. Ibid.
17. L.M. Lüthi, *The Sino–Soviet Split: Cold War in the Communist World* (Princeton: Princeton University Press, 2008).
18. T.W. Robinson, 'The Sino–Soviet Border Dispute: Background, Development, and the March 1969 Clashes', *American Political Science Review* 66, no. 4 (1972): 1175–1202.

19. Ibid. (11).
20. 'The Encirclement of China: The People's Daily 1 February 1966', *Survival* 8 no. 4 (1966): 128–129.
21. Ibid. (11).
22. Ibid. (11).
23. J. Mann, *The China Fantasy: Why Capitalism Will Not Bring Democracy to China* (New York: Penguin, 2008).
24. Ibid.
25. L. Menand, 'What Went Wrong in Vietnam', *The New Yorker* (19 February 2018); https://www.newyorker.com/magazine/2018/02/26/what-went-wrong-in-vietnam
26. 'Strategic Arms Limitations Talks/Treaty (SALT) I and II', Office of the Historian, Department of State, United States of America; https://history.state.gov/milestones/1969-1976/salt
27. J. Valenta, 'Soviet–Cuban Intervention in the Horn Of Africa: Impact and Lessons', *Journal of International Affairs* 34, no. 2 (1980): 353–367.
28. D.H. Noon, 'Cold War Revival: Neoconservatives and Historical Memory in the War on Terror', *American Studies* 48, no. 3 (2007): 75–99.
29. B. Naughton, 'Deng Xiaoping: The Economist', *China Quarterly* 135 (1993): 491–514.
30. M. Kubow, 'The Solidarity Movement in Poland: Its History and Meaning in Collective Memory', *Polish Review* 58, no. 2 (2013): 3–14.
31. E.M. Nimmo, 'United States Policy Regarding Technology Transfer to the People's Republic of China', *Northwestern Journal of International Law & Business* 6, no. 1(1984): 249–274.
32. Ibid.
33. 'East–West Technology Transfer: A Congressional Dialog with the Reagan Administration', Joint Economic Committee Congress of the United States (1984); https://www.jec.senate.gov/reports/98th%20Congress/East-West%20Technology%20Transfer%20(1305).pdf.
34. Ibid. (11).
35. '2 US Officials Went to Beijing Secretly in July', *The New York Times* (19 December 1989); https://www.nytimes.com/1989/12/19/world/2-us-officials-went-to-beijing-secretly-in-july.html

36. G. Segal, 'China and the Disintegration of the Soviet Union', *China Quarterly* 133 (1992): 1–26.
37. F. Jannuzi, 'Whatever Happened to Chinese Human Rights?', *Foreign Policy* (1 November 2012); https://foreignpolicy.com/2012/11/01/whatever-happened-to-chinese-human-rights/
38. Ibid.
39. B. Gellman, 'US and China Nearly Came to Blows in '96', *The Washington Post* (1998); https://www.washingtonpost.com/archive/politics/1998/06/21/us-and-china-nearly-came-to-blows-in-96/926d105f-1fd8-404c-9995-90984f86a613/
40. D. Williams, 'Missiles Hit Chinese Embassy', *The Washington Post* (1999); https://www.washingtonpost.com/wp-srv/inatl/longterm/balkans/stories/belgrade050899.htm
41. N.R. Lardy, 'Permanent Normal Trade Relations for China', Brookings (2000); https://www.brookings.edu/research/permanent-normal-trade-relations-for-china/
42. J. Kynge, 'China was the Real Victor of Asia's Financial Crisis', *Financial Times* (2017); https://www.ft.com/content/5cf22564-5f2a-11e7-8814-0ac7eb84e5f1
43. Henry Kissinger, *The White House Years* (New Delhi: Vikas Publishing House, 1979).
44. D. Acheson, 'Speech on the Far East', Central Intelligence Agency (1950); https://www.cia.gov/library/readingroom/docs/1950-01-12.pdf
45. H.R.2479—Taiwan Relations Act, US Congress (1979); https://www.congress.gov/bill/96th-congress/house-bill/2479#:~:text=Taiwan%20Relations%20Act%20%2D%20Declares%20it,other%20people%20of%20the%20Western
46. S.1678—Taiwan Allies International Protection and Enhancement Initiative (TAIPEI) Act of 2019, US Congress (2020); https://www.congress.gov/bill/116th-congress/senate-bill/1678/text
47. M. Goldstein, 'Tibet: After the Fall of Chamdo', *Tibet Journal* (1991): 58–95.
48. M. Goldstein, *The United States, Tibet, and the Cold War* (Cambridge: MIT Press, 2006).
49. 'Designation of a United States Special Coordinator for Tibetan Issues', US Department of State (2020); https://www.state.gov/designation-of-a-united-states-special-coordinator-for-tibetan-issues/

50. 'US–Hong Kong Policy Act Report', US Department of State (2003); https://2001-2009.state.gov/p/eap/rls/rpt/19562.htm.
51. 'Harsh Penalties, Vaguely Defined Crimes: Hong Kong's Security Law Explained', *The New York Times* (13 July 2020); https://www.nytimes.com/2020/06/30/world/asia/hong-kong-security-law-explain.html
52. S.1838—Hong Kong Human Rights and Democracy Act of 2019, US Congress (2019); https://www.congress.gov/bill/116th-congress/senate-bill/1838/text
53. 'Once Reluctant to Hit China on Human Rights, Trump Moves to Use the Issue as a Cudgel Amid Growing Tensions', *Washington Post* (9 August 2020); https://www.washingtonpost.com/politics/trump-china-human-rights/2020/08/08/b2d09172-d97b-11ea-930e-d88518c57dcc_story.html
54. Uyghur Human Rights Policy Act of 2020, US Congress (2020); https://www.congress.gov/116/plaws/publ145/PLAW-116publ145.pdf
55. 'US Position on Maritime Claims in the South China Sea', U.S. Department of State (2020); https://www.state.gov/u-s-position-on-maritime-claims-in-the-south-china-sea/
56. J.D. Stoffey, 'Lessons from History: The Han–Xiongnu War and Modern China', *Small Wars Journal* (2017); https://smallwarsjournal.com/jrnl/art/lessons-from-history-the-han-xiongnu-war-and-modern-china
57. Ibid. (11).
58. D. Lin, *The CCP's Exploitation of Confucianism and Legalism* (London: Routledge, 2017).
59. Xi Jinping, 'Xi Jinping's Speech in Commemoration of the 2,565th Anniversary of Confucius' Birth', *China US Focus* (2014); http://library.chinausfocus.com/article-1534.html
60. Ibid. (11).
61. 'Trump Cutting US Ties with World Health Organization Over Virus', Reuters (2020); https://www.reuters.com/article/us-health-coronavirus-trump-who-idUSKBN2352YJ
62. Mao Zedong, 'Speech at a Meeting of the Representatives of Sixty-four Communist and Workers' Parties' (edited by Mao), *Wilson Center Digital Archive* (1957); https://digitalarchive.wilsoncenter.org/document/121559.pdf?v=d41d8cd98f00b204e9800998ecf8427e
63. 'China Continuing to Outpace the US Economy, CFO Survey Reveals', CNBC (2020); https://www.cnbc.com/2020/12/02/china-continuing-to-outpace-the-us-economy-cfo-survey-reveals-.html

64. 'The People's Republic of China: US–China Trade Facts', Office of the United States Trade Representative (2020); https://ustr.gov/countries-regions/china-mongolia-taiwan/peoples-republic-china#:~:text=U.S.%20goods%20and%20services%20trade,was%20%24308.8%20billion%20in%202019
65. 'China's Spending on R&D Rises to Historic High', Xinhua (2020); http://www.xinhuanet.com/english/2020-08/27/c_139322217.htm
66. Ibid. (11).
67. 'Kissinger Warns Biden of US–China Catastrophe on Scale of WWI', Bloomberg (2020); https://www.bloomberg.com/news/articles/2020-11-16/kissinger-warns-biden-of-u-s-china-catastrophe-on-scale-of-wwi
68. W. Safire, 'Super Yalta', *The New York Times* (1975); https://www.nytimes.com/1975/07/28/archives/super-yalta-essay.html
69. Ibid. (11).
70. Ibid. (11).

9: Did Kissinger Wake the Dragon Up?

1. Michael R. Auslin, *Asia's New Geopolitics: Essays on Reshaping the Indo-Pacific* (Stanford: Hoover Institution Press, 2020), p. 22.
2. Ezra Vogel, *Deng Xiaoping and the Transformation of China* (Cambridge {Massachusetts}/London {England}: The Belknap Press, Harvard University Press, 2011), p. 49.
3. Henry Kissinger, *White House Years* (Boston: 1979), p. 165.
4. Winston Lord, *Nixon goes to China*, Oral history given to the Association for Diplomatic Studies and Training; https://adst.org/2013/02/nixon-goes-to-china/
5. Evelyn Goh, 'Nixon, Kissinger, and the "Soviet Card" in the U.S. Opening to China, 1971–1974', *Diplomatic History*, Vol. 29, Issue 3, June 2005.
6. *Joint Communiqué of the United States of American and the People's Republic of China*, 28 February 1972; http://www.taiwandocuments.org/communique01.htm
7. Raymon Aron, *Paix et guerre entre les nations* (Peace and war among nations) (Paris: Calmann-Levy, 1984), p. 63.

8. *Full Text of Clinton's Speech on China Trade Bill*, Johns Hopkins University, March 2000; https://www.iatp.org/sites/default/files/Full_Text_of_Clintons_Speech_on_China_Trade_Bi.htm
9. Ibid .
10. Ibid.
11. Ibid
12. Nicholas R. Lardy, *Integrating China into the Global Economy* (Washington, DC: Brookings Institution Press, 2002), p. 22.
13. *Full Text of Clinton's Speech on China Trade Bill*, op. cit.
14. Alain Peyrefitte, *Quand la Chine s'éveillera . . . le monde tremblera* (When China wakes up, the world will tremble) (Paris: Fayard, 1973).

10: The Kissinger Paradox

1. Sun Tzu, *The Art of War*, trans. John Minford (New York: Viking, 2002), p. 3.
2. William Burr, *Kissinger Transcripts: The Top Secret Talks with Beijing and Moscow* (Diane Publishing Co., 1999), chap. 1.
3. Pradip Baijal, *Containing The China Onslaught* (Gurugram: Quadrant, 2019), chap. 1.
4. Jairam Ramesh, *Kautilya Today* (New Delhi: India Research Press, 2002), p. 293.
5. Jonathan Spence, *The Search for Modern China* (W.W. Norton & Co., 1990), pp. 230–236.
6. Ibid., pp. 237–238.
7. Ibid., p. 383.
8. Ibid., p. 384.
9. Ibid., p. 380.
10. Ibid., pp. 381–382.
11. Ibid., pp. 382–386.
12. 'Asia's Power Pairs', *Time* (13 April 1998), p. 76.
13. Spence, *The Search for Modern China*, pp. 333–334.
14. Diana Lary, *China's Civil War: A Social History, 1945–1949* (Cambridge University Press, 2015), p. 80.
15. Walter Isaacson, *Kissinger: A Biography* (New York: Simon & Schuster, 1992), p. 333.

16. Ibid., pp. 107–108.
17. Ibid., p. 117.
18. Ibid., pp. 117–118.
19. Henry Kissinger, *White House Years* (Boston: Little Brown & Company, 1979), pp. 265–68.
20. Isaacson, *Kissinger: A Biography,* p. 118.
21. Ibid., pp. 169.
22. Frank Dikotter, *Mao's Great Famine* (Bloomsbury, 2010), pp. 6–7.
23. Edward Crankshaw, *Khrushchev: A Career* (New York: Avon Books, 1966), pp. 234–250.
24. Dikotter, *Mao's Great Famine*, p. 7.
25. Adi Ignatius, 'Clashing with the Soviet Ex-Master', *Time* (27 September 1999), p. 79.
26. Ibid.
27. James Bradley, *The Imperial Cruise: A Secret History of Empire and War* (Little Brown & Company, 2009), chap. 1.
28. Isaacson, *Kissinger: A Biography,* p. 333.
29. Ibid., p. 348.
30. Walter LaFeber, *The Clash: US-Japanese Relations Throughout History* (W.W Norton & Co.), pp. 336–356.
31. Nick Kapur, *Japan at the Crossroads: Conflict and Compromise after Anpo* (Harvard University Press, 2018), p. 66.
32. Spence, *The Search for Modern China*, pp. 666–667.
33. Ibid., pp. 670–671.
34. Isaacson, *Kissinger: A Biography,* p. 334.
35. Ministry of Defence, Government of Ukraine; https://www.mil.gov.ua/en/news/2020/07/24/natos-enhanced-opportunities-program-for-ukraine/ 2020-07-24
36. Alexander Thalis, 'Threat or Threatened? Russia in the Era of NATO Expansion', *Australian Institute of International Affairs* (2018); https://www.internationalaffairs.org.au/australianoutlook/threat-or-threatened-russian-foreign-policy-in-the-era-of-nato-expansion/
37. Ibid.
38. Isaacson, *Kissinger: A Biography,* pp. 239–241.

39. Patrick Wintour, 'Henry Kissinger says Brexit will bring Britain closer to the US', *The Guardian*, 27 June 2017. https://www.theguardian.com/politics/2017/jun/27/henry-kissinger-says-brexit-will-bring-britain-closer-to-the-us.
40. Ibid.
41. Jeffrey Goldberg, 'World Chaos and World Order: Conversations With Henry Kissinger', *The Atlantic* (10 November 2016); https://www.theatlantic.com/international/archive/2016/11/kissinger-order-and-chaos/506876/.
42. Isaacson, *Kissinger: A Biography*, p. 333.
43. Richard McGregor, *Asia's Reckoning: The Struggle for Global Dominance* (Penguin, 2017), chap. 1.
44. Isaacson, *Kissinger: A Biography*, p. 335.
45. Spence, *The Search for Modern China*, p. 658.
46. Ibid., pp. 673–674.
47. Michael Pillsbury, *The Hundred-Year Marathon: China's Secret Strategy to Replace America as the Global Superpower* (St. Martin's Griffin, 2019), chap. 1.
48. TCA Srinivasa Raghavan, 'India, US, Japan Should Put Up a United Fight against China', *Financial Express* (15 September 2019); https://www.financialexpress.com/lifestyle/containing-the-china-onslaught-india-us-japan-should-put-up-a-united-fight-against-china/1706429/
49. John M. Broder and Jim Mann, 'Clinton Reverses His Policy, Renews China Trade Status', *Los Angeles Times* (27 May 1994); https://www.latimes.com/archives/la-xpm-1994-05-27-mn-62877-story.html.
50. Susan A. Thornton, 'Is American Diplomacy with China Dead?', *Foreign Service Journal* (July–August, 2019); https://www.afsa.org/american-diplomacy-china-dead
51. Clive Hamilton and Mareike Ohlberg, *Hidden Hand: Exposing How the Chinese Communist Party Is Reshaping the World* (Oneworld, 2020), chap. 6.
52. Samir Saran, 'If the EU Fails, We Can Say Goodbye to the Liberal Order', *Observer Research Foundation* (17 November 2020); https://www.orfonline.org/expert-speak/if-the-eu-fails-we-can-say-goodbye-to-the-liberal-order/

53. Pillsbury, *The Hundred-Year Marathon*, chap. 1.
54. Lucian Pye and Nathan Leites, *Nuances in Chinese Political Culture* (Santa Monica: Rand Corporation, 1970); https://www.rand.org/pubs/papers/P4504.html.
55. Hamilton and Ohlberg, *Hidden Hand*, chap. 1.
56. Pillsbury, *The Hundred-Year Marathon, chap*. 1.

11: Kissinger in China, 1971–2021

1. Winston S. Churchill, *The Gathering Storm* (Cambridge: Riverside Press, 1948), p. 207–208.
2. See: A. Arbatov. *Transformation of Nuclear Deterrence.* — Mirovaya ekonomika i mezhdunarodnye otnosheniya, 2018, vol. 62, no. 7, pp. 5–16.
3. R. McNamara. *The Essence of Security: Reflections in Office,* NewYork: Harper&Row, 1968, p. 176.
4. Henry Kissinger. *Does America Need a Foreign Policy?: Toward a Diplomacy for the 21st Century* (New York: Simon and Schuster, 2001), p. 141.
5. A. Dobrynin. Strictly confidential (Moscow: Avtor, 1997), p. 188.
6. Ibid, pp. 189–190.
7. Bolo Lo. *Global order in the shadow of the coronavirus: China, Russia and the West*. Lowy Institute Analyses (July, 2020); https://www.lowyinstitute.org/publications/global-order-shadow-coronavirus-china-russia-and-west
8. Bobo Lo. *A Wary Embrace.* Lowy Institute Papers (April 2017), p. 8; https://www.lowyinstitute.org/publications/wary-embrace
9. David Wainer. Kissinger Warns US and China Must Set Limits to Avoid a Blow-up. — Bloomberg (7 October 2020); https://www.bloomberg.com/news/articles/2020-10-07/kissinger-warns-u-s-and-china-must-set-limits-to-avoid-a-blowup

12: Nixon's Outreach

1. https://www.nationalchurchillmuseum.org/10-07-13-lets-hope-churchill-was-wrong-about-americans.html

2. David C. Wolf, '"To Secure a Convenience": Britain Recognizes China – 1950', *Journal of Contemporary History*, vol. 18, no. 2 (1983), pp. 299–326; JSTOR, www.jstor.org/stable/260389
3. David C. Wolf, op cit.

13: China's Rise and Japan's Awakening

1. I learned a lot about the inside stories of Sino–Japanese relations from the following book: Sakutaro Tanino, *China, Asia and the Secret Story of Diplomacy: A China Hand's Memoirs* (in Japanese) (Tokyo: Toyo-Shinpo, 2017).

15: The Strategic Legacy in Southeast Asia

1. Evelyn Goh, *From Red Menace to Tacit Ally: Constructing the US Rapprochement with China, 1961–1974* (Cambridge: Cambridge University Press, 2004).
2. Kurt M. Campbell and Ely Ratner, 'The China Reckoning', *Foreign Affairs*, 30 November 2020; Mike Pompeo, 'Secretary Pompeo – The China Challenge', US Embassy in El Salvador (6 November 2019); Michael McFaul, 'Cold War Lessons and Fallacies for US-China Relations Today', *The Washington Quarterly* 43, no. 4 (December, 2020), pp. 7–39; Hoo Tiang Boon and Hannah Elyse Sworn, 'Strategic Ambiguity and the Trumpian Approach to China-Taiwan Relations', *International Affairs* 96, no. 6 (2020), pp. 1487–1508.
3. Laura Silver, Kat Devlin and Christine Huang, 'Unfavorable Views of China Reach Historic Highs in Many Countries', Pew Research Center's Global Attitudes Project (Pew Research Center, 6 October 2020); Laura Silver, Kat Devlin and Christine Huang, 'U.S. Views of China Amid Trade War Turn Sharply Negative', Pew Research Center's Global Attitudes Project (Pew Research Center, 13 August 2019).
4. Ang Cheng Guan, *Southeast Asia's Cold War: An Interpretive History* (Honolulu: University of Hawaii Press, 2018), p. 52.
5. Michael J. Montesano, 'Bandung 1955 and Washington's Southeast Asia', in *Bandung Revisited: The Legacy of the 1955 Asian-African Conference for International Order*, eds. Tan See Seng and Amitav Acharya (Singapore: NUS Press, 2008), Chapter 9.

6. Ang, *Southeast Asia's Cold War,* 53; Michael E. Latham, 'The Cold War in the Third World, 1963-1975', in *The Cambridge History of the Cold War Volume 2: Crises and Détente*, eds. Melvyn P. Leffler and Odd Arne Westad (Cambridge: Cambridge University Press, 2010), p. 266.
7. Chen Jian, 'China and the Bandung Conference: Changing Perceptions and Representations', in *Bandung Revisited: The Legacy of the 1955 Asian-African Conference for International Order*, eds. Tan See Seng and Amitav Acharya (Singapore: National University of Singapore Press, 2008), p. 140.
8. Latham, 'The Cold War in the Third World, 1963-1975', p. 266.
9. Jay Taylor, *China and Southeast Asia: Peking's Relations with Revolutionary Movements* (New York: Praeger, 1976); Charles B. Smith Jr., *The Burmese Communist Party in the 1980s* (Singapore: Regional Strategic Studies Programme, Institute of Southeast Asian Studies, 1984), p. 7.
10. Wen-Qing Ngoei, *Arc of Containment: Britain, The United States, and Anticommunism in Southeast Asia* (Ithaca: Cornell University Press, 2019), pp. 11–14.
11. Ang, *Southeast Asia's Cold War,* p. 64.
12. Corrine Phuangkasem, *Thailand's Foreign Relations: 1964-80* (Singapore: ISEAS, 1984), p. 38.
13. Ang Cheng Guan, *Ending the Vietnam War: The Vietnamese Communists' Perspective* (Florence: Taylor and Francis, 2014).
14. Sorpong Peou, *Intervention and Change in Cambodia: Towards Democracy?* (Singapore: Institute of Southeast Asian Studies, 2000), p. 124.
15. Chansambath Bong, 'Cambodia's Disastrous Dependence on China: A History Lesson', *The Diplomat* (4 December 2019).
16. Leo Suryadinata, *China and the ASEAN States: The Ethnic Chinese Dimension* (Singapore: Singapore University Press, 1985), pp. 24–58.
17. Suryadinata, *China and the ASEAN States*, pp. 59–66.
18. Leo Suryadinata, *Pribumi Indonesians, the Chinese Minority, and China* (Singapore: Heinemann Asia, 1992); Mary Somers Heidhues, 'Anti-Chinese Violence in Java during the Indonesian Revolution, 1945–49', *Journal of Genocide Research* 14, no. 3–4 (2012): pp. 381–401.
19. See, for example, Johanes Herlijanto, *Old Stereotypes, New Convictions: Pribumi Perceptions of Ethnic Chinese in Indonesia Today* (Singapore: ISEAS–Yusof Ishak Institute, 2019).

20. Dewi Fortuna Anwar, 'The Cold War and its impact on Indonesia: domestic politics and foreign policy', in *Southeast Asia and the Cold War*, ed. Albert Lau (London: Routledge, 2014), pp. 142–144.
21. Ngoei, *Arc of Containment*, pp. 114–148.
22. Ang, *Southeast Asia's Cold War*, pp. 140–141; Stuart-Fox, *A Short History of China and Southeast Asia*, p. 185.
23. Ngoei, *Arc of Containment*, pp. 149–176.
24. See, for example, Sergey Radchenko, 'The Sino–Soviet split', in *The Cambridge History of the Cold War Volume 2: Crises and Détente*, eds. Melvyn P. Leffler and Odd Arne Westad (Cambridge: Cambridge University Press, 2010), pp. 349–372; Ankur Shah, 'China, Russia, and the Legacy of Zhenbao Island', SupChina, 3 March 2020.
25. David S. Painter, *The Cold War: An International History* (London: Routledge, 1999), p. 69.
26. Chen Jian, *Mao's China and the Cold War* (North Carolina: University of North Carolina Press, 2001).
27. MacMillan, *Nixon and* Mao, pp. 174–175; Chen Jian, *Mao's China and the Cold War*, p. 255–256.
28. Kimball, 'The Nixon Doctrine: A Saga of Misunderstanding', p. 69.
29. See Nicholas Griffin, *Ping-Pong Diplomacy: Ivor Montagu and the Astonishing Story behind the Game That Changed the World* (London: Simon & Schuster, 2015).
30. Hoo Tiang Boon, *China's Global Identity: Considering the Responsibilities of Great Power* (Washington, DC: Georgetown University Press, 2018), p. 8–15.
31. Wayne C. McWilliams and Harry Piotrowski, *The World Since 1945: A History of International Relations* (Boulder, Colorado: Lynne Rienner Publishers, 2005), pp. 233–235; Chen Jian, 'China and the Cold War after Mao', *The Cambridge History of the Cold War Volume 3: Endings*, eds. Melvyn P. Leffler and Odd Arne Westad (Cambridge: Cambridge University Press, 2010), p. 186.
32. See, for example, Chen Jian, 'China and the Cold War after Mao', p. 184.
33. For example, D.R. SarDesai names it as one of the four most important events that shaped Southeast Asian international relations in *Southeast Asia: Past and Present (Fifth Edition)* (Boulder, Colorado: Westview Press, 2009), pp. 379–380; A. Doak Barnett writes that 'the repercussions of

all these events were immediate and far-reaching. Virtually all nations in Asia, large and small, were compelled to reassess their positions and policies' and 'virtually every nation in Asia was impelled to reexamine its security requirements', in 'The Changing Strategic Balance in Asia', in *Sino–American Détente and Its Policy Implications,* ed. Gene T. Hsiao (New York: Praeger, 1974), pp. 27–28; Gene Hsiao writes that 'by the yardstick of history, this remarkable development in Sino–American relations is undoubtably one of the most momentous events of the 20th century. Its impact on the course of history will be felt for many years to come' in 'Introduction', in *Sino–American Détente and Its Policy Implications,* ed. Gene T. Hsiao (New York: Praeger, 1974), p. xvi; Lorenz M. Lüthi and Chen Jian note that 'with Nixon's visit to the PRC in February 1972, the era of Sino–American antagonism and its reverberations throughout the Afro-Asian world came to an end. The impact of "the week that changed the world" was both symbolic and substantive ... In terms of its impact upon East Asia and the world, the breakthrough in Sino–American relations dramatically shifted the balance of power between the two conflicting superpowers in the Cold War.' In 'China's Turn to the World', in *The Regional Cold Wars in Europe, East Asia, and the Middle East: Crucial Periods and Turning Points,* ed. Lorenz M. Lüthi (Washington, D.C.: Woodrow Wilson Center Press, 2015), p. 161. There are many other such examples.

34. Alice D. Ba, *(Re)Negotiating East and Southeast Asia: Region, Regionalism, and the Association of Southeast Asian Nations* (Stanford, CA: Stanford University Press, 2009), p. 75.
35. Ngoei, *Arc of Containment,* p. 173.
36. See, for example, Alice D. Ba, 'China and Asean: Renavigating Relations for a 21st-Century Asia', *Asian Survey* 43, no. 4 (2003): pp. 622–647; and more.
37. Donald G. McCloud, *System and Process in Southeast Asia: The Evolution of a Region* (New York: Routledge, 2019), pp. 209–210; A. Doak Barnett, 'The Changing Strategic Balance in Asia', p. 28; and more.
38. SarDesai, *Southeast Asia,* p. 379.
39. SarDesai, *Southeast Asia,* p. 380.
40. Goh, *From Red Menace to Tacit Ally.*

41. See, for example, Donald E. Weatherbee, *International Relations in Southeast Asia: The Struggle for Autonomy* (Lanham: Rowman & Littlefield, 2015), p. 75; Donald E. Weatherbee, *Historical Dictionary of United States-Southeast Asia Relations* (Lanham, MD: Scarecrow Press, 2008), p. 15; SarDesai, *Southeast Asia*, p. 380.
42. Weatherbee, *International Relations in Southeast Asia,* p. 75.
43. Suryadinata, *China and the ASEAN States*, pp. 183–185, 198–200, 207–209.
44. Weatherbee, *International Relations in Southeast Asia,* p. 75.
45. Zheng Yongnian and Lim Wen Xin, 'Lee Kuan Yew: The Special Relationship with China', in *Singapore–China Relations: 50 Years*, eds. Zheng Yongnian and Liang Fook Lye (Singapore: World Scientific, 2015), p. 32.
46. Katherine Enright, 'A Historical Perspective on Singapore–China Relations 1965–1975', *Singapore Policy Journal*, 25 October 2019.
47. Richard Garratt Wilson, *The Neutralization of Southeast Asia: Foreword by G.T. Hsiao* (New York: Praeger, 1975).
48. Ang, *Ending the Vietnam War*, p. 85.
49. Chen Jian, 'China, the Vietnam War, and the Sino–American Rapprochement, 1968–1973' in *The Third Indochina War: Conflict between China, Vietnam and Cambodia, 1972–79*, eds. Odd Arne Westad and Sophie Quinn-Judge (London: Routledge, 2009), pp. 33–64; Lorenz M. Lüthi, 'Beyond Betrayal: Beijing, Moscow, and the Paris Negotiations, 1971–1973', *Journal of Cold War Studies* 11, no. 1 (2009): p. 68.
50. Ang, *Southeast Asia's Cold War,* p. 152; McCloud, *System and Process in Southeast Asia*, p. 197.
51. Ang, *Southeast Asia's Cold War,* p. 142–143.
52. Boon, *China's Global Identity*, pp. 162–165.
53. Transcript of speech by Minister for Foreign Affairs and Minister for Law K. Shanmugam at the American Jewish Committee Global Forum: East Asian Geopolitics, 13 May 2014.
54. Hoo Tiang Boon, 'Hardening the Hard, Softening the Soft: Assertiveness and China's Regional Strategy', *Journal of Strategic Studies* 40, no. 5 (2017), pp. 639–662.

55. For more on the concept of hedging, see Cheng-Chwee Kuik, 'How Do Weaker States Hedge? Unpacking ASEAN states' alignment behavior towards China', *Journal of Contemporary China*, 25, no. 100 (2016), pp. 500–514; Hoo Tiang Boon, 'The Hedging Prong in India's Evolving China Strategy', *Journal of Contemporary China* 25, no. 100 (2016), pp. 792–804.
56. It is not just ASEAN states that face this dilemma. In general, 'smaller' states with extensive economic links with China also face this conundrum. See Hoo Tiang Boon and Charles Ardy, 'China and Lilliputians: Small States in a Big Power's Evolving Foreign Policy', *Asian Security* 13, no. 2 (2017), pp. 116–131.

16: Triangulation and the Tilts

1. Conversation Among Nixon, Kissinger, and Haig, 12 December 1971, *Foreign Relations of the United States [hereafter FRUS] 1969–1976 vol. E-7: Documents on South Asia, 1969–1972* (Washington, DC: GPO, 2005), doc. 177.
2. British Embassy, Washington, to FCO, 14 December 1971, The National Archives, Kew Gardens, Surrey, UK, FCO 37/755, doc. 9.
3. 'Interview with Edward C. Ingraham', Association for Diplomatic Studies and Training Foreign Affairs Oral History Project (8 April 1991). http://www.adst.org/OH%20TOCs/Ingraham,%20Edward%20C.toc.pdf
4. The next two sections draw from the author's book, *Fateful Triangle: How China Shaped US–India Relations During the Cold War* (Gurugram: Penguin Random House India, 2020).
5. Dennis Merrill, *Bread and the Ballot: The United States and India's Economic Development, 1947–1963* (Chapel Hill: University of North Carolina Press, 1990), p. 147.
6. Richard M. Nixon, 'Asia after Viet Nam', *Foreign Affairs* 46, no. 1 (October 1967): pp. 111–125.
7. Raymond L. Garthoff, *Detente and Confrontation: American-Soviet Relations from Nixon to Reagan*, revised ed. (Washington, DC: Brookings Institution, 1994), p. 276.

8. HAK Talking Points re US China Policy for August 14, 1969 NSC Meeting, National Archive and Records Administration, Nixon Presidential Materials (hereafter cited as NPM), NSC Institutional Files, NSC Meetings, Box H-023, NSC Meeting (San Clemente) 8/14/69 Briefings.
9. Henry A. Kissinger, *White House Years*, 1st edition (Boston: Little, Brown & Company, 1979), pp. 853–854.
10. Margaret Macmillan, *Nixon and Mao: The Week that Changed the World* (New York: Random House, 2007), pp. 177–181.
11. See footnote 2 re Nixon's note on Kissinger memo, 28 April 1971, *FRUS 1969–1976 vol. XI, South Asia Crisis* (Washington, DC: GPO, 2005), p. 98.
12. Nixon–Kissinger–Keating Conversation, 15 June 1971, *FRUS 1969–76 vol. E-7*, doc. 137.
13. Tad Szulc, 'U.S. Says It Will Continue Aid to Pakistan Despite Cutoff Urged by Other Nations', *The New York Times* (29 June 1971), p. 2.; 'House Foreign Affairs Comes Alive', *The Washington Post* (20 July 1971), p. A18; 'More US Weapons Will Go to Pakistan', *The Washington Post* (30 June 1971), p. A17.
14. See Kissinger's accounts of his conversations with Chinese ambassador to France Huang Chen (16 August and 13 September) and Chinese PR to the UN Huang Hua (26 November) in *FRUS 1969–1976 vol. XVII: China, 1969–1972* (Washington, DC: GPO, 2006), pp. 475–484, pp. 595–598, and with Zhou (22 October), *FRUS 1969–1976 vol. E-13*, doc. 44.
15. Pakistani ambassador to China's comments in Summary of Discussions of Pakistan Ambassadors' Conference (Geneva), August 1971, Nehru Memorial Museum and Library (NMML), P.N. Haksar Papers (III), SF no. 220.
16. Consideration of Contingency Study on Pakistan by Senior Review Group: Briefing Memo, 5 March 1971, in Roedad Khan, ed., *American Papers: Secret and Confidential, India–Pakistan–Bangladesh Documents 1965–1973* (Karachi: Oxford University Press, 1999), pp. 502–517.
17. Memorandum of Conversation, Beijing, 11 July 1971, *FRUS 1969–1976 vol. XVII*, p. 452.
18. Kissinger, *White House Years*, p. 862.

19. Dennis Kux, *The United States and Pakistan, 1947–2000: Disenchanted Allies* (Washington, D.C: Woodrow Wilson Center Press, 2001), p. 203.
20. Conversation between Kissinger and Gov. Rockefeller, 3 November 1971, 7.00 p.m., NARA NPM, HAK Telcons, Chronological File, 1 November 1971– 24 January 1972, box 12.
21. NSC staff, 'Possible US Responses to Chinese Military Actions in South Asia', 7 October 1971, *FRUS 1969–1976 vol. XI*, p. 435.
22. John Burns, 'China Vows Support for Pakistan', *The Washington Post* (8 November 1971), p. A18; Kissinger to Nixon, November 1971, *FRUS 1969–1976 vol. XVII*, p. 550; Kissinger to Nixon, 26 November 1971, *FRUS 1969–1976 vol. XVII*, p. 597
23. Kissinger Conversation with Secretary of State Rogers (23 November 1971), *FRUS 1969–76 vol. E-7*, doc. 155.
24. Nixon–Kissinger Conversation (4 December 1971), NARA NPM HAK Telcons, Home File, July 1970–April 1972, box 29.
25. Memorandum of Conversation, New York (10 December 1971), *FRUS 1969–1976 vol. XVII*, p. 611.
26. Richard M. Nixon, *RN: The Memoirs of Richard Nixon* (New York: Grosset & Dunlap, 1978), p. 526. Also, Minutes of NSC Meeting (6 December 1971), *FRUS 1969–1976 vol. XI*, p. 672 and CIA Information Cable (7 December 1971), *FRUS 1969–1976 vol. XI*, p. 687; Lord Cromer, British ambassador to the US, to FCO (15 December 1971), NA doc. 19, FCO 37/755: US Policy Towards India and Pakistan, 1971.
27. Conversation between Nixon, Kissinger and Attorney General Mitchell, 8 December 1971, 4.20-5.01 p.m., *FRUS 1969–76 vol. E-7*, doc. 165.
28. Editorial Note re Nixon-Kissinger Conversation (9 December 1971), *FRUS 1969-76 Vol. XI*, Doc. 256.
29. 'Pakistan: In Search of Assurance', *American Papers* (27 September 1971), pp. 679–680, and 'French Actions in Regard to Indo-Pak Situation', *American Papers* (24 November 1971), pp. 724–725.
30. MemCons, New York (10 and 12 December 1971), *FRUS 1969–1976 vol. XVII*, p. 612, pp. 621–624.
31. Sulzberger, 'Mrs Gandhi Asserts India is Still a Nonaligned Nation', *The New York Times* (17 February 1972), p. 1.
32. Extracts from R. Bhandari (Indian chargé in Moscow) to D.P. Dhar (ambassador to the USSR) on 27 March 1969, NMML, PNH (III), SF no. 203.

33. Record of Gandhi–Kosygin Conversation, 6 May 1969, NMML, PNH (III), SF no. 140.
34. Record of Gromyko–Swaran Singh Conversations, Moscow (7 and 8 June 1971), NMML, PNH (III), SF no. 203.
35. Record of Kissinger–Jagjivan Ram (7 July 1971), NMML, PNH (III), SF No. 229.
36. Apa Pant (IndHicom London) to Kaul (23 March 1971), NMML, PNH (III), SF No. 276.
37. MemCon, New Delhi (7 July 1971), *FRUS 1969–1976 vol. XI*, p. 222.
38. Haksar's Note on Conversation with Kissinger, 6 July 1971, NMML, PNH (III), SF no. 229.
39. Gandhi to Nixon (7 August 1971), NMML, PNH (III), SF no. 170.
40. K. Subrahmanyam to Defence Minister, et al, (4 April 1971), enclosing paper on Bangla Desh: Policy Options for India, NMML, PNH (III), SF no. 276.
41. Helms (DCI) to Kissinger, 29 July 1971, *FRUS 1969–1976 vol. XI*, p. 291; Haksar, Points for PM's Conversations with Gromyko (8 August 1971), NMML, PNH (III), SF no. 170.
42. T.N. Kaul, Points for Consideration by FM and PM, 3 August 1971, NMML, PNH (I-II), SF no. 49.
43. Record of Kosygin–D.P. Dhar Conversation (5 August 1971), NMML, PNH (I-II). SF no. 51.
44. IIPO, 'A Study of International Images in Metropolitan Cities and a Trend Analysis: 1966–1971', *Monthly Public Opinion Survey* vol. XVI, no. 11, 12 (August and September, 1971), pp. 4–9.
45. 'Praise of Soviet Voiced in India', *The New York Times* (11 August 1971), p. 7.
46. MemCon of Jha–Kissinger Meeting (10 March 1972), *FRUS 1969–76 vol. E-7*, doc. 233.
47. Jha to Kaul (28 February 1972), NMML, PNH (III), SF no. 277.

18: Kissinger and the Rise of China: A South Asian Perspective

1. Henry Kissinger, *On China*, p. 224.

2. 'The Opening to China: A Discussion with Henry Kissinger', in conversation with Tom Brokaw (7 March 2012); https://www.nixonfoundation.org/kissinger-nixons-trip-china/
3. Memorandum for the President, *Policy Options Toward Pakistan*, Secret, p. 6. Includes Nixon's handwritten Nixon note, (NPMP, NSC Files, {28 April 1971}); https://nsarchive2.gwu.edu/NSAEBB/NSAEBB79/BEBB9.pdf
4. Srinath Raghavan, *1971: A Global History of the Creation of Bangladesh* (Cambridge: Harvard University Press, 2013).
5. India–Bhutan Treaty of Perpetual Peace and Friendship; https://mea.gov.in/bilateral-documents.htm?dtl/5242/treaty+or+perpetual+p
6. Triloki Nath Kaul, *Diplomacy in Peace and War: Reflections and Recollections* (New Delhi: Gyan Publishers, 2016), p. 93. The book was published posthumously after Kaul's death in 2000. Originally published by Vikas Publishing House, 1979.
7. Rishikesh Shaha, 'Nepal: Reflections on Issues and Events of 1971', *Asian Survey*, vol. 12, no. 2 (February, 1972).
8. *The Subcontinent of South Asia: Afghanistan, Ceylon, India, Nepal and Pakistan* (US Department of State Publication, 1959); https://books.google.co.in/books?id=0c5iAsJdbcwC&printsec=frontcover&source=gbs_ge_summary_r&cad=0#v=onepage&q&f=false
9. Balance of Power in International Relations Theory; https://www.britannica.com/topic/balance-of-power
10. 'India and Pakistan: Crisis and War, March–December 1971, Foreign Relations, 1969–1976', vol. E-7, Documents on South Asia, 1969–1972 (Office of the Historian US Department of State Archive); https://2001-2009.state.gov/r/pa/ho/frus/nixon/e7/48213.htm
11. Telegram 19600 from US Embassy in Delhi to Washington, 23 December 1971; https://2001-2009.state.gov/r/pa/ho/frus/nixon/e7txt/49219.htm
12. Conversation between President Nixon and his Assistant for National Security Affairs (Kissinger), Washington, 10 December 1971; https://2001-2009.state.gov/r/pa/ho/frus/nixon/e7/48542.htm
13. Suhasini Haidar, 'U.S., India Have "Close Cooperation" on LAC Action by China: Kenneth Juster', *The Hindu* (5 January 2021); https://www.thehindu.com/news/national/us-india-have-close-cooperation-on-lac-action-by- china-kenneth-juster/article33503654.ece

14. Fox Butterfield, 'Peking Signs Treaty on Trade with US', *The New York Times* (8 July 1979); https://www.nytimes.com/1979/07/08/archives/peking-signs-treaty-on-trade-with-us-looks-to-tariff-cut-carter.html
15. US–China Trade Facts, USTR; https://ustr.gov/countries-regions/china-mongolia-taiwan/peoples-republic-china
16. 'Nixon's China Game: Ping-Pong diplomacy'; https://www.pbs.org/wgbh/americanexperience/features/china-ping-pong/
17. Mao Zedong's interviews to Edgar Snow; https://newrepublic.com/article/119916/edgar-snow-interview-china-chairman-mao-zedong
18. 'Simla Agreement July 2, 1972'; https://mea.gov.in/in-focus-article.htm?19005/Simla+Agreement+July+2+1972
19. S. Jaishankar, *The India Way: Strategies for an Uncertain World* (Noida: HarperCollins, 2020).
20. Yubaraj Ghimire, 'Next Door Nepal: The Morning After', *The Indian Express*; https://indianexpress.com/article/opinion/columns/the-morning-after-nepal-elections-4987322/
21. Suhasini Haidar and Kallol Bhattacherjee, 'Nepal Inks Treaty with China', *The Hindu* (21 March 2016); https://www.thehindu.com/news/international/nepal-inks-transit-treaty-with-china-to-have-first-rail-link/article8381195.ece. Anil Giri, 'Nepal Signs Deal with China to Access Seven Ports', *Kathmandu Post* (30 April 2019); https://kathmandupost.com/national/2019/04/30/nepal-signs-deal-with-china-to-access-seven-chinese-sea-and-land-ports
22. Harsh V. Pant and Kabir Taneja, 'Looking Back, Looking Ahead: Foreign Policy in Transition under Modi', p. 21; https://www.orfonline.org/wp-content/uploads/2019/07/ORF_SpecialReport_93_ForeignPolicy-Modi_NEW25July.pdf
23. 'Travel South Asia: India's Tourism Connectivity with the Region'; https://www.brookings.edu/research/travel-south-asia-indias-tourism-connectivity-with-the-region/
24. Constantino Xavier, Aakshi Chaba and Geetika Dang, 'Is India Still the Neighbourhood's Education Hub?' (Brookings, 10 March 2020); https://www.brookings.edu/research/is-india-still-the-neighbourhoods-education-hub/
25. Lu Yang, 'BRI, RCEP Best Solution for South Asia and Southeast Asia Recovery', *Global Times* (23 December 2020); https://www.globaltimes.cn/page/202012/1210800.shtml

26. Suhasini Haidar, interview with Subrahmanyam Jaishankar in *The Hindu*; https://www.thehindu.com/news/national/lac-standoff-india-will-not-accept-less-than-bottom-line-in-talks-with-china-says-jaishankar/article33234296.ece
27. Joint Statement Following Discussions with Leaders of the People's Republic of China, Shanghai (27 February 1972); https://history.state.gov/historicaldocuments/frus1969-76v17/d203
28. Conversation between President Nixon and his Assistant for National Security Affairs (Kissinger), Washington (26 May 1971); https://2001-2009.state.gov/r/pa/ho/frus/nixon/e7/48585.htm
29. Henry Kissinger, *World Order: Reflections on the Character of Nations and the Course of History* (London: Allen Lane, 2014).

19: Balancing Powers

1. https://nsarchive2.gwu.edu/NSAEBB/NSAEBB70/doc27.pdf.
2. https://nsarchive2.gwu.edu/NSAEBB/NSAEBB70/doc26.pdf.
3. Ibid.
4. Samina Yasmeen, 'Chinese Economic and Military Aid to Pakistan, 1969–79' (working paper no. 6, Department of International Relations, Australian National University, Canberra, 1987), pp. 1–10.
5. Interview, 10 March 2021.
6. Australian Prime Minister E. G. Whitlam's discussion with Zhou Enlai (31 October – 3 November, 1973). Summary (Woodrow Wilson International Center for Scholars Archives, 30 April 1980).
7. Ciphered Telegram No. 68, Embassy of Hungary in Pakistan to the Hungarian Foreign Ministry (Woodrow Wilson International Center for Scholars Archives, 30 April 1980).
8. Kamran Khan, 'Pakistan Says It Is Studying Errant US Missile', *The Washington Post* (28 August 1998).
9. M. Ziauddin, 'And We Kept Missing the Bus', *Business Recorder* (17 March 2021).
10. 'Memorandum of Conversation between George H.W. Bush and Zhao Ziyang' (Woodrow Wilson International Center for Scholars Archives, 26 February 1989).

11. Interview with member of the Rand Corporation team (Washington, DC, June, 2000).
12. Interview, November 2002.
13. https://www.reuters.com/article/us-pakistan-uighurs-idUSBREA2D0PF20140314.
14. Kurt Campbell, *The Asia Pivot.*
15. 'Pakistan's Masood Azhar: China Blocks Bid to Call Militant Terrorist', *BBC Online* (14 March 2019).
16. Alex Vatanka, *Iran and Pakistan: Security, Diplomacy and American Influence* (New York: Bloomsbury, 2015).
17. Andrew Small, 'Returning to the Shadows: China, Pakistan and the Fate if CPEC' (report for the George Marshal Fund, 23 September 2020).
18. 'Pakistan Wants the US's Trust, Not Its Financial Assistance: COAS', *Dawn* (23 August 2017).
19. Natasha Tariq, 'Pakistan's Economic Vulnerability and the US South Asia Strategy in Light of CPEC' (paper for the Sustainable Development Policy Institute, 2019), pp. 3–5.

Contributors

Teresita Schaffer

Ambassador Teresita C. Schaffer was a US diplomat for thirty years, with postings in Israel, Pakistan, India, Bangladesh, and as ambassador to Sri Lanka. Her career focused on South Asia, in which she was one of the US government's principal experts, and on international economic affairs. Since retiring from government service, she has worked at two Washington think tanks and has published three books on the region, most recently *India at the Global High Table*, co-authored with her late husband, Howard Schaffer. She graduated from Bryn Mawr College, and did graduate studies in economics at Georgetown University. She is currently a senior advisor at McLarty Associates, a strategic advising firm based in Washington, DC. She also teaches a course on Practicing Diplomacy Abroad at Georgetown University.

Kishore Mahbubani

Kishore Mahbubani is Distinguished Fellow, Asia Research Institute, National University of Singapore. He has dedicated five decades of his life to public service. In his thirty-three years as a Singapore diplomat, Kishore took on many challenging assignments, serving for example in Phnom Penh, Cambodia, in 1973/74 during the war. He also served two stints as Singapore's Ambassador to the UN (1984–89 and 1998–2004) and held the position of Permanent Secretary of the Ministry of Foreign Affairs from 1994 to 1998. He was also conferred the Public Administration Medal (Gold) by the Singaporean Government in 1998. Kishore had an equally illustrious career in academia. He was appointed the Founding Dean of the Lee Kuan Yew School of Public Policy in August 2004. Despite his heavy administrative duties, Kishore has received global recognition for his intellectual contributions, having been listed several times in the list of top global thinkers by *Foreign Policy* and *Prospect* magazines, and is a prolific author. He has published eight books, including *Can Asians Think?* and *Has China Won?*.

Kanti Bajpai

Kanti Bajpai is Wilmar Professor of Asian Studies and Director, Centre on Asia and Globalisation, Lee Kuan Yew School of Public Policy, National University of Singapore. His research areas are Asian security, South Asia politics, and Indian foreign policy and national security. His most recent publications are *India versus China: Why They Are Not Friends* (Juggernaut, forthcoming) and the *Routledge Handbook of China–India Relations* (2020). He has taught at Maharajah Sayajirao University of Baroda, Jawaharlal Nehru University, and Oxford University. He has held fellowships at the Kroc Institute of International Peace Studies at the University of Notre Dame, the Brookings Institution, the Australian Defence Force Academy, the Institute of Defence and Strategic Analyses, New Delhi, and the Bellagio Center of the Rockefeller Foundation. He writes a regular column for *The Times of India*.

Rana Mitter

Rana Mitter, OBE FBA, is the Director of the University China Centre and Professor of the History and Politics of Modern China at the

University of Oxford. He is the author of several books, including *China's War with Japan, 1937-1945: The Struggle for Survival* (US title: *Forgotten Ally*, 2013), which won the 2014 RUSI/Duke of Westminster's Medal for Military Literature and was named a CHOICE Outstanding Academic Title and a Book of the Year in the *Financial Times* and *The Economist.* His latest book is *China's Good War: How World War II Is Shaping a Nationalist Future* (2020). He has commented regularly on China in media and forums around the world, including the World Economic Forum at Davos. His broadcast work includes the *BBC Sounds–Chinese Characters* (available online) for which he was named Best Presenter at the 2019 ACTA/Eastern Eye awards.

Chung Min Lee

Dr Chung Min Lee is a Senior Fellow at the Carnegie Endowment for International Peace and Chairman of the International Advisory Council of the International Institute for Strategic Studies. His most recent book is *The Hermit King: The Dangerous Game of Kim Jong Un (2019)* and *Beyond Pyongyang: South Korea's Defense Choices in the 2020s* (IISS, forthcoming in 2021). Dr Lee served as the Republic of Korea's Ambassador for National Security Affairs (2013–16) and Ambassador for International Security Affairs (2009–10). He taught for twenty years at the Graduate School of International Studies, Yonsei University, and was a visiting professor at the National University of Singapore and the Graduate Research Institute for Policy Studies (Tokyo). He also worked at the RAND Corporation, the Sejong Institute, and the National Institute for Defense Studies (Tokyo). Dr Lee has lived in ten countries.

Sanjaya Baru

Sanjaya Baru is Distinguished Fellow, M.P. Institute for Defence Studies & Analyses, India. He has been editor of India's major financial newspapers, *The Economic Times*, *Financial Express* and *Business Standard.* He was Media Advisor to Prime Minister Manmohan Singh and Director for Geo-economics and Strategy, International Institute of Strategic Studies, London. He was Visiting Professor, Lee Kuan Yew School of Public Policy, Singapore and has lectured at the Indian School of Business and the Indian School of Public Policy. He is a member of the Advisory Council of the Bharti Institute of Public Policy. He was a member of India's National Security Advisory Board in 1999–2001 and a member of the India-ASEAN Eminent Persons Group, 2010. He is Founder-Trustee, Forum for National Security Studies, India. His publications include *The Strategic Consequences of India's Economic Rise* (Routledge, 2006); *India and the World: Essays on Geo-economics and Foreign Policy* (Academic Foundation, 2016); *India's Power Elite: Caste, Class and a Cultural Revolution*, (Penguin, 2021).

Rahul Sharma

Rahul Sharma is a former newspaper editor (*The Khaleej Times*, Dubai and *The Hindustan Times,* New Delhi) and a former Reuters journalist in Asia, with deep interest in issues around foreign policy and global economy. A contributor to various newspapers and online portals, Sharma covered some of the biggest diplomatic, political and economic developments in Asia before transitioning to public affairs and policy advocacy and spends time advising global companies on business, strategy, policy, and communications. He is the co-founder and former president of the Public Affairs Forum of India, a body of public affairs professionals. In his free time, as part of his readings, he curates *www.lookingbeyondborders.com*, which tracks global foreign policy and economic news.

Sujan Chinoy

Sujan R. Chinoy is Director General, Manohar Parrikar Institute for Defence Studies and Analyses, New Delhi. A career diplomat of the Indian Foreign Service, he was India's Ambassador to Japan and Mexico. Chinoy has extensive experience of East Asia, having served at Indian Missions in Hong Kong, Beijing, and Shanghai. He has an advanced diploma in

Chinese (Mandarin) from the New Asia Yale-in-China Chinese Language Centre of the Chinese University of Hong Kong. He also served as India's representative to the First Committee at the United Nations dealing with Disarmament and International Security Affairs. Chinoy was seconded to the Indian National Security Council Secretariat in the Prime Minister's Office, where he worked on internal and external national security policy and anchored strategic dialogues with key interlocutors around the world.

Frédéric Grare

Dr Frédéric Grare is Senior Policy Fellow at the European Council on Foreign Relations (ECFR) where he works on Indo-Pacific issues, and Non-resident Senior Fellow at the Carnegie Endowment for International Peace. At Carnegie, his research focuses on Indo-Pacific dynamics, the search for a security architecture, and South Asia Security issues. Prior to joining Carnegie, Grare served as Advisor at the Center for Analysis, forecasting and strategy at the French Ministry of Foreign Affairs, and as head of the Asia bureau at the Directorate for Strategic Affairs in the French Ministry of Defense. He also served at the French embassy in Pakistan and, from 1999 to 2003, as director of the Centre for Social Sciences and Humanities in New Delhi. Grare has written extensively on security issues in Asia, in particular South Asia. His msot recent book is *India Turns East: International Engagement and US–China Rivalry.*

Samir Saran

Samir Saran is the President of Observer Research Foundation (ORF), one of Asia's most influential think tanks. His research focuses on issues of global governance, climate change and energy policy, technology and new media, and India's foreign policy. He curates the Raisina Dialogue, India's annual flagship platform on geopolitics and geo-economics, and chairs CyFy, India's annual conference on cybersecurity and internet governance. He spearheads the foundation's efforts to foster new international partnerships and globalize its platforms. Samir is a Commissioner of the

Global Commission on the Stability of Cyberspace, a member of the Regional Action Group of the World Economic Forum (WEF) and sits on the Board of Microsoft's Digital Peace Now initiative. His published works include *The New World Disorder and the Indian Imperative* with Shashi Tharoor and *Pax Sinica: Implications for the Indian Dawn* with Akhil Deo.

Kalpit A. Mankikar

Kalpit A. Mankikar is Fellow with Strategic Studies Programme, and is based out of ORF's Mumbai centre. His research focuses on China, specifically looking at its rise—its domestic politics, diplomacy, and techno-nationalism. Kalpit was selected for the Kautilya Fellowship in 2020, and for 'Learning to Lead: Leadership Development' from the Oxford Global Leadership Initiative at the London School of Economics and Political Science (LSE) in 2019. He is a 2015 Reuters Fellow where he was selected for 'Editorial Judgment' training. Kalpit has written extensively for *International Business Times, The Times of India, Swarajya, India–China Business Chronicle*, among others.

Igor Yurgens

Igor Yurgens is the President of the All-Russian Insurance Association and the President of the Russian Association of Motor Insurers, the President of National Union of Liability Insurers, the Chairman of the Management Board of the Institute of Contemporary Development (INSOR), a member of the Management Board of the Russian Union of Industrialists and Entrepreneurs, a member of the Presidential Council for Civil Society Institutions and Human Rights, a member of Russian Council on International Affairs, a member of the Council of the International Institute for Strategic Studies (IISS), and a member of the Advisory Board of the Centre for European Reform (CER). Born in Moscow in 1952, Yurgens graduated from the Economics Department of Moscow State University in 1974. He is a professor of the Higher School of Economics and author of numerous articles and monographs, and honorary consul general of Monaco in Moscow.

Bill Emmott

Bill Emmott is a writer best known for his thirteen years as editor-in-chief of *The Economist* in 1993–2006, a publication he first joined in 1980. He is now co-director of the Global Commission for Post-Pandemic Policy, and chair of the International Institute for Strategic Studies, Trinity College Dublin's Long Room Hub for Arts & Humanities Research Institute, and the Japan Society of the UK. In 2016, the Japanese government awarded him the 'Order of the Rising Sun: Gold Rays with Neck Ribbon'. He was a visiting fellow at All Souls College in Oxford in 2017–18 and is an Ushioda Fellow at Tokyo College, University of Tokyo. Bill is the author of fourteen books on Japan, Asia, the twentieth century, and Italy, and co-wrote a documentary on Italy, *Girlfriend in a Coma* (2013). His most recent books have been *The Fate of the West* (2017) and *Japan's Far More Female Future* (2020).

Tsutomu Kikuchi

Dr Tsutomu Kikuchi is Professor and former Vice-President at Aoyama Gakuin University and Senior Adjunct Fellow at the Japan Institute of International Affairs (JIIA), both in Tokyo. He now heads a research group on Indo-Pacific strategy supported by the Japanese Ministry of Foreign Affairs. He was a visiting fellow at the Australian National University (ANU) and the Institute of Southeast Asian Studies (ISEAS), a visiting professor at the University of British Columbia, Canada, and a consultant of the Asian Development Bank (ADB). He has deeply engaged in the Track-2 activities in the Asia-Pacific at such institutions as PECC (Pacific Economic Cooperation Council) and CSCAP (Council for Security Cooperation in the Asia-Pacific). He specializes in international relations of the Indo-Pacific. He obtained a doctoral degree from Hitotsubashi University, Tokyo.

Peter Varghese

Peter Varghese is Chancellor of the University of Queensland. He was Secretary of the Australian Department of Foreign Affairs and Trade (2012–16) and has also served as High Commissioner to India (2009–12), High Commissioner to Malaysia (2000–02), Director-General of Australia's peak intelligence agency, the Office of National Assessments (2004–09), and Senior Advisor (International) to Prime Minister John Howard (2003). Varghese was the author of a comprehensive India Economic Strategy to 2035 commissioned by the Australian Prime Minister and submitted in July 2018. He is chair of the Asialink Advisory Council and sits on the boards of CARE Australia and North Queensland Airports. He is also on the international governing board of the Rajaratnum School of International Studies in Singapore.

Hoo Tiang Boon

Dr Hoo Tiang Boon is Assistant Professor and Coordinator of the Masters in Asian Studies Programme at the S. Rajaratnam School of International Studies, Nanyang Technological University (NTU), Singapore. He is also a US-ASEAN Fulbright Scholar, as well as a Faculty Fellow with NTU's University Scholars Programme. He holds a DPhil in International Relations from the University of Oxford. Dr Hoo is the author of several publications on China and US–China relations. His latest books include: *China's Global Identity: Considering the Responsibilities of Great Power* (Georgetown University Press, 2018); *Chinese Foreign Policy Under Xi* (Routledge, 2017); and *Chinese Regionalism in Asia* (Routledge, forthcoming in 2021). Dr Hoo has been involved in several diplomatic initiatives, including the Singapore–US Strategic Dialogue, the Singapore–France Dialogue on China, the Korea–Singapore Forum and the Network of ASEAN Defence and Security Institutions.

Quah Say Jye

Quah Say Jye is Research Assistant at the S. Rajaratnam School of International Studies, Nanyang Technological University (NTU), Singapore. His publications include articles in the *Singapore Policy Journal*, *The Journal of International and Public Affairs*, and *The Spectrum*.

Tanvi Madan

Tanvi Madan is the Director of the India Project and a Senior Fellow in the Foreign Policy program at the Brookings Institution. Her work explores India's role in the world and its foreign policy, focusing in particular on India's relations with China and the US, and its approach in the Indo-Pacific. Madan is the author of *Fateful Triangle: How China Shaped US-India Relations During the Cold War* (Brookings Institution Press, 2020). Her ongoing work includes a book project on the recent past, present and future of the China–India–US triangle, and a monograph on India's foreign policy diversification strategy.

C. Raja Mohan

C. Raja Mohan is Director, Institute of South Asian Studies, National University of Singapore. Earlier, he was the founding director of Carnegie India, Delhi. A leading analyst of India's foreign policy, Mohan also works on South Asian security, great-power relations in Asia, and arms control. He is the foreign affairs columnist for *The Indian Express*. He was a member of India's National Security Advisory Board from 2009 to 2010 and the Henry Alfred Kissinger Chair in Foreign Policy and International Relations at the Library of Congress. Previously, he was a professor of South Asian studies at the Jawaharlal Nehru University in New Delhi and the Rajaratnam School of International Studies in Singapore. He also served as the diplomatic editor and Washington correspondent for *The Hindu*. Mohan's most recent books are *India's Naval Strategy and Asian*

Security; *Modi's World: Expanding India's Sphere of Influence*; and *The Handbook on Indian Foreign Policy*. His earlier books include *Samudra Manthan: Sino-Indian Rivalry in the Indo-Pacific*; *Impossible Allies: Nuclear India, US and the Global Order*; and *Crossing the Rubicon: The Shaping of India's New Foreign Policy*.

Suhasini Haidar

Suhasini Haidar is the diplomatic and national editor of *The Hindu*, one of India's most widely read and respected national dailies, where she writes regularly on foreign policy issues. Over the course of her twenty-five-year-old reporting career, Suhasini has covered the most challenging stories and conflicts from the most diverse regions including Pakistan, Sri Lanka, Libya, Lebanon, and Syria, covered several prime ministerial visits worldwide, and interviewed a number of global leaders on the biggest stories of the time. Prior to this, Suhasini was foreign affairs editor and prime time anchor for English news channel CNN-IBN (2005–14), and Correspondent for CNN International's New Delhi bureau (1995–2005). Suhasini has contributed to many publications, and her essays have been included in books on Indian foreign policy, the Kashmir conflict, and the India–China rivalry in South Asia.

Ayesha Siddiqa

Ayesha Siddiqa is a Ph.D. in war studies, currently associated with the Centre for International Studies and Diplomacy (CISD) at the School of Oriental and African Studies (SOAS), London, as a research associate. She is a former Woodrow Wilson, Ford and Charles Wallace fellow and author of *Pakistan's Arms Procurement and Military Buildup, 1979-99: In Search of a Policy* (Palgrave Press, 2001) and *Military Inc: Inside Pakistan's Military Economy* (Pluto Press, 2007).

Index

About the Editors

Sanjaya Baru is a political commentator, author, former newspaper editor and policy analyst. He is now a Distinguished Fellow at the Manohar Parrikar Institute for Defence Studies and Analyses, New Delhi.

Rahul Sharma is a former newspaper editor who heads the India business of APCO Worldwide, a Washington-based global communications advisory firm. He has a deep interest in international affairs and runs a foreign policy blog.

30 Years *of*

HarperCollins *Publishers* India

At HarperCollins, we believe in telling the best stories and finding the widest possible readership for our books in every format possible. We started publishing 30 years ago; a great deal has changed since then, but what has remained constant is the passion with which our authors write their books, the love with which readers receive them, and the sheer joy and excitement that we as publishers feel in being a part of the publishing process.

Over the years, we've had the pleasure of publishing some of the finest writing from the subcontinent and around the world, and some of the biggest bestsellers in India's publishing history. Our books and authors have won a phenomenal range of awards, and we ourselves have been named Publisher of the Year the greatest number of times. But nothing has meant more to us than the fact that millions of people have read the books we published, and somewhere, a book of ours might have made a difference.

As we step into our fourth decade, we go back to that one word – a word which has been a driving force for us all these years.

Read.

Harper Collins · 4th · HARPER PERENNIAL · HARPER BUSINESS · HARPER BLACK · हार्पर हिन्दी

HarperCollins *Children'sBooks* · HARPER DESIGN · HARPER VANTAGE · Harper Sport